PLATO'S GHOST

PLATO'S GHOST
Minus Links and Liminality in Psychoanalytic Practice

Nilofer Kaul

PHOENIX
PUBLISHING HOUSE
firing the mind

First published in 2022 by
Phoenix Publishing House Ltd
62 Bucknell Road
Bicester
Oxfordshire OX26 2DS

British Library Cataloguing in Publication Data

A C.I.P. for this book is available from the British Library

ISBN-13: 978-1-912691-97-5

Typeset by Medlar Publishing Solutions Pvt Ltd, India

www.firingthemind.com

To

Raj and Damyanti who started me off

It was Prometheus the father of a new race that formed Truth, so justice may be dispensed among mankind. While he was still forming it, he was summarily called away by Jove. Thereupon he left his workshop in the charge of the treacherous Cunning, his new apprentice. It was this same Cunning who formed such a clever likeness of Truth that none could have told them apart. He then found he had no clay left to make the feet. His master returned and was struck by the brilliant imitation. Wanting credit for both, he baked them in his great furnace and breathed life into them. Sacred Truth walked with modest gait, while its imitation remained rooted on the spot. This spurious copy got named Mendacity because it had no feet—a charge to which I must agree.

—Phaedrus. Prometheus and Cunning. Fable IV

In: H. T. Riley (Ed.), *The Comedies of Terence: And the Fables of Phædrus*. Adapted from a translation by H. T. Riley & C. Smart. London: G. Bell & Sons, 1887.

Contents

Part II: Vertices

Acknowledgements

This is the page that I most wanted to write even before I began to imagine this book.

It was a book dreamt of by Dr Salman Akhtar. I had not imagined I had a book in me. But I was moved by his faith and I knew I could not fail him. To his faith, I owe this enterprise. Thank you for giving me such an unlooked-for gift. For your unwavering faith and unasked-for generosity.

I then began to frantically hunt in my essays for a "figure in the carpet" (Geertz, 1973). Like Banquo's ghost at the banquet, it turned out that what had hovered around me was the inherently liminal nature of psychoanalysis. I am filled with the need to justify a project that might after all be yet another set of essays of an uneven quality, lumped together under a rubric. And yet, here I am trying to see what this particular label might have to offer. It is hard, given that every time I have thought of something, I realise that it is a pale echo of one's teachers and psychoanalytic parents—Freud, Klein, Bion, Meltzer, Winnicott, Tustin—of the ones so ahead of their time and who left behind such a trove that it would require me many lifetimes to explore. They are followed by the teachers who continue to expand the work of these: in no particular order—John Steiner, Ruth Stein, Jean Laplanche, Giuseppe Civitarese, Dana Amir, Anne Alvarez, Thomas Ogden, Christopher Bollas, Adam Phillips, and many, many others. But most of all, it is Avner Bergstein who breathed life into Bion's cryptic prose—through readings and patient supervision—to whom I owe the deepest debt and gratitude.

To Mallika Akbar, my analyst, mentor, friend, colleague, and much else, I owe my psychic birth, my life as I know it now. And to our little reading group of three—Mallika, Vinita, and myself—where we have read Bion together on Saturday afternoons, through happy and dark hours.

To my patients and my students for bringing me material, for trusting me with their minds and hearts. For teaching me and taking me to places in myself that I may never have seen. Chapters published earlier have had to be modified because of the incredibly rich material that just keeps flying in.

To Kate—my gracious editor who took me on without knowing me and who remained warm, attentive, and patient through the terrible times. Her name in my inbox was the one that lit up the moment of wakening to Covid news. I would also like to thank Kate's wonderful team, especially James and Nick. They were patient and prompt.

To my supervisees and patients for having faith in me even as they continue to teach me.

To Micky who adopted me in the Mumbai family and through whom I found a community that continues to teach me. To my colleagues, from and with whom I continue to enjoy learning, especially Gouri and Micky. And supervision by Mrs Dastur who extended her support to include me and the fledgling group we have in Delhi. I am also very happy to have found Malika Verma and the peer supervision group with Banu and Mrs Bharucha.

To my friends over long years—Farida, Abha, Chitra, Isha, Neeladri, Shalini, Rana, Ben, Rajiv, Tani, Sunita, Suvritta, Mukul, Prabhu, Maitri, Namita, and Bill who is no more with us.

To Alan and Lucy, dearest friends of my father—who continue to go beyond the call of friendship and duty and who allowed Firdaus to taste a bit of grandparental love.

To Vinod Mubayi—my cousin who of all my family held me in his mind through the years. And all the Mubayis for letting me retain links with the family past.

To Vannajam Ravindran who is no longer here, but who filled me with passion for poetry that shaped my taste.

To Amir, Saloni, and Jalal—our extended family in LA.

To Uday who encourages me to read far beyond my comfort, and to write, and for bearing with many rough drafts over the years.

To my oldest friend and sister Madhvi who kept at bay my sense of being orphaned, for letting me hang on to a sense of having a family. To Madhvi and her family—Jacob and Naima. Needless to say Jacob's acerbic comments on my introduction were most helpful.

To Urvashi—friend, sister, family—for encouraging me proudly.

To my son Firdaus—my *raison d'être*. You had to share this page, because I am not sure there will be another.

And above all, to Pankaj for collaborating with me in creating a life that feels richer as we grow older, and for always putting me ahead of himself, for encouraging me to change, to grow. For enduring me.

Permissions

I am grateful to the Frances Tustin Fund for the generous award in 2018. The paper is republished here as Chapter 5. The generosity of Alina Schellkes has been a source of warmth and solace.

Likewise the *British Journal of Psychotherapy* for allowing me to publish an article in 2018, "Rehearsed Language of Psychoanalysis: Camouflage, Masquerade, ventriloquism". Ann was extremely patient with my redrafts. The paper is republished as Chapter 1 and leads into the book.

I have also been given permission by Karnac to republish "On Regret and Plato's Ghost" which is Chapter 3. Routledge has given permission to republish "Literary Portrayals of Arrogance". It appears here as Chapter 4.

I have Faber's permission to use T. S. Eliot for my concluding paragraph.

All the papers that have been republished have also been revised, keeping the theme of negative links in mind.

About the author

Nilofer Kaul, PhD, is a Delhi-based training and supervising analyst. Until recently she taught English literature at an undergraduate college in Delhi University. She won the Frances Tustin Prize in 2018. This is her first book. Her monograph *Fearful Asymmetries* is forthcoming with Zubaan, New Delhi. She lives in Delhi with her partner Pankaj Butalia and their son Firdaus.

Prologue

... a dim and undetermined sense of unknown modes of being ...
—Wordsworth, *The Prelude, Book 1,* 1798

Liminal spaces

Psychoanalysis may well have sprung up from unoccupied spaces in the mind that remain inaccessible to thinking. And yet, human imagination has often endeavoured to give shape to such areas of blindness that may have been suppressed, dreaded, denied, or dimly recognised. Such indeterminate spaces may be undecided, unknowable, ineffable, and often create an experience of impotency. Such affective states press for their own language and what erupts is a language for the unconscious. This may often intersect with what has come to be recognised as the language of psychoanalysis.

We may see a kind of prehistory of the relationship with the intermediate in mythology, literature, and religion—that feeds the language of psychoanalysis. To use Bion's (1962) idea, such harbingers of liminality could be read as what preceded Freud—the "preconceptions" he inherited, that "mated" with his mind and led to the "conception" of psychoanalysis (p. 91). Psychoanalysis is created through what I would like to term the "uncannisation" of the stable contours of life. As we both court and evade these states in our sessions, we forge links that are truthful as well as those that are untruthful.

Uncannising language

Freud's idea of the "contact barrier" (1950a) as the permeable divide between the conscious and the unconscious provides a good visual for the shaky contact the psyche has with "reality". Writing in 1895, Freud imagines this barrier as a moveable line that enables repression. This latter being essential to deal with the overwhelming data the world inundates us with, some editing must happen unconsciously. This permeable divide then enables the formation of the "unconscious". The mind requires to consign some of the overwhelming data into the vast unconscious. Thus "… an uncanny effect often arises when the boundary between fantasy and reality is blurred, when we are faced with the reality of something that we have until now considered imaginary …" (Freud, 1919h, p. 150). Freud thinks of the destabilising experience of the uncanny ("familiar" rendered "unfamiliar") as an affective experience where that which has been banished by the mind revisits it; albeit in a way that the divide instilled between known and unknown is jolted.

Furthermore, the whole experience of reading "The Uncanny" embodies the aesthetic tension that recurs through this book—the inadequacy of language to capture emotional experience and the compulsion to use it. Or the sense of awe at the unknowability of the universe and the creation of messiahs and "strange gods" that give an assurance of access. This unusual paper locates a body of sensations that signal an inchoate experience which destabilises the quotidian texture of our lives. The affect Freud locates exceeds the interpretations, creating an estrangement from the quotidian but in doing so he gives words to an experience that is immense and exceeds verbal language. This tension is at the heart of Freud's paper as well as this book.

More importantly, he is creating a vocabulary for the unconscious and this paper is significant in the relationship Freud creates between language and meaning. The free associative style where meanings emerge fleetingly and are then replaced is a template for writing psychoanalytically.

Old, familiar words are revitalised with new meanings and associations. This thus embodies the process of meaning-making that is the work of psychoanalysis. It would be fair to say then that the language of psychoanalysis, whether it is about time, memory, or dreams, attempts to "un-consciousise" (Bion, 1992, p. 353; Civitarese, 2011, p. 277) language. Bion (1962) draws our attention to the idea that the unconscious is not an already existing entity, but psychic work enables it. Overwhelmed as we are by stimulating elements, the mind relies for its survival on the process of unconsciousising. To extend this, the "uncanny" may also be seen as the reservoir of the language of psychoanalysis. Some of the building blocks of this are considered.

Spectral time

The timelessness of the unconscious Freud demonstrated variously in his work on dreams that disregard chronology, in transference where both time and space are suspended. In fact *Nachträglichkeit*, transference, and repetition compulsion are just a few of the very many ways in which Freud creates a vocabulary for psychic time. The psychic experience of time can be either an evasion of the now, or a suspension of transience. But emotionally we understand the psychic significance of *nunc stans* (or abiding time).

Time itself becomes elusive as the patient is full of memory (melancholy, regret) and desire (future, anxiety) but is situated in the present. It seems however that we would rather dwell in what Bion (1965) calls the "ghosts of the past" or the "ghosts of the future" (p. 95)—than to inhabit the present, the here and the now.

Memories which are presumed to be the keepers of time, the way Freud writes about them repeatedly, are both chronicles and alibis; both revealing and concealing; meaningful and unknowable. Straddling the past, present, and future, they are timeless and historical, weaving inextricably terrors and desires. Through his writings, Freud examines the whimsical nature of truth in remembering, thereby creating an emotional logic that is peculiarly psychoanalytic. For instance, the hysteric that he encounters is an uncanny figure who seems to suffer from uncontrollable memories (Freud, 1916–17, p. 43). We may argue that hysterics suffer from undigested, unprocessed thoughts. Is it that they strain the bearer who cannot digest them? Is it about a refusal to mourn? The hysteric evades pain by slipping away from it into a kind of melancholic past. But what is radical is that apparently somatic symptoms are caused by "whimsical remembering" and not the events themselves. This is radical subjectivity and emotions are at the heart of this.

"The Mystic Writing-Pad" (Freud, 1925a) suggests another model of the mind to him that is certainly not a blank slate. In fact emotional events leave behind traces. Akin to what he says about transference, he suggests that while the original memory is lost, it will get revivified in a way to resonate with the moment. Extending spectrality, Freud (1926e) suggests that in the transference the analyst is like a witch doctor who exorcises the ghosts in the room or "evil spirits" (Civitarese, 2011). Loewald (1960) extends Freud's idea, where he says that the unconscious is a "crowd of ghosts" and these ancestors haunt the present generation with their afterlife. Here is the passage that is memorable not just for its prose but also for the poetics of transference and which I quote because it is always a pleasure to reread:

> Transference is pathological in so far as the unconscious is a crowd of ghosts, and this is the beginning of the transference neurosis in analysis: ghosts of the unconscious, imprisoned by defences but haunting the patient in the dark of his defences and symptoms, are allowed to taste blood, are let loose. In the daylight of analysis the ghosts of the unconscious are laid and led to rest as ancestors whose power is taken over and transformed into the newer intensity of present life, of the secondary process and contemporary objects. (p. 29)

While Freud introduces this spectral dimension to transference, we see Loewald in the passage above elaborating the uncanny aspect of the field: blood, old ghosts, shadow-life, crowd of ghosts, haunting, imprisoned, let loose, and taste blood. This is the vocabulary that seems befitting to Freud's conception of psychoanalysis, which in the daytime world of goals and treatments we tend to forget all too often.

Working with the Wolf Man's (1918b) "memories", Freud realises a counter-movement. "Memories" are being created, he suggests (radically inverting his earlier work), in the present to resonate with the experience of the here and now. Memories—which refer us to the past or even the future, are in fact the "remembered present" (Edelman, 1989) and almost indistinguishable from dreams. When we are able to function analytically, we can listen to them oneirically. Needless to say, we may find ourselves listening concretely (as to facts), or with envy or contempt, and so on—which brings us to the idea of minus links.

Dreams

The belief and construction of emotional logic is evident when Freud places dreams at the heart of psychoanalysis. In doing so, he de-centres the daytime, rational universe by placing the apparently nonsensical topsy-turvy sleep fragments as Hansel's breadcrumbs that would lead the way to the unconscious. He reads dreams like unconscious poems that might give us clues to our underworld. Some of the time they can be like puzzles that can be put together through associations. These free associations are somewhat like a medium conducting a seance—they bring messages from the unknown world and we make what sense we can of them.

In this sense, free associations arise from a liminal space between sleep and waking, between conscious and unconscious. The building blocks are the repressed past, the recent past, and their relationship with the wishes of the present. The unconscious dissolves some obligations to the cold world of facts (temporality and spatiality) to be able to marry its memory to desires. There is a tense haiku here. As he de-centres rationality of the mind, he creates a rationale for the irrational mind. But in this somewhat supple crossfire, there emerges the idea of the "unknown navel" (1899a) of the dream. This unknowable knot defies penetration and remains perhaps the best signifier of the psychoanalytic project.

If dream analysis in a classical sense lays emphasis on associative patterns, Bionian metapsychology breaks down the distinction between dreaming and waking states. We can be "awake" but dreaming, as also "sleeping" but without having the sleep apparatus at work. Bion introduces reverie as fundamental to the capacity for thinking, when he imagines a bipersonal field with mother and baby. The mother who can think about the baby's experiences for him displays a capacity for reverie (1962). She can drift into her baby's mind and step out of it. She is labile and amphibian—she can swim in baby's mind and she can walk on the ground outside it. This is a capacity of the mind that the baby may be able to introject. This "reverie" is like a waking dream. The mind is aware that it is dreaming and is able to come out of it. On the other hand, Bion (1957) writes of psychotic patients who speak of the concrete world in a way that sounds like the "furniture of dreams" (p. 268). The contact barrier has collapsed and what should have been a dream is experienced as nightmarish reality.

The analyst is accordingly required to be in suspense (literally, to hover, to doubt) and treat the patient's presence like a dream. This induced state of "hallucinosis" can be facilitated by the analyst's eschewing of memory and desire. The past and the future are coordinates that anchor us too firmly and inhibit dreaming. So we see how dream/waking in Bion's writing becomes dream⇌waking. I am using here the reversible arrows to indicate the bidirectionality implicit in Bion's thinking. Dreaming and waking states often punctuate one another and do not require sleep to cleave them apart. In the caesural space between them lie reveries, delusions, hallucinations, and hallucinosis. The analyst needs to mobilise his psychotic part to receive the patient's state of mind, and also when she needs to become the patient's double (Botella & Botella, 2005) and become his experience.

Psychoanalysis defamiliarises familiar words like time, memories, sleep, and dreams to create a psychic lexicon for what is an uncanny experience. Into this slippery and indefinable space between analyst and analysand, all movement and exchange can either be towards emotional truth or away from it. The path to the truth of the analytic link is paved with dangers. However, the links between the analyst and herself, or between her and the analysand may not always be truthful. Pain, shame, fear, incomprehensibility may all obtrude on the link and take it towards untruth.

Introduction

liminal, a.('lɪmɪnəl) [f. L. līmin-, līmen threshold + -al1.]
a.a gen. Of or pertaining to the threshold or initial stage of a process.
rare. b.b spec. in Psychol. Of or pertaining to a 'limen' or 'threshold'.
—OED, 2009

Plunged into terrifying and primitive states of unknowability in a Covid-struck universe, it seems all the more pressing for psychoanalysis to insist on its commitment to what Keats (1818) famously referred to as "negative capability"—a capacity for enduring the incertitude of life, the singular absence of foreknowledge. This book is dedicated to a reiteration of unknowability, paradox, gaps, synapses, and aporias as well as the minus links that may spring in the space of the in-between. I have used the idea of liminality to broad-brush these openings that spring between monoliths—large faults as well as small crevices, caesuras, and colons. Bion uses the idea of synapses or the space between nerve endings to delineate a synaptic model (1962) of the mind. In the same way as the openings between the nerve endings transmit messages that reach the brain, it is the dynamic field of the analytic link that shapes the course of the analysis.

This may have a certain resonance in the times we live in where denial, disavowal, lies, and propaganda invade us virtually and we have to set up apps to filter the news for us.

Liminality

The concept of the "liminal" was developed by the eminent anthropologist Victor Turner (1969), who borrowed and modified Arnold van Gennep's (1960) *The Rites of Passage*. While the latter used the term to refer to a specific set of rites of passage required for boys to transition into becoming men, Turner and the post-structuralist turn gave what was the idea of a middle, a certain indeterminacy, and an infinite sense of suspension. He identified rituals, carnivals, plays as liminal spaces where the time and space dimensions of our lives—the grid that upholds the quotidian rhythm of our life—collapses its dominant grip. It is not just middle, but "betwixt and between", it is both and neither. Spatially we can think of it as borders, boundaries, margins, highways. These lines separate, but somewhat like an accordion, fold in and expand, making it a dynamic rather than fixed concept.

This space that opens up between bifurcated entities is the space where transformation is potentially possible. Most fundamentally it is the space between the analyst's unconscious and that of the analysand. It seems that the space that springs up between life and death, dreams and waking, god and man is a dynamic one, much like Freud's "contact barrier". When spaces open up between such bifurcated entities (death/life, sleep/waking, terror/beauty) they are marked by a dynamic, shifting liminal quality. These spaces are akin to what has been expanded by Bion (1977) into what Freud called caesura (1916a). This is both a space break and a continuity.

It may be a dramatic collective trauma like the Covid-19 pandemic or a terrible personal rupture—it is always a space of unpredictable change. This may be symbolised imaginatively with patients when we can dream and/or create a language to communicate with. Or it may only gesture towards the ineffable as we see when we cannot forge a language with patients, or with whom the link feels sterile or dead. Through the unknowable whispers and wordless exchanges, psychoanalysis opens a space for reading. This dynamic space between the text (session) and

reader (analyst) offers itself up for making meaning and thereby transformations. It is in such caesural spaces that transformative thinking
may happen, but it is also where minus links can be forged.

Caesura

When Freud (1916a) famously writes of how the continuity between life
inside and outside the womb is greater than the impressive "caesura" of
birth suggests, his emphasis is, as we know, on the continuity through
the separation. The baby is forever severed from the womb, but he retains
a lifelong link with mother. Freud uses the term "caesura"—a term used
in prosody which indicates a pause between two phrases. It is usually
indicated by a comma, a period, or an ellipsis. It is not the end of a sentence, but it is the middle which allows a breath, a rest, a halting space.
The relationship to this space is linked with the way we make meaning
of the world and our objects.

Bion expands Freud's use here by imagining it as a model for thinking and for emotional growth:

> The caesura of birth is the model of the birth of every new
> thought. Just as the caesura of birth makes one insensitive to the
> persistence of more primitive forms of knowledge and levels of
> the mind, so every new idea establishes a new caesura, a barrier,
> an obstacle to other ideas, which are thrust back into a cone of
> shadow, if not positively killed: A foetal idea can kill itself or be
> killed, and that is not a metaphor only. (Bion, 1977, p. 417)

Bion's use of the term indicates an indefinable gap between two momentous movements. This is a space charged with potency and the possibility of change. It is itself unsettled and therefore unsettling. The analytic
mind can drown at this meeting place, and it can also collaborate in
a perverse link. For instance, Meg Harris Williams (2005) in *The Vale
of Soul Making* writes of how the value of pain is not just to endure it
but to make meaning of suffering. This clarifies the distinction between
the analyst's masochistic submission to the analysand, and a more
tumultuous experience through which a depressive position may be
arrived at.

Minus links

Michaelangelo's "Birth of Adam" moves us because the hand reaching out is left yearningly unmet. God in that immortal gesture puts out his hand but their hands are unable to touch. This gives a visual representation of the enigmatic void—perhaps places in our mind that never became thoughts, for it awaits another to touch that part of our mind. The need to give order and form to this "void" comes from an experience that is of being lost or being without a mind that is adequate. When the mind is able to "suffer" loneliness and tolerate the void, it may experience what has been called the "sublime" or the oceanic feeling. However, this vision may be neither borne, nor succumbed to, but perverted. A third possibility opens when the mind is confronted with unbearable anguish. This third possibility may include false prophets and cult leaders who forge a minus link with the group.

The figure of the messiah in different religions (Dante's Virgil included) seems to promise an accessibility to the dread of this "formless void". The messiah figure in many religions stands between god and man, a promise of a medium, one who knows the overlord; a passage to the inaccessible. The messiah promises to fill in this gap, to traverse the threateningly indeterminate space. Christ straddles both mortal and immortal worlds by being both Son of Man and Son of God. The epiphanic truth is borne by the messiah for the group.

A profane version of this would be the séance and the medium—not to mention the psychoanalyst in the throes of transference. Such a figure promises access to truth and knowledge, but mainly promises to straddle the turbulent middle space. When writing about the mystic's relationship to the group, Bion (1970) suggests that the messiah seems to be born from the group's inability to bear this gap. This is analogous for him with how the thinker is born from a pressure of thoughts. This reverses the dominant philosophical tradition which posits the Cartesian cogito, and a mind that is the font of thoughts. In Bion's vocabulary, thoughts are largely unprocessed bits of data the mind is overwhelmed by. These bits of information are about the world outside as well as the one inside. To deal with this constant pressure, these thoughts demand a thinker and these are the conditions that are conducive for the mind/thinker to be born; but this latter is by no means inevitable. Analogously groups (especially the ones that cohere on the dependency model) await and even create their messiahs. There is often the negative possibility and a frequent outcome is the perversion of this role. False prophets and demagogues, fascists and fanatics use their capacity to take in group projections (charisma) and offer a group identity that is based on hate, propaganda, and lies, rather than truth. Demagogues who promise a golden age but through ethnic and religious cleansing, proffer hatred as knowledge, and violence as martyrdom.

Perversion offers a way of evading the breakdown without renouncing the power. Psychosis, prophesy, and perversion then become three possibilities. In such perverse relationships with truth, delusion replaces knowledge. We now look at how terror can find a pseudo-container in horror, mourning can be endlessly deferred as melancholia, equivocation can imitate the syntax of paradox, and autistic spaces can imitate transitional spaces as they replace spontaneous and creative relationships with repetitive "fantasying" (Winnicott, 1971, pp. 35–50). In this section I juxtapose links with their minus versions. This is a prelude to the exercise involved in analytic work. Do we have a truthful link with the analysand? Are we colluding with his melancholic narcissism to evade the painful work of mourning? Are we making interpretations that dilute the terror or are we really giving shape to it? Are we equivocating with the analysand or are we enabling a paradoxical state of mind? And finally, given how we have all had to work virtually during Covid-19, was the virtual space being used as a transitional space or an autistic one?

The nervous system communicates messages through the spaces that lie between nerve endings, or the synapses. Likewise the analytic field resembles the space of a synapse where two minds link. Bion seems to suggest an almost exclusive focus on the link between the analyst and analysand. It is only through the expansion of these spaces that the mind's capacity to experience, to think, and to give meaning can be expanded. This "caesural" space (between the analyst and analysand) is congruent with the "synaptic model of psychoanalysis" (Bergstein, 2013; Bion, 1962). The emotionally transformative encounter between two minds requires a "transcending of the caesura" (Bergstein, 2013; Bion, 1976). The submerging into the caesura, the failure to link may be an attack or a deficit (Alvarez, 1998). All too often the analyst may experience the patient's drive to communicate as an attack on linking (Bergstein, 2015).

Thus the link between the two minds can also become the space for destruction, perversion, evacuation, regression, and stasis. The area that lies between the mind of the analyst and that of the analysand is thus the liminal area of psychoanalysis—of growth, change, turbulence as well as that of impasse, bastion, and failure. This latter is perhaps what Bion (1962) meant about minus links.

Bion (1962) identifies the three emotional links possible between the analyst and analysand as being L, H, and K, that is, love, hate, and knowledge.

While it is K that is desirable as a link between the analyst and analysand, Bion recognises that there can also be the negative version of each of these possibilities. Using algebraic grammar, he then expands the idea of "minus links" between analyst and analysand. Meltzer and Williams (1988) elaborate:

> Many objects and events arouse one or the other; we love this, hate that, wish to understand the other. Our passions are not engaged. Our interest is in abeyance; we wish to engage with the object of love, to avoid or destroy the object of hate, to master the object that challenges our understanding. (pp. 143–144)

In my experience, minus links include not just anti-linkages, but often the mimicked, the travesties, the obverse of true emotional links. For instance, it is often a patina of empathy/concern that works as a smokescreen and conceals the ongoing emotional truth of the link. And a masochistic surrender often acts as an alibi for containment. This breeds a popular misconception in the cultural unconscious of the analyst as some kind of martyred mother—"murtyr"—and may become a source of great and secret narcissistic resource for the analyst. Bion suggests that the "-K link in analysis tells the story of an internal object relationship saturated with envy and hate between mother and infant" (Bergstein 2019, p. 101). There can be a "perverse" link that is based on an untruth -K (Bion, 1962, pp. 66–71) that can prevail in the analytic relationship. There is an incipient experience of curiosity, arrogance, and stupidity—simultaneously or by turns. This link is related to the negative of knowledge. The capacity to give meaning is all too often in peril.

André Green's idea of the negative in *The Work of the Negative* (1999) gives a conceptual history of psychoanalysis through the idea of the negative. He uses the negative as Ariadne's thread that runs through psychoanalytic concepts. The study of the unconscious can be seen as the history of the negative, the absent, the blank, and the unrepresented. Green writes about the analysand's blank mourning and negative hallucinations, blank psychosis, and psychically dead mothers. He concurs with Bion's -K as manifest in moments when the patient refuses elaboration of meaning (p. 9).

This has a certain resemblance to Bion's ideas. But while Green is more concerned with giving shape to objectless states of mind, Bion is more interested in the emotional links between minds (as well as the link between us and our own emotions). It is not just the analyst or analysand that Bion dwells on, but the links between the two. His formulation of reveries, for instance, is a good example of the link in that the Bionian reverie inhabits this "caesarean"—the cutting off of the umbilical cord, with a mother continuing to dream for him, till he can dream for himself.

What Bion means by -L and -H is hard to grasp. Maiello (2000) suggests that,

> Hatred (H) is viewed by Bion as the other face of love (L). … that behaviour that is inspired by the mental state of H corresponds to aggression as described by Riviere, whereas destructive violence would be the equivalent of Bion's -H, i.e. a form of hate that has lost its object and has become incomprehensible and incommunicable. Its inaccessibility to K could be due to the effect of the attacks on linking in the mental apparatus of the perpetrator of violence. (p. 8)

Maiello feels that intense violence and hatred where the object is lost could well be what Bion meant by -H and -L. For Maiello, it is the intensity that distinguishes H from -H.

Extending Maiello, to me it appears that (if L and H are two sides of the same powerful emotional link, then they are located on the same side of his grid) the negative side of the grid may be read as a state of mind where all categories have been inverted and travestied. Here emotions have been hollowed out and the links retain the form of emotions but are emptied of substance. This may be captured in what Bion (1965) calls "ghosts of departed quantities" (p. 157)—or absences such as "no-breast" (1970, p. 16) that define powerful psychic entities. Absence, he argues, has a very potent psychic presence. The breast (or the mind) that can not be available to the terrified infant becomes in Yeats' term, a "terrible beauty" (1921).

As Bion tends to bring the focus on the analytic functioning, we can perhaps see how to recognise minus links in the analytic field. For instance when the analyst experiences the absence of love or the absence of hate. Such an absence of vitality may be hidden behind a mechanical "sense of duty". This may conceal indifference or boredom or a rustled up empathy. The negative of love and hate it seems to me could well be the deadened responses by the analyst—dutiful concern and empathy appear to be frequently reported responses in supervision. Boredom may overwhelm the link, blurring the edges of righteousness and contempt the analyst fails to recognise in herself. I am suggesting that the links of L, H, and K can be psychically strenuous, and that unconsciously the impostor versions of these may replace them. Dutiful responses such as concern and protectiveness often form a patina that is the negative of L and H. An absence of curiosity at one end and prurience at the other end can form -K.

Does this patina indicate a perversion of the truth because the analyst has mastered the evasion of emotions, or is it an inevitable wall that we are all unable to scale in ourselves? Perhaps it is hard to tell the difference, but this absence of vital links, or the "second skin" that forms a layer on the link, makes the spontaneous emotion inaccessible and is closer to what I imagine as a minus link. Our hatred and dread of analysis surfaces in the way we unconsciously evade the intolerable atmosphere of being with patients: our aversion to pain, our inability to bear envy, the attack on our narcissism, the impotency from our inability to help them, the mind's unavailability for what appears so foreign—a kind of psychic xenophobia. It is this "unbearability" that enables the forging of minus links which are in danger of becoming a kind of "minus psychoanalysis".

Based on this template, this book attempts to expand liminal spaces between the language of the unconscious and that of psychoanalysis

(Chapter 1). This demands attentiveness to the gap between vocabulary and syntax (Chapter 2). Where for instance, false sentimentality replaces emotionality (Chapter 3). This is a crucial instance of the distinction between L, H, and -L, -H. Other chapters look at the presumed binaries between mind and body and pride and arrogance. Eventually the discussion around parasitism takes us to a creation of autistic islands which may well be when the analysis either ends or fails (impasses, bastions).

For me, the titles of the chapters echo the Eliotesque shadow that falls in "The Hollow Men" (1925) between "idea and reality", "motion and act", "conception and creation", and so on. Somewhat later to my surprise (and dismay) I discovered how creatively Tustin (1986) has used Eliot's poem while describing autistic mechanisms. Writing about the unpleasant experience of the infant when he confronts disappointing reality, Tustin gives to the Freudian shadow an added meaning: the constant sulk of disappointment that lurks all too often in us. In deference to this poignant expression of the rather eternal caesura between "the idea and the reality", I quote this to enlarge the area of shadows:

> This unpleasant experience has aroused a profound sulk, which Eliot calls the "shadow". This sulk of disappointment—this umbrage—which comes between "the idea and the reality" is the result of the discrepancy between what was expected and what actually occurred ... (p. 163)

When Bion (1962) first writes of minus links, he relates this to an absence of containment and to unbearable psychic pain that must be evaded. The psychotic part of the personality functions to protect the mind by a flight from truth. But when the Botellas (2005) write about the "work of figurability", it is not so much about evasion as it is about the inaccessibility and the irrepresentability of the unconscious. There appears to be an implicit causality in writing of minus links as strategies of evasion. It is of course not possible to know when it is "evasion" and when it is "beyond the spectrum" (Bergstein, 2014), but it is worth keeping these two paradigms in mind. It is also worth keeping in mind Bergstein's (2019) observation that minus links may not merely be "attacks on linking", but may be coming from a "drive to communicate" (p. 101). He suggests that these are perceived by us as attacks, but, from another vertex, these are also communications—maybe ones that we are unable to translate. Either way, this is difficult to distinguish and lies in a liminal space. But it is a salutary reminder against analytic complacency of knowing the truth.

It seems to me that at all times there is a force that acts against the recognition of truth and which eludes us much of the time. How can we expand our thinking of negative links between the analyst and the analysand—negative links encompassing both "perverse" obfuscations (lies and propaganda) as well as what the novelist Coetzee (1992) calls the "unimaginable", when he writes, "… the task becomes imagining this unimaginable, imagining a form of address that permits the play of writing to start taking place" (pp. 67–68).

Elaborating on Bion's idea of the caesura as his discourse on method, Civitarese (2008) writes:

> However, to what caesuras is Bion referring? One need only read the text, which enumerates a whole series of them: between foetal and postnatal life; between body and psyche (Bion [*A Memoir of the Future*], p. 449); … and hence between direct and indirect evidence; between past and present …; between the language of the analyst and that of the patient; between words worn out by daily use but absolutely suited to the formulation of an interpretation, on the one hand, and specialist jargon, on the other; … between mature and primitive levels of the mind … (p. 1131)

While Civitarese opens up the term caesura here, my own use of the caesural space is more specifically aimed at the subversion of the truthful link. Before we look at the chapters, I want to give examples of concepts plotted on the positive and negative grid. These spaces are marked by the opening of different possibilities: the move towards knowledge and growth, the retention of stasis, or the devolvement into chaos and hell. Often this is a site for where analytic functioning breaks down, while there is apparent harmony. This area where the link is not "truthful", or the analytic couple is unable to discern or tolerate the emotional truth is common to all minus links. It is forms of untruthfulness we slide into that drives my exploration of such liminality.

Mourning or melancholia

"Carrion Comfort" (1885, Hopkins & Smith, 1976), like many of Hopkins' poems, is a violent struggle with the difficulty of keeping faith. This includes not falling to despair. He speaks of despair as being the "carrion" against which he wrestles to keep his faith. At the end, there is a release:

> That night, that year
> Of now done darkness I wretch lay wrestling with (my God!) my God.

Hopkins seems to escape despair which represents a perverse temptation. Hopkins' despair scavenges on pain, rather than bears it. This "feast on despair" is a Christian sin that resembles Freudian melancholia. Melancholia, Freud (1917e) seems to suggest, is an evasion of mourning. Here Freud makes a distinction that strikes at the very heart of this. He distinguishes between two ways of responding to object loss—melancholia, where the relationship with the lost object is not relinquished, and mourning, where after a prolonged struggle the relationship with the lost object changes—some thing is relinquished, while other things are introjected. Either loss is experienced so profoundly as a loss of a part of oneself that one never recovers oneself, or else, over time there is a relinquishing through introjection (keeping parts of the object by identifying with the lost object). When the psyche encounters some unexpected pain or threat, it may resort to either "fight or flight" (Bion, 1961).

Mourning is in this sense a fight, while melancholia is a flight from transformative suffering. Dante's purgatory can be read as a melancholic space—in that the souls are perennially waiting for their lost object (Paradise, Promised Land). Perhaps one could stretch this to say that melancholia can be the negative of mourning? The melancholic is in pain, while the mourner is suffering it? Is melancholia always indicative of a narcissistic relation to its lost object? Or could it also include blank mourning states, as André Green refers to them, or other forms of unrepresentable pain?

Here as elsewhere, we see that this space which offers itself for transforming suffering does so only through volcanic eruptions of unanticipated pain. These spaces can then stagnate or turn sterile. Turbulence itself may become a refuge from transformation. A good example of this is Bollas' (1984) paper on "Loving Hate". The patients described here are addicted to turbulence. In order to evade psychic pain, all links may be perverted. The analytic space, as Bollas illustrates in the paper, can be eroticised and recruited in favour of "psychic equilibrium", as opposed to "psychic change" (Joseph, 1989).

Imagination may be used to create music from suffering, as it can be used to escape from it. Both impulses coexist in poetry as well as in analysis. The work in analysis often entails unpicking mourning from melancholia, masochistic submission from suffering, paradoxical states from equivocatory elisions. I next look at how the language of paradox captures the rhythms of the unconscious in the way that it allows contradictions to coexist. This is often mimicked by equivocation, which is the grammar of perversion.

Paradox or equivocation

It is not new to argue that the psychoanalytic aim is quintessentially paradoxical in that it is both an acknowledgement of the ineffable, and an attempt to give it form—as a way of containing the magnitude of this helplessness. This paradoxical state generates a grammar that is at once an attempt to estrange the quotidian as well as to make acquaintance with the alien and unknown.

In Winnicott's (1971, p. xii) inimitable words:

> My contribution is to ask for a paradox to be accepted and tolerated and respected, and for it not to be resolved. By flight to split-off intellectual functioning it is possible to resolve the paradox, but the price of this is the loss of the value of the paradox itself.

There is an enrichment in the state of the paradox, albeit an enrichment through the renunciation of a fixed meaning. This area of paradox is also the area of playing and it is also the place for psychoanalysis. Here Winnicott is writing about transitional spaces where the playing child is described. For him the game is both real and not. This paves the way for a paradoxical state of mind in which we listen. By "real" he means as concrete as marbles and as fictional as a story. Transposed into relationships, the object is both under my omnipotent control and separate. Transitional space, or the intermediate area between reality and fantasy—is the concept of an emotional space that is real and imaginary—it is both and neither. Mother's shawl is both mother and not her. Stories move us as though they are real even while we know they are not.

When Freud first dreamt of the psyche as a conflicted zone, he saw the ego as occupying an embattled space—dynamic, moving about, ingratiating, disguising, never still. The ego it seems survives by equivocating with us. Yet persistent equivocation creates a syntax of disavowal. This is best seen in "Fetishism" (1927e) where he mentions two young men who lost their fathers when young. He thinks they have scotomised (literally, scotoma means blind spot) this but then realises his mistake. One current in the mind is still waiting for father, while the other current behaves as his heir. They both believe and do not believe. This realisation of Freud's made him recant on his earlier distinction between neurosis and psychosis (pp. 155–156). I refer to this as the syntax of equivocation.

The paradoxical state of mind is one where two contradictory truths are held together emotionally, without resolution. But in borderline and psychotic states, we can see that the syntax becomes equivocatory. This may resemble paradox, but is in fact a disjunction of the sentence. Paradox requires the renunciation of control (tolerating our inability to control emotional complexity); while equivocation is driven by deceit. In the latter, the mind "pretends" to believe the painful truth, but secretly holds on to the lie.

Equivocation is to evade the truth and psychic pain, while paradox is an expression of psychic complexity and often a surrender to it. The resemblance between paradox and equivocation corresponds to another preoccupation in the book—that is, the capacity of the mind to mime a language adhesively either to beguile or to allay the analytic process. These roadblocks are discussed in Chapter 1.

In a now forgotten paper, "Borderline Phenomena", Sailesh Kapadia (1998) elaborates the grammar of borderline states. He uses the Trishanku myth—about a king who wanted to reach heaven but without dying. In this impossible quest he goes to two rival sages, and while one refuses this, the other encourages this delusion. Eventually he finds himself in the space between heaven and earth. He is always reaching out and getting thrust back. "Trishanku's final suspended state depicts the subjective experience of a borderline patient" (p. 513). The motion sickness of the borderline state is captured imaginatively here by Kapadia. The syntax resembles that of a paradoxical state of mind, but its grammar is entirely different. It appears to accept both, but its relationship to contraries is one of shuttling and/or evading the pain rather than mourning it. Trishanku can neither bear to die nor to forego heaven. Between the Scylla of unbearable pain and the Charybdis of psychic death, the borderline patient cycles slowly and painfully so as to avoid a breakdown. These states are not fixed or frozen but oscillate between deadness and unbearable pain; between being asleep and awake. However, besides these two possibilities (accepting and denying), one can argue for a third relationship with reality.

Steiner (1993), elaborating on Freud's ideas on fetishistic disavowal, suggests that such persons have perversely disavowed the "facts of life" (Money-Kyrle, 1978). These being "the recognition of the breast as a supremely good object, the recognition of the parents' intercourse as a supremely creative act, and the recognition of the inevitability of time and ultimately death" (p. 443). Taking from this, disavowal may be read as a perverse relationship with reality.

Steiner clarifies that it is not simply the coexistence of contradiction which is perverse:

> The perversion arises as integration begins, and lies in the attempt to find a false reconciliation between the contradictory views which become difficult to keep separate as integration proceeds. Such a reconciliation is not necessary when splitting keeps the contradictory views totally separate and unable to influence each other. The problem only arises as the split begins to lessen and an attempt is made to integrate the two views. (1993, p. 93)

At this juncture, the patient may resort to a psychic retreat, that is neither psychosis nor acceptance of reality, but a third place situated in the middle.

In his discussion of the different models of psychoanalysis, Steiner (1989) writes about the model of perversion. His use of "perverse" harks back to its original meaning of something that was good but has taken a wrong turn. What is perverted here is the relationship with truth and reality. The perverse patient does take in the analyst, but in ways that twist and distort psychic knowledge.

> I believe that some patients adopt such an attitude to a whole area of reality which they find unacceptable, and that they retreat to a kind of borderline state ... which reality is not completely denied and is also not completely accepted. (p. 118)

The script in front of patient and analyst is the same, but they read it from opposite ends of the glass. One is looking at the image straight, the other at its inverse form. Bion (1962) refers to this as "reversible perspective".

Steiner's idea of perversion seems to me to be continuous with Bion's idea of minus links. The analyst is often unable to tolerate the emotions the patient arouses. Rather than tolerate this not know-ing, we find ourselves over-listening to words, taking recourse to our favourite psychoanalytic concepts, colluding in different ways with patients because of our own personal terrors—our unanalysed and unreachable limits.

In such encounters, we may collude with our patients in mistaking melancholia for mourning, horror for terror, fear for respect, paradox for a perverse equivocation, masochism for endurance, obsequiousness for gratitude, flattery for love, and so on.

I mention the language of paradox being mimicked by the syntax of equivocation. In politics this may be seen when the state justifies its violence in terms of false equivalence rather than a true recognition of equal rights. This is yet another reason that reliance on verbal com-munication is misleading. The perverse parts of the mind can adopt the stance of the depressive position. But this is in fact another way of perpetuating delusions and falsehoods. To use a political analogy, states that avow electoral democracy find ways of subverting its sig-nificance through the hollowing out of its content, while retaining its form. This is another form of perversion. Unlike a paradox that expands the mind by its refusal to resolve, equivocation maintains the psychic economy by evading the pain. The relationship between para-dox and equivocation is discussed as paradigmatic of that between K and -K.

Transitional or autistic spaces

In the post-Covid era the analytic omnipotence over the setting has been completely overthrown. We have had to work on phones, Zoom, Skype. The connections have been unstable, the asymmetry less stark. How did this enormous change affect us? I am only going to mention one point which emerges from the concerns here. The virtual space that opened up provided a transitional space for us to continue despite the sudden breakdown of all familiar contours (Civitarese & Ferro, 2013, p. 127). However, even though the virtual medium lends itself to Winnicott's transitional space, it also does so to Tustin's autistic space. If Winnicott's transitional space offers an imaginative freedom to create (paradoxically only possible when it is recognised as fantasy), Tustin's autistic space is a retreat into a delusional omnipotence (where fantasy takes centre stage by shutting out reality). The autistic part of the psyche can retreat more easily into its enclave.

Also the virtual world opens up different kinds of spaces: between delusion and reality; between fiction and metafiction; virtual spaces can create confusional spaces where the paradox can slip into delusion.

Here I mention a small vignette. Maya is a young woman about twenty-two years old. She wore little girls' dresses and spoke in soft cadences. Her eyes looked half-closed. She tended to stay indoors, no matter where in the world father was posted. She said she had never had friends. Stepping out meant being bullied, so she did not go out of her house. Instead she remained in cyberspace, playing a storytelling game. This involved telling a story about fictional characters who would acquire a shape online. These characters would go into the "world", unlike Maya. Here they would meet other characters created by other storytellers. One of her characters (a young woman) went on dates with someone else's character (a man). She would whisper how terrified she was. I could feel the menace. This man looked like a rapist. But her character was insisting on going ahead. He lived in M (a country considered unsafe) and she had bought her tickets. This space she lived in was not strictly delusional, nor did it acknowledge itself as fictional; instead it was breaching both frames—the fictional and the delusional. What had begun as a fictional impulse had now become "hyperreal". But in not being able to sustain the intermediarity of this experience, in crossing over and becoming her character, Maya (who now took over from her character) was going to fly across continents and meet a man who like herself was also crossing the line from creating fiction to inhabiting it. In doing so, the author became a character. Bion writes of thoughts needing a thinker, but in Maya's case, the thinker abandons thinking and instead becomes a wild thought. This could be read as an instance of transformation but one that goes towards delusion, rather than towards thinking/reality.

This resembles the -K that could all too easily become the link between the analyst and the analysand. The hyperreality here is emblematic of a compelling world of fantasy where the analyst can only too easily be drawn into being recruited as a co-author and where the distinctions that patrol analytic functioning get confused and collapse, taking the dyad into a collaboration that appears to be knowledge, but is steadily moving towards a folie à deux.

About the chapters

"Language", Bion (1954) writes, "is employed by the schizophrenic in three ways; as a mode of action, as a method of communication, and as a mode of thought" (p. 24). The lexical use of words is only one dimension then. Bion demonstrates how the patient experiences words as concrete things that can either kill or engulf; consequently he feels invaded and attacks them in turn. Interpreting the content of the speech gives way to the location of it, and the affects in the field. Meltzer (Meltzer et al., 1986) takes this even further: when he observes his patient "lalling" (making imperfect, infantile sounds) he feels that there is a "buccal" (in the cheeks and mouth) theatre that is prior to the stage where words (or sound combinations) get linked to meaning and get used to communicate thoughts and feelings. This is, he thinks, "a developmental space that is neither internal nor external in its implications, the 'Buccal Theatre for Generating Meaning', tracing its implications both for speech development and for character" (pp. 181–182).

This kind of communication may be evacuative, but it is still a form of proto-speech and an instance of how when the communication is non-lexical, the chances are that we miss it. On a similar note, Betty Joseph (1982) writes of "chuntering" and Ignes Sodre (2015) of "chantering". In each instance, the patient's semantic communication is meaningless, while it is in the detection of the way in which sounds are used that we can reach closer to where the patient is located. The use of language may also have a quality which is monotonous or lulling, that invites the analyst to snooze, or else to restore some quiet in his noisy mind through monotonous clucking or a mechanical clearing of his throat.

The book follows Bion's separation of language from communication, and verbal language from non-verbal language, and lexical from non-lexical content such as tone, sounds, rhythm. Here is Civitarese's (2016) eloquent distinction between words and meaning:

> Word representation provides a walkway that stops us from falling into the abyss of infinity and the infinite differences of things in nature ... the word 'closes' the meaning, but since it is itself conveyed by what is called the signifier it can never 'close' it completely ... Thought comes into being in this fissure as the more or less successful attempt to bridge it. (p. 147)

The impulse to communicate, it seems, is searching for a vehicle to convey it. The words both carry and "miscarry" these communications which are often unformulated. Can we try to retrieve some of what is lost in this movement from experience to words?

Chapter 1 opens by looking at the relationship between language and psychoanalysis. Taking up Bion's (1957) idea of a continuum between the psychotic and non-psychotic parts of the mind, this opening chapter looks at clinical moments where the primitive part—psychotic and "autistic-contiguous" (Ogden, 1992)—mimes language and takes over the analytic field. It is an exploration of rehearsed languages that form "bastions" (Baranger & Baranger, 2008)—in the way patient and analyst collude in semantic exchanges that deceive both about the nature of the analytic treatment going on. The patients discussed seem to intuit the analyst's blind spots and a pseudo-language takes over as primitive parts of the patient collude with mine, but where I am unable to stir myself out of these dark holes. In my work writing became the rope, holding onto which I sometimes managed to return.

Chapter 2 looks at the gap between the vocabulary of psychoanalysis and the prearranged syntax of existing language. Concepts of development incipiently enter clinical spaces and this may shape the form of the analysis. Psychoanalytic clinical writing is not always able to depart from a certain kind of narrativising. This is somewhat akin to what Bion borrowing again from Keats was to call the distinction between the "Language of Achievement" (which is poetic and closer to dreaming) and the "Language of Substitution" which is like a prose translation of the poetic (Bion, 1970). This gap is important because the linearity of writing that underwires our case histories makes the outcome a dominant force in the session.

Chapter 3 looks at the difference between sentimentality (-L, -H) and emotionality (turbulence). In the stories discussed here we explore aspects of non-lexical communication that may bring us closer to emotional truth, rather than lose orbit through screen memories, nostalgia, and melancholia. The word "regret" is explored not just in the content of the stories but in its different components such as ellipses, tone, syntax, tense, and form. We look at the history of the word as it has historically travelled from "bewailing" to a more narcissistic state, devoid of affect. The different stories discussed here are contrasted as nostalgic (sentimentality, -L, -H) versus truthfully emotional (turbulence is always jostling between L and H). Eventually Coetzee's novel *Disgrace* (2000) tells of a man who is unable to experience feelings till he undergoes his disgrace. The undergoing of a true emotional experience appears to be in itself humbling. It is the -L and -H at the beginning of the novel that painfully gives way through humiliation, and defeat gives way to L, H, and finally K. The contrast between sentimentality and emotionality emerges as analogous to that of screen memory and truth in Freudian terms.

Chapter 4 explores arrogance as a possible link that destroys analysis. It begins by looking at narratives that respond to arrogance either by acknowledging or rejecting it. It seems that while the register of tragedy accepts it, that of Christianity forbids it. Stories seem to be born out of the tension between the flight to grandiosity and its inevitable crashing. Invisible shields of omnipotence promise an escape from unbearable helplessness. The omnipotence of arrogant postures is discussed as a recurrent, almost quintessential trope in myths and while narratives seek to abjure it, recurrence points to its inevitability. The skirmish between its stubborn return and the subsequent fallout seems to engender narrative itself. A look at literary narratives reveals the ubiquity of a syntax that is born out of a tussle with arrogance and yet language itself seems to collapse into some assertion of it, some form of omnipotence. Is it possible to create narrative without traces of arrogance/omnipotence? Samuel Beckett's "The End" (1946) presents yet another landscape of death-in-life. The abjection of the protagonist and his complete indifference to life create an idiom as remote as possible from arrogance. This effacing of meaning and the negating of the self engender an anti-narrative. And except for stray moments, we can see nothing but the debris of a self. Is this the other to arrogance?

Finally it is with Bion's description of the link between patient and analyst that we see arrogance brought to our door. A small clinical vignette demonstrates that the analytic couple colludes in perpetuating this. Frequently the patient brings the thoughts he is unable to think: this may be seized upon by the analyst, who may in this moment take on the role of the messiah, rather than someone who can enable thinking. This can make for stupidity and arrogance in the link; yet another kind of minus link.

Chapter 5 on parasitism expands on Bion's idea of the parasitic link in analysis. Parasitism has a malignant ring and has been thought of mostly in an intrapsychic way. While this is not without its justification, this perspective could be seen as paranoid from other "vertices". Bearing in mind the discourse of natural sciences, this chapter sees more primitive aspects of what drives parasitism in a "bipersonal field" (Baranger & Baranger, 2008) and attempts a "binocular" (Bion 1962, p. 86) reading towards that. It is suggested that the womb–foetus link may be used paradigmatically to map parasitic relations which could be emerging from an encounter of autistic parts of the patient and analyst. But fundamentally it is about recognising the still "encapsulated" (Tustin, 1986; Bergstein, 2009) parts of our mind that collaborate in the formation of autistic islands. The idea of an ectopic pregnancy which is discussed here imagines the parasitic psyche in some situations as unable to find a place in the womb. It clings to any surface it finds. This space outside the womb but inside the body adds another layer to this effort to theorise minus links.

The first four chapters focus on the limitations of language, while Chapter 5 embodies "multiocular vertices" (Bergstein, 2019, p. 167). Bion seems to suggest vertices as enabling analytic listening. The term vertices is derived from geometry where it is defined as angular points of polygons and other such figures. The term provides an alternative to perspectives. Clinically, "vertices" (Bion, 1965, p. 90)—which are more dynamic versions of perspectives—place emphasis on lability, attentive movements, and the ever changing moods and tones of the session. In order to retain an emotional link with the patient, the analyst needs to be willing to change the locations from where he listens. This shifting of the vertex is in itself expansive for the mind and it fuels the analytic link.

Unlike ideas of genealogy and history that tend to take away from the dynamic of the ongoing rhythm, the here and now is the best instance of the transient but middle space of the present tense—that lies between the genealogical (preoccupied with the trellis of the past) and the prophetic (projecting onto the future from material of the past). Accordingly, the next chapter will focus on expanding the spaces for thinking and they each happen to use multiocular vertices.

In Chapter 6 it is suggested that the autoimmune system may offer another dimension to the relationship between mind and body. This chapter attempts to supplement Bion's ideas on the mental process resembling the alimentary, respiratory, and muscular systems; it suggests that autoimmune systems seem to be prior to the splitting of mind and body, and seem to correspond to the protomental apparatus proposed by Bion. This apparatus may help us think about the "irrational" outbreaks of symptoms that defy causality. This may also further problems of technique when confronted by primitive forms of communication, where the body is unable to form distinct symptoms, but is suffused by alien sensations.

One of the recurrent themes of the book has been the finite language of psychoanalysis that cannot contain the vision of the unconscious. Truth and lies, failure and success, writing and ineffability remain the tense poles of the axes that criss-cross the body of psychoanalysis. Chapter 7 examines the area between untruth and failure. What constitutes "un-success"? Do we tend to shy away from writing about it? Are we haunted by the outcomes? Is there a way we can think beyond outcomes? These are questions I have raised for further thinking. When what we are fundamentally interested in is the unknowable and wordless unconscious, how do we define truth and untruth?

If at the core of analytic stuckness lie knots of proto-emotions and proto-thoughts, then how are we to redefine the shape of the truth we are in search of? To what extent does our linguistic limitation bind us to the language of narratives, failures, and success? In this context, I look at instances of "failure" in analysis to trace analytic untruth as a part of the ordinary limitations of the analytic mind. This is opposed to the unconscious omniscience and omnipotence that we carry despite all our commitment to incertitude and fallibility.

If psychoanalysis is concerned with emotional growth, this book considers obstructions to truth in the emotional relationship between the analyst and the analysand. Among these would be analytic allegiance to our particular schools, our inability to forge a technique in the face of the protomental apparatus which can breed arrogance, our complacent use of language, the gaps between our theoretical allegiance and our technique, and finally, all too often our unwillingness to get in touch with our truth. Most fundamentally I would like to think of beginning to write more incisively about the dailiness of failures and limitations—not as exceptions or rescued just in time, but abject failure as well as quotidian failure. The concluding chapter ends with an elegy to loneliness that such thinking about our feelings demands.

With this introduction I hope to have defined the preoccupation with the nature of links that may be forged in liminal spaces that impede thinking. The chapters that follow will hopefully expand on different locations of stunted, obstructed, and perverted thinking. By no means comprehensive, the book only hopes to expand on how we may turn a blind eye to what may be going on in our analytic life.

Part I

Language

CHAPTER 1

The unconscious and psychoanalysis

We must, however, bear in mind that free association is not really free. The patient remains under the influence of the analytic situation even though he is not directing his mental activities on to a particular subject.

—Freud, 1925d, p. 39

"By the term borderline case", Winnicott (1969) writes somewhat disturbingly,

I mean the kind of case in which the core of the patient's disturbance is psychotic, but the patient has enough psychoneurotic organisation always to be able to present psychoneurosis ... In such cases the psychoanalyst may collude for years with the patient's need to be psychoneurotic ... we are inwardly troubled when the madness that is there remains undiscovered and unmet. (p. 711)

From a different perspective, Bion (1957) writes,

3

Since contact with reality is never entirely lost, the phenomena which we are accustomed to associate with the neuroses are never absent and serve to complicate the analysis, when sufficient progress has been made, by their presence amidst psychotic material. On this fact, that the ego retains contact with reality, depends the existence of a non-psychotic personality parallel with, but obscured by, the psychotic personality. (p. 62)

Through these borrowed thoughts, I have attempted to draw attention to how language can beguile, and how words may clarify, obscure, or sometimes mimic. Following classical psychoanalysis, Winnicott (1969) assumes the idea of disease masked adeptly by health, while Bion (1957) reverses this psychic geometry by suggesting that there is some sanity even when least suspected. Winnicott seems to warn us we can be deceived, while Bion holds out hope of reaching even the most unreachable. Either way we may be attuned to one register of communication and miss another, or we may hear the words and miss the "music of what happens" (Ogden, 1998, p. 428, quoting Seamus Heaney).

In this chapter I want to examine moments where I feel I have been betrayed by my capacity to think and have felt allured by the words but failed to "hear the music". My other concern is that the language of psychoanalysis is oversaturated and patients come to us with a "preformed transference" attempting to impose the role of "psycho-analyst" as derived from reading, films, rumour, and phantasy (Meltzer, 1967, p. 6). Templates of narratives told to therapists are ever present in popular culture, and communication is overdetermined. Patients carry inherited ideas about what is spoken about in analysis, such as abuse, perversion, parents. Our clues come from the tiredness of hearing overused words. Under the circumstances, free association feels difficult especially with patients who have jumped the analytic theory-cart before riding the analytic practice-horse.

I have tried to delineate how primitive parts of patient and analyst may come together to evade pain through a shared language. This chapter is however not so much about why learning is avoided, as it is about the different kinds of collusions that may take shape depending on the particular analytic dyad. I use three clinical vignettes to support my argument. The patients discussed here are highly intelligent with tremendous semantic skills, know more than two languages, and uncannily tapped into my own love for words.

Language offers familiar moulds of communication mediated by psychoanalytic language rather than spontaneous associations. Ways of telling our stories, and language itself, have templates that precede our telling. Oedipus' story has already framed our narratives, as have many others. These may obstruct spontaneous associations. Similarly symbols, metaphors, paradoxes, as well as psychoanalytic tropes (dreams, primal scenes) may also be a part of our linguistic inheritance, rather than free associations. However, there could be other building blocks of communication which could help convey the internal world more reliably. For instance, syntax whether straight, winding, or circular may help map our object relations. Tone and density may well reveal the grammar of internal objects. So it seems that primitive experience gets obscured by learned languages, and the barrier in analysis may be caused by the gap between an over-evolved language and the specificity of experience. Primitive parts of the mind may nestle in these moulds that then defend against psychic change.

At the end, I will try to sum up technical variations that helped as more classical technique floundered.

Dina

Dina brought an overabundance of rich-looking material that promised much, but eluded meaning. She filled me with a dread that I could not put a name to. I felt that if my interpretations were not accurately chiselled, she would collapse. What I experienced felt uncanny, like psychic goosebumps; as if some big secret was withheld. Strangely I found myself mimicking her gestures. I'd brush this off, along with other unthought feelings. It took a while before I realised I was identifying adhesively with her. I would remember the jumbled flow of her chaotic words long after the sessions, as if stretching my skin to hold them together.

Waking dreams

With some patients dreams can be so thin that one wonders why they should be called dreams. Not so with Dina who has dense, overcrowded dreams, "symbols" knocking each other down like skittles. But awake too, her words sound like "waking dreams" (Ferro, 2002). There is a very interesting line in Bion (1970) where he departs from Klein's idea on symbol formation. He writes,

> For example, the psychotic patient does not always behave as if he is incapable of symbol formation. Indeed, he often talks or behaves as if he is convinced that certain actions, which to me are innocent of any symbolic significance, are obviously symbolic. (p. 65)

The psychotic patient is using the symbol but not in a way that marks symbolisation; instead he assumes that this symbol is universal and transparent, not idiosyncratic and translated.

Her dead father's eyes followed her around in recurrent dreams. Terrifying as it sounded to me, her voice would remain soothing. Her responses did not correspond to the experiences she spoke of. By "surprising" me thus, she seemed to stay ahead of me.

In retrospect I realised I was not reflecting on why she decided to speak of recurrent dreams, or how an acquaintance with the language of psychoanalysis (which she had) could obtrude on the language of the unconscious. In a dream she brought after my vacation, she said she was in a fairground where colours were oversaturated and it was "timeless".

In the dream she asked me (I appeared in a bubble) when she could get back, but I told her that time no longer existed so "when" was no longer a valid category. This disturbed me, but her tone was even.

The panic of collapsing because of my absence was all mine. We spoke of this again, some weeks later. She said her world was like that fairground, oversaturated: "My world looks like yours—it has cars, houses, streets ... but it's different."

It certainly felt topsy-turvy. All my "associations" seemed turned on their head. This seemed to be a peculiarity of the primitive part—a kind of gratification derived from toppling associative logic. Beckett (1946) embodies this:

> Personally I have no bone to pick with graveyards. I take the air there willingly, perhaps more willingly than elsewhere, when take the air I must. The smell of corpses, distinctly perceptible

under those of grass and humus mingled, I do not find unpleasant, a trifle on the sweet side perhaps, a trifle heady, but how infinitely preferable to what the living emit with their feet, teeth …
ovules. (p. 65)

Like a Beckettian character, Dina too appeared to be saying, "The world
I see is upside-down and you must feel the disorientation I feel, it is my
disregard for life I want you to hear. You are so allied to life, but death
has the last laugh." She had a kind of unimpressed air that made me want
to be deferential. This spurred me on to furiously follow the impossible
twists of logic, my interpretative speed going into overdrive, images proliferating dizzyingly, my mind unable to sort, process, to have reveries.
I would rush in to ride the storm, rather than to observe it. My palpable
anxiety would be about being able to match the velocity of her associations, as if I were trying to keep pace rather than contain. This "keeping
pace" is a folie à deux that I entered. The terror of internal disarray being
unbearable to her, she evacuated it in a frenzy, all the time looking back
to see if I was "following" her, Orpheus to her Eurydice. Like Orpheus,
I seemed to be reassuring her that she was not alone, and in so doing,
dooming us. By soothing her with interpretations of the content that
"sounded" correct, I left this terror well alone. Perhaps for both of us.

Primitive parts of the mind, it seems, camouflage disorganised sensations as free associations; the raw beauty of her words disguised hallucinatory incoherence—poignant but meaningless. I would find myself
riveted, in terrified stillness, rather than evenly suspended attention. As
she spoke, her scattered words dazzled me, the gesture with which she
wiped her tears filled me with cathartic relief, her flooding me with dis-
jointed "bizarre objects" drawing me into an over-attentive, tense mind
(Bion, 1957). It did not occur to me that when "evenly suspended attention" is disabled, then the verbal register is already redundant and holding onto it is for my sake, rather than hers.

Ersatz symbols

Dina's associations were overwrought with ersatz symbols or symbolic
equations (Segal, 1957); metonymy (contiguity) posing as metaphor
(substitution). "Sometimes," she said, "one part of the room seems to
grow big. Like my foot—it becomes giant. Here it is my head that keeps

growing. When I go out from here, the head shrinks. Outside I would not recognise you. I only hear your voice, and when I go out, my head shrinks and I can't remember anything. It feels as if the distance between my head and my feet is very great."

My head would swim with engulfing and encysting objects. But I would stay away from this confusion engulfing me. Sometimes I managed to observe and establish separateness: "You find it hard to think."

But at other moments her unravelling would overflow into me: "I can never stitch anything. You know how in the old days there would be these machines which you operated with your legs? One tight metal ball sits inside my stomach or heart … it's either very big or very small. Like a virus, like a mosquito …"

This seemed to begin like a conceit but proliferates so infinitely that after a while, one could not distinguish between the "tenor" and "vehicle" (Richards, 1936). When she says, "It feels like …" it suggests a symbol but there is in fact no language to express the concreteness of this experience. It is not "like" the foot is growing, but the foot actually shrinks and grows, a nightmare world: Alice's wonderland. Here we are confronted again by deceptively symbolic language that is not "learned by experience" (Bion, 1962). Language can either be learned from experience or it may be mimicked. Dina has learned ideas of time and knowledge from watching people but feels quite removed from "other people's world".

She was able to tell me that she is removed because perhaps she would sense a synapse open between us that would allow our dissociated parts to merge. I seemed to know what a timeless world feels like and how hard it can be to tell the difference between dreaming and reality in moments. She seemed to remain an outsider to the world of reality, in Neverland. Her world would feel like an oversaturated, noisy, thrill-driven version, continents away from the quotidian world. This distance was frightening, but the terror of the world she was excluded from was greater. She would over-hear, over-see, over-feel things and as an eavesdropper, she could use the language she heard but was unable to find her own.

In hindsight, I should have observed the grinding speed at which her mind was proliferating images. Instead of which I was collaborating with it: "It feels as if some virus has mutated inside you." I could have said: "It feels frightening to have such strange things going on inside."

Unlike Alvarez's (2012, p. 62) patient who cannot use the conjunctives, Dina is trapped by an overused symbolic language, and the evocative use of the conjunctive camouflages the graininess of experiences. The false conjunctions lack the substitution that defines symbols, but are evacuated feelings, "kaleidoscope eyes", where the words in themselves do not "mean" but stick together to recreate an experience. Language as it is spoken by her and heard by me is already organised—it has a pre-existing grammar.

Perhaps the volume of communication is a better indicator of the "level of functioning" and hence of determining whether we make a "why because" interpretation or use the "psychoanalysis of description" (Alvarez, 2010, p. 863). Often, in primitive states, there are very few pauses that allow thinking to happen. This could be because there is an acceptance of substitution in symbols, but this part is unable to sustain any distinction between inside/outside, self/other, real/fantasised, and imbues the object with so much of its own parts that the representational function of language collapses; the representation becomes inseparably intertwined with the thing. With Dina, analogies acquire a life of their own. They start out as anchors and are held on to with ferocity, so the boat does not capsize.

If metaphors enable us to coalesce thoughts, the literal offers no such relief; it gives no corners to huddle in, staring back at us without consolation. A metaphor can be a refuge, and reassure the suffering, non-psychotic part with a (re)semblance of sanity. The primitive part kicks away the element of substitution by devouring the metaphoric and rendering it concrete. This then gets lodged in the mind adding to the dreadful, bizarre objects. In this world, the quotidian disintegrates and the debris floats alongside hostile internal objects forming a bizarre colony.

"I got late coming up because I am very bad with directions, I looked in my GPS. It kept sending me round and about. Finally I stopped and asked this car cleaner to help me find your house. I said I am not going to lie, I am not from these parts. I am from outside." I felt an eerie tingle at her losing her way after all these years.

She felt like an outsider to the world of reality. Every time she encountered reality, she feels the sense of having seen a ghost. The object in whom she has placed a part of herself then stands outside of her, deriding her sense of control over it: "The empty glass taunts me." I have learned with her that verbalising the experience is more helpful than interpreting the content. This gives priority to the loneliness of the bizarre experience. And for this, I must shake off the dread that engulfs me.

Pseudo-containers

If the primitive part learns the idioms of speech and replicates it to mask incoherence, then pseudo-containers promise to explain and give coherence to the experience of psychosis. Primal scenes are an instance of such pseudo-containment. There would be a ghostly shudder in Dina's haunted face, the images of long, hot afternoons with mother whispering secrets about father, grandmother's strangeness, "father's perverse acts in the woods behind …" Her paintings were haunted by a sense of the secrets withheld. But recently she wondered if she "manufactured these memories".

I would feel something uncanny, which perhaps came from the violence of her being forever refused entry into mother's mind, left to cope with too many unbearable sensations and feelings, all of which take on the shape of cryptic hieroglyphs.

The pursuit of a secret felt like a trail that kept her in a zone without a complete outbreak of psychosis. In Dina's case, the trail would lead not to knowledge but frustration. The terrified mind tries desperately to assuage these fears and searches for potent ideas that can carry the terrors of internal glaring objects. The perverse primal scene has the capacity to provide this: "At night I always lay frightened of the noises that would come from their bedroom." Perverse secrets allow her to match the bizarreness of the inside or a heavy enough peg to hang her terrors onto.

I am reminded of Amir (2010) writing of the child joining in with mother through a psychotic discourse that is founded on a denial of separateness, suggesting that this comes from an incestuous wish to be one with mother (p. 37). Certainly a denial of separateness alleviates the fear of being left alone with psychosis. I am moved when Dina says: "Sometimes I wish someone would tell me she is not my mother. That would be a relief." With Dina, my collusion sustains the illusion that we are indistinct from each other. The most potent force is a kind of suction which pulls me into protecting her from the knowledge of separateness and thus of aloneness. The adhesive response in me was perhaps me stretching myself to form a second skin for her.

The writing of her case became a symptom of this adhesiveness as pronouns would get enmeshed. It was hard to see which of us was speaking. It is essential for me to separate myself from her internal objects to free her from someone who is blocking her entry (mother) or pouring dreadful contents into her (grandmother). In order to do this I needed to separate her words from her feelings, but more importantly her from me. This was not a "seduction" in the sense of her "leading me astray", but rather her touching upon something in me that made us fuse. It felt as if she sensed potential spaces in me that also wanted to be sought out.

Dreaming in the here and now

Over time, I found that tracking Dina's changing responses through the session was helpful. For instance at the beginning of the session she brought in an ominous "dream" of a bird sitting on her chest (she finds birds very sinister), and we arrived at how the bird could be me watching her "eagle-eyed" to ensure she does not slip away. But as the session moved on, the mood changes the valence of the bird.

I said: "I see how the image of a bird is not so terrifying when we look at it together." She smiles.

After this she mentioned a dream about father that had a new dimension of tenderness. I observed this new "character in the field" (Ferro, 1999). She goes on to tell me how in fact father was kind to her that morning. I said: "Perhaps sometimes you have to be able to dream of something before you can receive it. Like a camera needs the right light to record the image." Her eyes moisten. Here I listened and spoke in the transference but not wishing to overwhelm her, did not allude to the here and now by avoiding direct pronouns "I" and "you" (Bergstein, personal communication, 2017).

I find myself using dreams as props to wade through different states of mind in the here and now. Dina continues to teach me how to use them as a way of navigating the session; so rather than a "meta-interpretation" once, I learn to revisit images through different moments in the session. It helps her to experience the possibility of change in the "furniture of dreams" (Bion, 1957, p. 268).

Her over-stimulated mind, unable to contain its overflow, finds an entry into mine; as if she senses both my own dissociated mind and my welcoming of hers. Somewhat reminiscent of Bromberg (1998), there is an odd feeling of peace between us when I am attuned to her dissociated state. The feeling I have is of spaces opening in myself. The uncanny feeling of being "one with her" is when in one of her dreams she dreams of something intensely sad in my life which she could not have known of. It is when I speak from this place that I find her at peace, her body relaxing and I can say: "You feel very in tune with me." The adhesiveness I spoke of at the beginning appears to make sense. Looking back, I think my being unable to separate myself from her allowed me to get in tune with her, after which I could begin to observe her from a distance. So even though I "colluded", it feels like it helped to assuage the intense loneliness of residing with objects who did not have room for this oversensitive baby.

Recently she said, "Now somehow I can imagine that you have another life besides this …".

Rehana

Rehana (who we will meet again in Chapter 7) believed she was god, not godlike; every collision with reality shatters. She had no memories and only felt vitriolic hatred. She regularly cut herself through the first two years of our work. The predominant sense I would have is of someone who experienced the expulsion from the womb as an unpardonable betrayal. As if, by comparison to the wondrous womb, life felt "too much" and the contrast between the womb and outside was itself felt as a storm. So birth had felt like being left to die, a mismatch between an overwhelming baby and an overwhelmed mother. The thinness of internal objects makes for raging storms in a barren desert.

Manic see-saw

There are small moments of "rest" but if I was not wary, the compulsively manic part swoops down and hijacks such moments. She savoured words that felt refreshing but they also get used as crutches she held onto, so she did not dissipate. Initially she would always tell me that I "vaporised" over the gaps. This was followed by a phase when she would scribble things in her notebook as we spoke, as if she had some vestigial hope of keeping me. She talked about one of the women she dated: "I can't be with her. I have to hide how much I don't want her." I felt I was being pared down, as if I were the sum of my words, while my words were being used autistically—to hold something concrete as she felt herself vaporise. With sensuous delight she repeated some phrase that caught her fancy, like the word "ordinary" to adhesively stick to. She would then use words as things to stave off being blown away, for otherwise her thoughts would whiz about as attacking objects. Manic glee swooped down on such an autistic object, hoping words could substitute for life. Mostly she scorns life, shreds memory, refutes causation, and swerves dizzyingly from mania to depression, leaving me riveted by this spectacular dismissal of life. Life is devalued as the refuge of the mediocre; while death is heroic. Cutting seems like desperate bids to experience something in lieu of feelings which are inaccessible.

Countertransference

Curiously I would feel an intense rush of tender affection even as she'd repeatedly tell me how I was just a shadow. Perhaps she needed to arouse this feeling in me, an intense rush of love that can swallow and place her back in the foetal waters. This appears to be an urgent need. She says it is like a bodily need: "I want to dissolve inside." Her body language, of a hapless, disoriented infant is used to seduce me into re-opening the birth canal and letting her back in, to undo the "caesura of birth" (Freud, 1926d, p. 137).

All reminders of reality sound like death knells. She often chants hypnotically: "I am sorry, sorry …" As if pleading to be let in, back into the womb.

In Rehana's case, language is appropriated by the primitive desires to provide a shape and give form to this inchoate self. This need not be synonymous with a death wish per se. In this sense, death itself represents the limits of language. And in its turn this leads us back to a thin internal object who cannot take in terrifying projections because of her own terrors.

Now in the fourth year of our work she has brought me to a barren desert. Having broken up with her girlfriend she tells me how she feels "no sadness, I care for nobody and nothing. I have no feelings. It's a relief I no longer need to pretend I care. I have always known I had a secret. I realise that I have been feigning normalcy so nobody finds that out. Truth is I don't fucking care about anyone: you, parents, lovers, men, women. I just pretend. I would write down notes here but outside they made no sense. You and I created stories about the beauty of ordinariness—a good story."

Finding myself quite shaken, I try to discourage my desire to contradict her. Instead I let myself be moved by the landscape of an uninhabited desert where she has had to raise storms in order to "feel" experiences. I had mentioned how ordinariness was embarrassing for her. This seemed to resonate. She had whispered the word caressingly in soft undertones to herself, as she tends to in such moments. But slowly ordinariness took on an "Aphroditean" (a character she identifies with) dimension. For her, ideas took the place of feelings. I have to stay here in the desert. The barrenness of evacuated objects feels very hard to bear, and she has had to create storms all her life. Her relief is palpable when I relax to explore the desert.

I: You have nothing to say to me and no desire to come sometimes.
She: It's true. Sometimes I feel nothing, I don't want to talk, sometimes I feel curious about what I will say, sometimes I feel fatigued and hopeless and I feel you really don't get it …
I: You are surprised that your feelings about coming to me change all the time.
She: I felt our connection has been broken for a while now.
I: Did you feel I was not there?
She: About 75% there … I wondered if I wasn't being able to communicate. Then I felt angry, whatever …

I recall being preoccupied at the time she felt our disconnection, and I realise how attuned she was to my absence, and how she could sense even a flicker of tuning out. She cannot refind these vaporised objects.

A few sessions later she tells me she noticed her father was ageing and how it "hurt". For the first time she was moved to gift something to her father. It also felt like the gift was born from a sadness that she could bear, rather than run away from. It was revelatory for her to realise that feelings were different from ideas, that they were not inherently inconstant and "spontaneous".

Observing the mechanisms of thinking has had a containing effect.

For instance she talks of a sudden outburst of hate and an incident that does not "warrant this rage". She says it has been difficult for her not to speak about it, as it is someone else's secret. I see her struggling to accommodate it. Geographically there is no storage area inside the head.

"You feel like you have swallowed without biting, masticating." Interventions like this give shape to an apparatus that is yet only erratically present. My despondency helps me connect to a very thin internal object that gives up easily on a distressed child.

Recently when she went on a new date she said that there was no "profound connection". She worries about our connection. Perhaps she fears I will have no role to play when she can think her own thoughts.

She acquiesced. "Yes I do wonder about us. It has changed—it was more dense earlier and it's thinner now. Now I tell you more about ordinary things I didn't dare to. I come to things myself now." She is afraid of discarding me. But every step forward is fraught with dangers of flight into grandiosity.

Being extremely sensitive to language, she can feel gathered together by words if they ring true, but on the flip side, she disperses when they sound jaded. I found that happened recently and I was feeling her withdrawal from me. And I said, "When I carry a memory from an older state, it feels there's nothing holding you in place." Klein writes, "I would also say that the early ego lacks cohesiveness and that a tendency towards integration alternates with a tendency towards disintegration, a falling into bits" (1946, p. 100).

I am able to bring her back now that I address the experience of getting dispersed and not the mechanism of why it happens. I say that she feels herself falling off the map, unable to locate herself because of a "moveable", easily dispersed self and how she needs me to move along with that. Sometimes a word comes to our rescue, when I have been really pushed into finding the aptly contoured shell to hold her in that moment. And if I am able to find such a word, say "thin", she will take it with so much joy and repeat it for weeks now and then, as if she has discovered a depth to a word that felt shallow. I find myself always sharing this delight.

Mohan

Mohan, a thirty-five-year-old translator, comes with panic and a history of self-harming. He is rigidly sealed. In an early session we associate with the Tin Man. He appears like a clockwork toy with awkward, robotic gestures. His tone doesn't waver and he speaks in monotonous spurts. It has been two years now and though he does not experience the same panic, the sessions are wordy and affectless. Frustrated by our conversations, he has a strong experience of boredom. It is this boredom that has driven him to cut himself, and now to analysis.

Psychic disguises

Huddled rather than scattered, he defeats language in his own way, by getting under my skin and speaking from inside my head, rather than his own. The sessions feel correctly analytic—fees, punctuality, "transference" dreams—everything seems "perfect", but sterile.

Initially he brought dreams full of "psychoanalytic" material: Hitchcock-type images with dead bodies, pools, and staircases. I fell into "unmasking" these images. The fact is that he could find the most evocative lines of poetry that pulled me into a blinding collusion. But it began to feel "too pat"; as if we were avoiding real contact. My interpretations were not necessarily incorrect but too distant, arrived at intellectually. Joseph (1985) writes,

> … having heard certain of my interpretations and their meaning correctly, he used the words and thoughts not to think with, but unconsciously to act with, to get into and try to involve me in this activity, spinning words but not really communicating with them. (p. 452)

This then became one more weapon in his armoury.

He would talk about panic in a voice hollowed of emotions: "Something is stopping me. There is a frenzy somewhere …"

Most communication is in the passive voice and even if it is not, as in "bring today to you panic that belongs nowhere", the doer/done-to distinction seems missing; the language would be highly literary but emotionally remote: "Virgil to my Dante, Prospero to Ariel." I would try to tease out meaning from these allusions: "So am I leading you out of blindness? Is this a safe conduit out of the storm?"

I observed the weaving of poetry: "Something felt amiss—as if while we both wrote poetry together, the pain stayed untouched." He nods. This compliance continues to be paralysing: "Yes there is something that stops me. It debars me from thinking. Starts from a point here (pinches his fore-arm) … strikes a note, changes music … something ingrown …"

Speech

Mohan's voice is stripped of urgency, the syntax is passive, and personal pronouns are inaudible: "desire chooses an object … that has nothing to offer and gets nourished". Sentences are often dispersed with distant pronouns: "It is as if somebody somewhere will not be able to tolerate it." The syntax is so convoluted that if there was any meaning, it is gnarled out of shape: circular rather than linear.

He: "Am I oppressed because of something that oppresses me or because I think I must be oppressed? Is it the idea of oppression that oppresses me?" I now resist being sucked into wordplay by observing the distance between us.

He also often uses antitheses like duty and dread, reassuring and alien. But more than the paradoxical nature of truth itself, it feels like miming the rhythm of thinking. Paradoxes represent the unresolvably contrary nature of emotions, but become handmaidens of his fortress against his truth. They are pseudo-paradoxes that resemble emotional conundrums, but are in fact more like equivocations that capture his liminal position in life; akin to Steiner's "psychic retreats", Mohan lives on the fence between psychic life and death.

Negatives proliferate: "Can't just say I don't care about this feeling that I can't walk away from. Can't tell you what I am feeling, don't know how to break down. Can't drop it or myself." These grind away at any possibility of meaning. It feels as if we are in the presence of a negating object. I am reminded of a mother too depressed to bear her baby's alive-ness. And so when he turns to me, he experiences a void. As if he sensed I was not editing the story he wrote for me, but something tangential, he said: "I am bored of myself."

Ventriloquism

I had this slightly eerie sense that he reads what he imagines I read, to avoid contact with himself and then finds the sessions boring.

"The problem," he said, "is that I can become a part of someone else's head, so I never know who I am or what it is that I am feeling." He talks of his one-sided "frenzied love affairs" which have an entirely predictable pattern, and cloning seems to be the only paradigm as all "affairs" have an identical trajectory.

I sense precociousness, as if he had experienced things before his time. It turned out he was a premature baby. An avalanche of images of eggs, leaking, the unformed, follows; gratifying, but only in the moment. Speaking to him is like giving him a cue which his overdeveloped intelligence incorporates into his psychic vocabulary and which mimes life. This is, then, a premature patient. A person yet unable to suffer the pain of analysis, but who hopes to bypass it through a learned language. There seems to be a puppet who is saying someone else's words: ventriloquising rather than talking.

His survival instincts are extremely strong and pitted against life with all its vagaries. As he says, "I see people relax and I copy them."

He has turned things on their head and made a virtue of his terribly desolate world, but by cocking a snook at life. When we talk about this he agrees: "Photographs are better than life, free of ups and downs, while life is uncanny, unreliable." He refers to Hitchcock's *Psycho* as his model of love: an object he can kill, stuff and then ventriloquise rather than talk to. This is an accurate description of what he attempts with me in the sessions, by draining my words of life, by making our encounter into a meaningless ritual. But pointing this out makes him more supercilious with me. "It is too difficult to take the risk of actually hearing me ..." is perhaps better.

In this landscape of rituals, feelings do not "surge", there is no authentic feeling and empathy feels manufactured. There is a flatness to this robotic world, where simulated cars and phantom lovers substitute for real ones. These tether him and he knows no other anchor. He says: "I will never bring myself to the black hole and what saves me from that is the sense of self I have built. I don't really believe you have helped me. I have done everything." But the loneliness and sheer boredom of living inside an autistic shell would drive him to seek painful and dangerous sensations—to smoke, drink without restraint—to alleviate the numbness. Sensations become substitutes for feelings. The panic is threatening to go and this bothers him. As Tustin (1991) observes about autistic states "in which the symptoms may act as bodily containers or a second skin" (p. 587), the panic was like his "second skin".

He comes punctiliously, but ritualistically, speaking in rehearsed tongues, mimicking the language of psychoanalysis. Every session demands a newness that surprises him and prevents him from miming. His is not language used either to communicate or evacuate, but to mimic other voices, to camouflage the death-in-life; ventriloquism as a form of omnipotent control. As his words fail to rouse me from my dummy state, I imagine the hands that held him felt wooden, perfect but mechanised, and a robotic internal object that can only be echoed.

Pseudo-transference dreams

Initially he brings dreams about me repeatedly—missing sessions, dreaming of me dressed in his grandmother's saris, forgetting sessions, about lying on my "chest", which to me sound like the "dried fruit" he eats, stripped of comfort, of life. There's a baby I am holding in my arms. The next session he brings a dream in which a child has died and he says in falsetto: "Oh no, I killed the baby." I feel an agonising boredom at the mechanical interpretations that rush in to my head. I could speak of the analytic baby being killed. Dreams often become a substitute for, rather than a means of real communication. Many hours have been spent "decoding". I might have said how the dream reassured him that he was untouched by feelings. His disdain for life feels impenetrable. I observe that he cared a lot about preserving himself. He was jolted into a silence. What stares at me is that he is as helpless as I am because of having over-developed his capacity to get under the skin of others. "If you told me how to feel, I would. I am always gauging how to feel." I imagine a womb impatient to be rid of the foetus.

Mohan's disconnection with the world does not engender dread (Dina) or panic (Rehana). It feels barren like a long trudge in a desert. Languages are learned to mimic relationships, and obfuscate communication. Psycho-analysis is one such language he seeks to learn. He topples, but regains his balance, adding that to his array of defences. New idioms will be learned and incorporated as a tic; no longer useful. I have to keep waiting—perhaps be an incubator—and find new languages to surprise him with.

On technique

With Dina I realise how the quantum of material was more telling than the content because interpreting the content encouraged a deluge of chaos. I distance myself from the content and observe the fluctuations of mood and tone in the session. Rather than make an abiding interpretation of the dream, it helps to look at the changing valence of the symbols during the course of the session: "Look how the bird is not so frightening now." Dina responds well to my observing her infantile states without condescension: "Every time I speak, I am reminded of how a baby tests a morsel in its mouth, just in case a small bit is unmashed." A similar intervention does not work well with Mohan who adeptly picks up on "infantile states" and incorporates them in his parodic armoury.

But both show me that prearranged narratives, including psychoanalytic ones, obstruct the forging of a meaningful link. The story about the dreadful primal noises from the parents' room, while not necessarily untrue, is more revealing of the need for a metaphor that encapsulates a state of mind. Metaphors and dreams fail to give the space to exhale when you pause and say "it is as if".

Common to all three is the abundance of the "perverse" as an alibi for disorder. Popular culture (movies, sitcoms) encourages this facile cause-and-effect narrative. Perversions often indicate a furious search of the psyche to find a shell wherein it can nestle safely. With Rehana, what often helps her feel consolidated is an acknowledgement: "You are unable to arrange your thoughts." Also to point out how she drains words of feelings. To unobtrusively break down the components of thinking enables her to rearrange her haphazard (pulverised with cruelty) internal objects.

"You are unable to digest what has happened because you could not do this alone." I am learning to speak of "ideas" that blind like Aladdin's cave. She has a dream where her headphones have been smashed and she has been carried away by a secret society. It seems like the secret (grandiose) part is hijacking the sane part. This happens a lot; she speaks mostly as if she has "turned over a new leaf". I find it helpful to observe changes so as not to crush hope, while I might say how impatient she is to be well, which forewarns a sudden flight into the manic. I might not always interpret how she wants me to believe she is fine now. Through her dreams she seems to demand from me how improved she is and not remain in this position of dependency which makes her subservient.

Likewise, Mohan's saying, "I am always excited by the woman's presence in a man's life, that is when desire grips," has an un-refreshing tonality. Usually I let the tiredness simmer for a bit and might say: "You need to keep this 'arranged desire' intact—its circularity is reassuring," and he might respond: "Yes it is like a scaffold." My interpretations are responses to the tone or the syntax: "You prefer winding roads to straight ones." His responses have the air of non sequiturs: "I resist feeding." I try not to respond to the parts that sound rehearsed, instead of which I might say: "Your communication seems to be to repel affection." He always assents to indicting comments: "People are stupid." This impulse to invite harsh comments succeeds. Then I find his old arrogance replaced by a meeker stance: "I don't like to take up space in the world." I observe the change of tone and how he must fear having lost me by repeatedly devaluing me. That he is suddenly scared. Observing tonal shifts through the session seems to make this space and our relationship more real than "hallucinatory". As also my tone which I use both to startle and soothe. When he begins to drone, I try to surprise him by saying something quite concrete in a louder voice than usual: "Oh, so you take the Metro to come here!" Such moments force him to see me as a real person which he finds very discomfiting.

With Mohan I would wait for moments when he could be ambushed by his own wish to live (a wish he disavows), or for any unguarded moment where I could "surprise" him. When he speaks of "replaying scenes of abandonment" in his head, I do not wheel back into what works like a trap, but say: "You are desperate to feel something." He evades through circuitousness. Then I step on the gas: "I feel like you need me to keep throwing the ball to feel my presence, but you want it to bounce back, not catch it. It is important that I keep throwing it though."

He: "When you don't speak my eyes have nothing to focus on, it feels all blurry. Like driving through a foggy window."

We are silent as I feel his blurriness. I feel rewarded when he says, "These days I get the feeling that light comes out of black holes."

Conclusion

This is a chapter about the nature of language in analysis and how reliance on verbal language may obscure rather than clarify. I have looked at three patients and their idiosyncratic use of language which "made me" stray away from what was actually going on.

Retrospectively I see my straying away as a collusion which came from a shared and perhaps an adhesive love for words. I began writing this with the idea of psychic disguises that "hoodwink" and even "seduce" the analyst, but came to see this in more bipersonal terms where I was not being led astray but where shared blind spots flourished in camouflaged language.

I have mostly retained a focus on how this shared language obtruded on the analytic process, creating a collusion between the unmentalized parts of both patient and analyst. The unbearability of emotional truth which forms the primitive core may deploy language to serve in its army, nevertheless it is the latter and not the former that I focus on. Or as Eliot would say, "Go, go, go, said the bird: human kind/Cannot bear very much reality" ("Four Quartets", 1935, in 1962, p. 190). What cannot be borne by both patient and analyst may become "bastions", then organise pseudo-thoughts which gang up to fortify the illness (Baranger & Baranger, 2008). The kaleidoscopic internal world is hidden with a surfeit of intellectual skills that are adhesively acquired. These defences keep many patients on the verge of psychosis, without allowing a descent into unravelling terrors that emotional experiences represent. The use of language helps keep at bay such terrors through sticking to the surface of words. The patients discussed speak of an indifference to life, but death may represent the limits of language and hence the unthinkable. Primitive mechanisms often seem to abjure life in order to stave off death and ensure survival.

Mohan once said: "I feel like a kitten that has gone up a tree and is howling because it's stuck." I took this to mean that while he has come for the analysis, he doesn't know how to go through with it without the pain involved. But I feel like the cat too. So how do I go through with what was embarked upon—given the prison-house of a "learned" language? The path to the unconscious may be strewn by false clues embedded in the matrix of language and collusions such as these perhaps attempt to obfuscate our own terror of madness. It is the idiosyncratic grammar that our patients use that often brings us closer to their states of mind. "There is not a conjunction or a preposition, and hardly an adverbial phrase, syntactic form, or inflection of voice in human speech, that does not express some shading or other which we at some moment actually feel to exist ..." (Ogden, 1997, p. 16, quoting William James). I have given instances of when I could have observed how "thoughts were getting ahead of themselves, pushing each other, toppling each other down" (Alvarez, 2010, p. 866), but failed to separate myself from the forceful collusion.

When I say "collusion", I mean unconscious processes of participation, which while inevitable are inherently neither desirable nor recommended. I have rethought this chapter from a more bipersonal point of view, where perhaps the patient senses or touches upon something in the analyst and they move towards a space that is shared and unexplored. Dissociation may enable this and sometimes this may give shape to an unformulated experience. Mostly it goes unnoticed, but occasionally we catch it and retrospectively give meaning to what may have been going on.

Some of them, it may be argued, served a purpose. Each collusion was different: Dina's fragments seemed to be waiting to be cohered through attunement. With Rehana, it was sharing her joy in discovering interesting depths in ordinary words. With Mohan's mimicry, my collusion was adhesive, and only rigidified the sealed boundaries. Each of them invited me to play a part in a familiar orchestra, handing me an instrument they felt I could play. And I did. Some of it helped for a bit, but much of it just happened and this chapter is about giving meaning to what happened retrospectively. My own dissociation may have enabled this and sometimes may have given shape to a yet inchoate experience. This chapter attempts to capture both the experience of collusion and the realisation of it later. It also moves from the idea of being seduced to having colluded. The writing of this attempts to capture this rhythm of the work through a "thick description" so that the reading allows a feel of the sessions.

CHAPTER 2

Vocabulary and syntax

Autonomy: casting a spell

"My dear Eliot, I am v. glad to have 'The Wasteland'," George Faber wrote. He goes on to wonder if he is "specially stupid. Is it that you are using a language of which I have learnt only the vocabulary but not the syntax?" (May 28, 1925).

Taking off from Faber's scribble here, this chapter looks at the caesura between the vocabulary of psychoanalytic ideas and the syntax used in working with and writing about them. It is argued that often our work and thinking get shaped by a developmental syntax. Some of this is congruent with the notion of autonomy that is briefly considered in the first part of this chapter. We look at a few instances where the analytic project appears as aiding the path towards man's quest for autonomy over his neurosis, his fractured being, and the idea of a repressed ego. The psychoanalytic project also happens to coincide historically with the nineteenth-century novel and in particular, the narrative of coming of age, the *Bildungsroman* (*Bildung* = education, *Roman* = novel).

Perhaps the grammar of development with its implicit assumption of autonomy is inevitable, but it does seem to force a sort of foreclosure

(premature exclusion) that goes against the messiness of the unconscious. It also feels collusive in terms of psychoanalytic omnipotence
and mastery. However, the *Bildungsroman* has its moments of rupture,
just as Freud does. These anticipate the fragmentary narratives that
we have come to call Modernist. Bion restores Freud's intimations of
a spectral unconscious—the vast unknowable area which is right there
throbbing at the very centre of psychoanalysis. Doing away with linearity and sequentiality—without "memory and desire" (Bion, 1967; Eliot,
1922) is just one such radical departure from older syntax.

At the end we will look at an alternative syntax that abjures the psychic momentum of such teleological syntax. Bion (1970) describes the
role of attention in psychoanalysis. The analyst is "arrested" by some
experience and then wants to draw the attention of the analysand. In
order to draw his attention, the analyst

> must employ the Language of Achievement. That is to say, he
> must employ methods which have the counterpart of durability
> or extension in a domain where there is no time or space as those
> terms are used in the world of sense. (p. 2)

This is the language that coincides with myths, dreaming, and paradoxes. But in speaking of it, it changes into the Language of Substitution.
This is a paradox that we can try to bear, or irritably resolve. Writing
about our work with patients often involves navigating between these
two languages.

This chapter will trace some thinkers who follow, and those who
move away from autonomy as telos. Klein and the idea of internal objects
and splitting mechanisms muddy the waters of autonomy. However, the
writing often remains embedded in the developmental syntax. We will
look at Bion who radically departs from the language of both autonomy
and development, and who breaks away at the syntactic filiation.

Meltzer (Meltzer et al., 1986) traces a line of thinking from Langer,
Wittgenstein, Cassirer, and Chomsky, where language came to be
thought of as two-tiered, as having "a primitive song-and-dance level
(the most primitive form of symbol-formation) for the purpose of communication of emotional states of mind by means of the non-patholog-
ical use of the mechanism of projective identification", and upon this

"deep grammar", denotative language with its lexical level, is superimposed (p. 181). Psychoanalysis is concerned with finding its way to this "deep grammar".

Also, the discursive practice of psychoanalysis can be seen as an attempt to be autonomous both of science and rationality on the one hand, and of religious practices on the other hand. In this sense, psychoanalytic writing embodies a liminal position of a mind freed from allegiances, without "memory or desire". It seeks to be at once free from dogma, religion, and desires—both nostalgic and utopic. As Freud's unconscious exploded what remained of rationality and its assumptions, he deployed a method that used rationalising as its modus operandi. Here lies a caesura. Meltzer (Meltzer et al., 1986) neatly sums it up:

> The history of speculation about the nature of the therapeutic function of analysis has, from Freud onwards, been divided between opinions in favour of the corrective emotional experience and development of insight. "Remembering, Repeating, and Working Through" (… 1914g) tells the one story, while "Analysis, Terminable and Interminable" (1937c) tells the other. (p. 74)

The former gives a linear structure, while the latter does not.

The "working through" model is compatible with a classic "interpretation"—arguably an instance of using the master's tools to dismantle the master's shed. Early on Freud (1900a) seems to say, we will try to "give meaning" (*Deutung*) to what has appeared hitherto incomprehensible. This striving to give meaning to something that appears quite incomprehensible may be read as an attempt to master an incomprehensible world and thereby make man autonomous in his relationship to the world. The *OED* defines the word autonomy as freedom to govern oneself—a body, biological or political, that is governed by its own laws. Kant speaks of it as an attempt to function "ethically without coercion". His idea of autonomy is one where "there are … no considerations of pleasure or pain influencing the will" (quoted by Coleridge, 1817 in *OED*, 2009).

How can psychoanalysis, which imagines the psyche to be split and moreover governed by the unconscious which is unknowable, ever conceive of "autonomy" without diluting its fundamentals? And given

Freud's own residence in the liminal unconscious seeking both mastery and death, how do we think of the relationship to autonomy?

In fact Western thought from the time of Aristotle has one or another notion of autonomy. To what extent are we autonomous when we do good? Are we doing good because we want to or because we are afraid of doing bad? Augustinian thought would question if good was God's will or our own. Rousseau might have encouraged passion and freedom to be who we are inclined to be. On the other hand, Strenger (1989) writes,

> Kant is profoundly suspicious of human nature to the extent that it is not governed by reason …. The romantic and classic vision[s] in the 18th and 19th centuries have one value in common: that of autonomy … Hegel … sees autonomy in the individual's rec- ognition that he is but one aspect of the general structure of reality and the submission to the laws of the whole. As opposed to that, Kierkegaard, one of the great figures of the romantic view, considers autonomy in the individual's ability to attain his own subjective truth … (pp. 595–596)

So even as both endorse autonomy, they are at odds. We can see both strains in Freud and in psychoanalytic narratives in general.

The legacy of this idea of autonomy is bequeathed to psychoanalysis. It is an important concept in Freud, Klein, and in developmental psy- chology. The romantic notion is most obvious in Laing, Winnicott, Bion, and Meltzer. Even as perhaps each of them brings different strands of Romanticism, they de-emphasise the normative streak within the body of psychoanalysis. Freud imagines the psyche as a battleground between the superego (which resembles Kant's Categorical Imperative) and the id (note the Romantic idea of subjectivity as associated with freedom and hope).

Freud imagines the baby bursting with heady infantile omnipotence, seeking to establish mastery over the world. This illusion is fostered by his dyadic fusion, the experience of undifferentiated bliss with mother. Nevertheless, he has disappointments aplenty lying in store. Father and siblings will interrupt and destroy his illusions. Thereafter, he will strug- gle to master this unruly universe. He will be disillusioned, but he will not necessarily accept this.

In this narrative, it is possible to read all our struggles as emerging from our inability to renounce our omnipotence. Man struggles against his body and its ageing, against external reality, against the forces of the id that want to give in to each impulse, against the commands of the superego that seeks to subjugate his impulses, and against his wish not to change. The emphasis in different schools of psychoanalysis falls on the need to renounce—whether it is sexual desire for primary objects, or omnipotence. Thus the psychoanalytic narrative ineluctably moves towards development (whether realised or desired).

Freud's idea of autonomy would refer to the ego's autonomy over the id and the superego. The child as Freud conceives him, mostly, is struggling with both instinctual needs that seek gratification and super-ego commands that subjugate him and curtail his wishes. This Faustian man seeks autonomy from his id and superego in varying and different degrees. Ideally the ego would like to be "autonomous" of both tyrants. But this sad, forked creature is not master in his own house. When man is thus divided against himself, he may seek to be free but freedom from one tyrant may enslave him to another. In one reading, psychoanalysis may embody relief from this tyranny. The ego "enslav'd so many ways" (Marvell, 1681) is strengthened, through a "working through", giving "autonomy" to the ego. This would coincide with genitality in another paradigm. This also coincides with maturation processes and the idea of psychic development that is the basis for the *Bildungsroman*.

Freud (1914g) writes: "Not only some but all of what is essential from childhood has been retained in these [screen] memories. It is simply a question of knowing how to extract it out of them by analysis."

His tone is decisive here and this echoes the popular version of psy-choanalysis as archaeological excavation with a telos: of filling the gaps of knowledge. Knowledge can be retrieved and conflicts can be "worked through". This is also the logic of the psychoanalytic narrative looked at in some of the writers considered next. This idea of a developmen-tal narrative is everywhere in psychoanalysis—implicitly or explicitly. Heinz Hartmann (1894–1970), Anna Freud (1895–1982), Erik Erikson (1902–1994), and Margaret Mahler (1897–1985) are some of the more important figures who carried forward the legacy of the more positivist Freud with an emphasis on development phases and the ego's striving towards autonomy. So while one strand in Freud identifies man as a forked creature, he makes this bearer of the forked ego allegorically represent man's constant battle between his impulses and his dread of succumbing to them. This image of man as battling himself lifelong occupies much of Freud's writing. Some of his writings (1937c) embody the convoluted nature of such untrammelled faith in recovery.

But there are also periodic references to different stages of psychosexual development. This latter thread in Freud has often been used as a basis for more developmentally oriented psychologists and psychoanalysts. In this paradigm, we could argue that autonomy could be impeded by a fixation at the oral, anal, or phallic stages, while to somehow make one's way to genitality would imply greater autonomy. The structural model of the psyche that Freud proposed has mostly emphasised the unruliness of the unconscious, but ego psychology took the adaptive functions of the ego and worked towards ridding the psyche of conflict.

Anna Freud viewed Hartmann's hypotheses with suspicion initially but saw his work as continuing Freud's ideas on developmental stages. We see the similarity when for instance, she (1963) writes,

> To serve as the prototype for all others, there is one basic developmental line which has received attention from analysts from the beginning. This is the sequence which leads from the newborn's utter dependence on maternal care to the young adult's emotional and material self-reliance—a sequence for which the successive stages of libido development (oral, anal, phallic) merely form the inborn, maturational base. (pp. 246–247)

She then divides these phases as eventually paving the way to a final separation. This "genital triumph" could well be seen as one way in which autonomy was imagined.

Following Freud's somewhat sociological thread, Erikson (1946) describes the field of psychoanalysis as being first occupied with man's enslavement by id, followed by the autonomous ego and superego strivings. He locates archaic mechanisms as the chief forces that come in the way of the ego's autonomy. "For the individual's mastery over his neurosis begins where he is put in a position to accept the historical necessity which made him what he is" (Erikson, p. 394). Erikson seems to imply the need to master the archaic mechanisms. "Psychoanalysis came to emphasise the individual and regressive rather than the collective-supportive aspects of these statements. It was concerned with only half the story" (p. 379).

Erikson (1995) sees the formation of autonomy as negotiated through interpersonal relationships. The wish for autonomy conflicts with group regulation. Members of a family, for instance, regulate each other's need for autonomy. One way in which this is redressed is by finding areas outside a shared space where autonomy may be exercised. The child may turn to his own body or auto-erotic practices where he uses his own organs to control sadomasochistically the others who control him (p. 60). Interestingly, Bion will invert this completely by arguing that a regression into groups—family being one—is symptomatic of the archaic mechanisms. This view sees groups not as an external "roadblock" but a symptom of the primitive part of the psyche.

In the pregenital phase, Erikson locates the child who is faced with the capacity for autonomy. He imagines that the child who experiences, in this anal stage, an inner goodness, will arrive at autonomy through a basic trust in himself and his world. "Muscular maturation", Erikson notes, brings two capacities: "holding on and letting go" (p. 226). A failure in establishing trust would inhibit autonomy and anal musculature would be forever linked with shame and doubt (p. 74).

The emphasis in this writing is on the environmental failure in the child's life, the underlying impulse is corrective, even didactic, and the paradigm seems to be repression. We observe here Erikson's wish to "complete the story" of psychoanalysis, and the assumption in his narrative is the establishment of the goal of mastery, which is through the removal of obstacles on the path of ego autonomy. He studies "other" cultures and through these differences culls out the features that enable such a mastery. It seems implicit that mastery is desirable, attainable, and even essential to acquiring autonomy. And it also feels that psychoanalysis, by restricting itself to the individual and the regressed, seems to be telling an incomplete story.

Erikson here seems to hold cultural taboos as causal rather than symptomatic. He elaborates on Freud's (1916–17) ideas of developmental stages and regressions and fixations, but while the structure resembles Freud, the emphasis shifts from Freud's intrapsychic state to a more socially driven, normative register. It seems as if the underlying syntax is that human nature itself could be fixed, if we brought in elements from different cultural observations.

Cultural studies have inspired a whole line of thinking that sees autonomy as often shaped by cultural variations. What haunts most of this writing is that autonomy is the desired end product of a particular Euro-American tradition which has assumed a universalist dimension. This forms the flip side of positivistic thinking. The theme of cultural otherness is riven with difficulties and often assumes the very universalism it sets out to critique.

Mahler's emphasis returns to the psychic but a psyche shaped very much by the presence of the actual mother and the advent of physical and cognitive skills. For instance, she writes (1958) of how locomotion (and the acquisition of cognitive skills) paves the way for autonomy. Many toddlers delight in the ability to walk unassisted while others respond with greater clinginess to this new growth spurt. This "adverse response" (p. 15) seems to indicate a denial of separateness and perhaps a dread of what may follow.

The emphasis in these passages is on the child's rapidly changing capacities which mother needs to be sensitive to. Perhaps greet them with joy or welcome them; instead there may be a disturbance here. Mahler (1971) imagines the child in his first three years gradually separating from a symbiotic tie towards autonomy. The state of symbiotic closeness envelops the baby and creates the security essential for him to be able to separate and feel autonomous:

> Two characteristic patterns of behaviour—the shadowing of mother and the darting away from her with the expectation of being chased and swept into her arms—indicate the toddler's wish for reunion with the love object, and, side-by-side with this, also a fear of re-engulfment. One can continually observe the warding-off pattern against impingement upon the toddler's recently achieved autonomy. Moreover, the incipient fear of loss of love represents an element of the conflict on the way to internalisation. Some toddlers of rapprochement age already seem to be rather sensitive to disapproval. Autonomy is defended by the

"no" as well as by the increased aggression and negativism of the anal phase … In most mother–toddler pairs, these rapprochement conflicts, … do finally come to an end. This is helped by the developmental spurt of the conflict-free parts of the autonomous ego. (Hartmann, 1939, p. 411)

The normal child's early defensive struggle against interferences with his autonomy was, however, amply exemplified by Sammy. He valiantly struggled, from an early age, in fact, from the fifth month on and attempted to extricate himself from the smothering grip of his mother. (Ibid. p. 407)

Or

One cannot emphasise too strongly the importance of the optimal emotional availability of the mother during this subphase. (Ibid. p. 409)

This emphasis on the optimal distance remains through much of Mahler's (1974) rather astute observations of the child's response to mother: "We also observed in this early period of practicing that the 'would-be fledgling' likes to indulge in his budding relationship with the 'other-than-mother' world" (p. 300).

She writes:

… the optimal psychological distance in this early practicing subphase would seem to be one that allows the moving, exploring child freedom and opportunity for exploration at some physical distance from the mother. It should be noted, however, that during the entire practicing sub-phase the mother continues to be needed as a stable point, a "home base" to fulfill the need for "refueling" through physical contact … It is easy to observe how the wilting and fatigued infant almost immediately "perks up" following such contact; then he quickly goes on with his explorations, and once again becomes absorbed in his pleasure in functioning. (Ibid. p. 300)

Akhtar (2002) summarises pithily Mahler's (1975)

> ... description of the maternal resilience during the child's rap-
> prochement sub-phase touches upon this issue. The child's mad-
> deningly contradictory demands for closeness and distance,
> protection and freedom, and intimacy and autonomy are met
> by the mother with a non-retaliatory stance. Her containment of
> the aggression mobilised within her allows the child to gradually
> see her as neither engulfing nor abandoning, and him- or herself
> as neither a passive lap baby nor an omnipotent conqueror of
> the world. A deeper, more realistic view of mother is now inter-
> nalised. With this, external dependency upon her diminishes.
> The contradictory selfimages are also mended ... (p. 185)

While the relationship between saying no and establishing a sense of
autonomy is shrewdly observed and quite undeniable, there remains
through much of this writing a great emphasis on the "optimal", which
is more within the realm of the conscious, rather than unconscious,
and the underlying tone tends to get somewhat prescriptive, if not
moralising.

In this section, psychoanalysis remains tied to the centrality of repression. But repression does not have the same meaning it has in Freud.
It appears weakened by this understanding of autonomy. The inability
to "grant" it is a matter of some failure, rather than governed by the
unknown brute gods in the unconscious.

It follows that autonomy from id and superego necessitates the
strengthening of the ego. Most of the writing here, whether it is a focus
on defence mechanisms (Anna Freud), cultural taboos (Erikson), or
failure to allow individuation by the environment (Mahler), is addressing ways to strengthen the ego, reduce the conflict, and usher in greater
coherence and integration and thereby enable autonomy. There is an
optimism in this writing—its latent syntax is one of leading man towards
light through an engagement with darkness. This syntax embodies a
fantasy which Akhtar (1996) in another context calls "if only". (Mahler's
location of the ambivalence around autonomy overlaps with Tustin's
writing discussed later.)

Autonomy: breaking the spell

Meltzer (Meltzer et al., 1986) writes incisively about why the "field model" is more appropriate than the "phase model". He writes,

> Taking this panoramic view of personality functioning the question must arise, pertaining to the model of personality development, whether we are to follow the tradition in psychoanalysis and speak of phases (primary narcissism, symbiotic phase, autistic phase, etc.) or elect a field theory as our preferred mode of thought. Such a debate cannot aim at establishing the question of "correctness" since we are not dealing with an area in which causality is seen to operate, the field being infinite and essentially creative. (p. 14)

Benjamin (1990) writes,

> The telos of this process [separation–individuation] is the creation of psychic structure through internalisation of the object in the service of greater independence. As a result, separation–individuation theory focuses on the structural residue of the child's interaction with the mother as object; it leaves the aspects of engagement, connection and active assertion that occur with the mother as other in the unexamined background. (p. 35)

Perhaps what Benjamin feels is omitted in this account is the particularity of the connection, not a theoretical mother, but the specific dynamic between this mother and this baby.

Many rights activists also speak of autonomy in a different register. For instance, feminism, gay rights, and lesbian rights all claim rights of autonomy over the body. In Catholic Ireland, women's rights for abortion must be framed as a demand for autonomy. Judith Butler does not dispute this. But she speaks of the body as both intensely private as well as public. In the following passage she eloquently locates the denial of the not-me that shapes our relationship to our bodies over which we can only aspire to have autonomy:

The body implies mortality, vulnerability, agency: the skin and the flesh expose us to the gaze of others, but also to touch, and to violence, and bodies put us at risk of becoming the agency and instrument of all these as well. Although we struggle for rights over our own bodies, the very bodies for which we struggle are not quite ever only our own. The body has its invariably public dimension. Constituted as a social phenomenon in the public sphere, my body is and is not mine. Given over from the start to the world of others, it bears their imprint, is formed within the crucible of social life; only later, and with some uncertainty, do I lay claim to my body as my own, if, in fact, I ever do. (2003, pp. 14–15)

The experience of autonomy which is seen in the discourse of human rights and other freedom movements feels like it is obstructed by some external agency, but in the passage above, Butler nuances the binaries of public and private bodies by speaking of bodies that are inherently shaped by and carry other presences. It is a salutary reminder of how autonomy is not an individual's "choice" nor is it prohibited by others. In the next section, I will look at the *Bildungsroman* which corresponds to the unconscious structure we tend to adhere to in our writing. The two instances I have chosen retract from the realisation of such a trajectory.

Bildungsroman and the psychoanalytic narrative

A particular kind of story—the coming-of-age story or the *Bildungsroman*—thrived in the nineteenth century in the Western imagination. The peculiarity of the social context where there is a movement from the country to city corresponds with the structure of many such stories where the hero must leave home to forge a life in the bigger world. Like the epic hero, the hero in a *Bildungsroman* must have his own adventures, but there is more powerfully present the idea that the home is a dangerous place to linger in. That the primary attachments will always come in the way of growing up and moving on. The underlying narrative for which we can borrow Flaubert's term "sentimental education" serves as a kind of template for narrativising. There is in this form a faith in attaining a certain integration which is close to the idea of autonomy. This syntax is seen in case histories which often read like developmental narratives.

The nineteenth century is usually hailed as the age of the great realist novel. But its underside, the ghost story with its gothic tropes—spectres, doubles, ominous secrets—flourishes alongside this. Such figures as the double which function as floating signifiers are however insistently recursive. Perhaps the shadow always follows the body; Romanticism and the *Bildungsroman* find their dark double in the gothic, deriving as they both do from a reaction to Classicism.

However, the *Bildungsroman* also ruptures its own form. I locate a few disruptive moments where it turns upon itself as an anti-narrative. This is in order to highlight the gap between the interrogation of growth and the form that already exists that enforces a certain structure. The limits of such arrangements of grammar—be it syntax or form—may often force certain ways of looking and rigidify a particular vertex.

In this narrative form, there seems to be an underlying connection between separating from originary homes and autonomy. Much of this narrative emerges from this psychic ovule residing in the space between fusion and separation. In this sense we can see much of this genre anticipates Mahler's formulation of separation–individuation. I could easily have picked any Dickens or Austen or even George Eliot—but these broadly conform to the structure of maturation and emotional development. Instead we look at two instances where the trajectory is more obviously ruptured.

In D. H. Lawrence's *Bildungsroman, Sons and Lovers* (1948), Paul Morel has to kill his mother to wrench himself free, so tenaciously does she hold on to her life and to him. Paul attempts different kinds of relationships with women, but the looming maternal presence lures and forbids and both his relationships fail. In an intimate conversation with his mother, she tries to comfort him: "You haven't met the right woman." Paul is quick to respond: "And I never shall meet the right woman while you live" (p. 427). Suffocated by the impossibility of his forked desires, he nurses her devotedly, but in a chilling culmination he finally mixes morphine in her milk, in order to be able to survive.

In the final chapter, hauntingly called "The Derelict", Paul after his mother's death walks through the night, leaving behind his old mining town, into the "phosphorescence" of London that beckons with luminous uncertainty and a wistful sadness that both promises and does not. This violent rupture does not translate as a promising beginning. Paul seems haunted, derelict, inhabited by ghosts. The book shifts its vertex constantly from father to mother to son. This slippery, mobile, rhythmic shifting creates dark, brooding coal mines which are like foreboding presences. Paul tries to get away but is paralysed by the tenacity of the emotional force.

These are "failures" to mourn. Mourning would imply a separation and instead there is a melancholia (Bion might have thought of this as pain that cannot be suffered). Implicitly, the structure of a *Bildungsroman* demands the renouncing of a desire for merger with oedipal objects, a mourning, and then a capacity to withstand the aloneness and differences from the loved object, and an attempt to disentangle this psychic knot seems to propel this kind of narrative. This may take different forms—matricide as in *Sons and Lovers* (the internal killing of the engulfing object which is literally carried out by Paul) and incest (*Oedipus Rex*) are at least two such possibilities. The failure of the (oedipal) narrative here can be seen as embodying the movement from early ideas of autonomy to Freud's distance from this positivism and a movement towards the death drive discussed in the next section.

It is suggested that the "death drive" can be seen as representing the unthinkable—for Freud is flummoxed by the seeking of the unpleasurable. Unable to find an explanation for it, he postulates a dark double of the pleasure principle. We can see how the *Bildungsroman* often ends with the death of the heroine (Maggie Tulliver, Anna Karenina, Emma Bovary).

I will now turn to a relatively obscure little novel called *Summer* by Edith Wharton (1917). The heroine here is named Charity by her foster parents (self-aggrandisingly naming their act of benevolence) who live in an isolated village, North Dormer. Her estrangement from the foster father is made acute by the latter's importunate advances. Her aversion to this threatened incest and the hatred of her foster home propels her into the arms of a kindly stranger, and through him into exploring her mountain origins. This lover, Lucius Harney, encourages her to weave a romantic origin for herself, much after the fashion of a "family romance" but with a twist. He encourages in her a desire to find her biological parents as a more desirable alternative to her guardians.

This movement is a variant of Oedipus'—purportedly. The quest for true parents is however disappointing. Like most romances, this too emerges as both inevitable and doomed to failure. While she is still awaiting her lover's avowal and fending off the guardian, she finds herself pregnant, her lover betrays her by returning to his fiancée, the family romance proves squalid and depressing, and she has no money for an abortion. As these disasters close in on her, she finds Mr Royall, her foster father, coming to her rescue, willing to make reparation. This story closes the circuit, as Charity chooses incest over separation. Wharton's novel in question here ends with marriage, like *Jane Eyre* (1847) or any of Jane Austen's novels. Except it is to the "father" and while she carries an "illicit" child. The closing in of the novel, the movement back into the home makes circular what is usually a linear trajectory.

The ultimate goal of the woman's version of a *Bildungsroman* (which ends in either marriage or death) is formally realised, but in fact it is a dark travesty, a resolutely ambivalent end where both father and daughter are transformed, and the relationship which had been entirely transactional transforms through reparation into a redemptive love but is tainted by its incestuousness. In the way it is structured, *Summer* promises a movement away from the incestuous (foster) home but ends with an incestuous marriage. Read thus, this story flips over and becomes the dark underside of the kind of story it sets out to be, the repressed double of the story of growing up. It becomes the negative of the growth, an anti-*Bildungsroman* where linearity gives way to circularity and both the repressed and the protagonist return. If marriage is a transferring from primary objects to new objects, then this story reveals the sameness and repetition of the new object.

So in this rupturing of the form lies a caesura, which reveals the failure of development, linearity, causality, and growth. Binaries of separation–merger and exogamy–endogamy fold in on themselves. Genres cut away at themselves, revealing scepticism about their assumptions. *Oedipus Rex* may be the urtext of the *Bildungsroman* or the arch anti-*Bildungsroman*, or better still, the first failed *Bildungsroman*. The hero leaves home and has an adventure by protecting the imperilled kingdom and as a reward, marries the queen. Except that everything is moving in the negative direction. To use Bion's symbols it is -L and -K. It is like the dark twin of the classic epic. If psychoanalytic

aims intersect at moments with ideas of autonomy, growth, development, and mastery (like the *Bildungsroman*), the unconscious cuts away
at such notions. However, the form of psychoanalytic writing seems to
foreclose this messiness. What I have given instances here of are how
a failed *Bildungsroman* embodies this caesura—it is both striving for
autonomy and failing. Yet there is no alternative form available, much
like our clinical writing.

Freud's double, summoning ghosts, and the aesthetics of incertitude

In Freud we can see increasingly that the headiness of mastery takes a
back seat, giving way to alleys and tunnels leading to pain and loss. The
Freudian narrative gets punctuated by tidings of death and destruction.
Man will struggle to stay alive and sane, against his own will to die. He
is not at war with external reality or the law of the father, he is doomed
by his own pull towards homeostasis. This "striving for homeostasis"
is always going to be at war with the wish to conquer the universe. As
Freud's voice moves from Manichean to tragic (from the duality of the
instincts to a more resigned fatalism), the shadow idea of autonomy that
emerges in his earlier writing begins to fade away. For instance, in an
interesting passage (1920g) where he writes of repetition, he talks of it in
terms of mastery (which leads the way to autonomy) but he also speaks
of a "daemonic force" (death wish):

> The manifestations of a compulsion to repeat (which we have
> described as occurring in the early activities of infantile mental
> life as well as among the events of psycho-analytic treatment)
> exhibit to a high degree an instinctual character and, when they
> act in opposition to the pleasure principle, give the appearance
> of some "daemonic" force at work. In the case of children's play
> we seemed to see that children repeat unpleasurable experiences
> for the additional reason that they can master a powerful impres-
> sion far more thoroughly by being active than they could by
> merely experiencing it passively. Each fresh repetition seems to
> strengthen the mastery they are in search of. Nor can children
> have their pleasurable experiences repeated often enough, and

> they are inexorable in their insistence that the repetition shall be
> an identical one … (p. 34)

The "mastery" Freud refers to in the passage above seems to be over the possibility of change and therefore that of loss. Repetition is not about pleasure in any simple sense, because there is also a repetition of unpleasurable activities. Perhaps repetition gives the reassurance of predictability: this story is exactly the same, so is mother who reads it every night. There is no change and loss is denied momentarily, till the story ends, as it must. Thus mastery is sought—but over pain. Repetition may in this sense be seen as an undoing of painful sensations, thoughts, and feelings. This notion of mastery is different from the mastery that is linked in ego and developmental psychology as working towards autonomy. The latter is Lockean in its idea of moving towards a coherent self through self-realisation.

In a search for its own shape, the ego/self attempts to "free" itself from the earliest objects. This requires accepting change and loss which involves mourning one's loved objects, and accepting both our limitations in loving them and the changing nature of relationships. This impulse we see constitutes the spine of much traditional Western narrative, which holds that in order to grow psychically it is essential to relinquish omnipotent control over one's objects. The further difficulty with the idea of autonomy is in the way the Freudian ego is not imagined only as a structurally embattled entity (1933a):

> Hardly have we familiarised ourselves with the idea of a super-ego
> like this which enjoys a certain degree of autonomy, follows its own
> intentions and is independent of the ego for its supply of energy,
> than a clinical picture forces itself on our notice which throws a
> striking light on the severity of this agency and indeed its cru-
> elty, and on its changing relations to the ego. I am thinking of the
> condition of melancholia … is the way in which the super-ego—
> "conscience", you may call it, quietly—treats the ego. (p. 59)

The Freudian ego is not just a playground of drives but affectively an "accretion" of abandoned and lost love objects (p. 453) and what we mean when we speak of "our ghosts".

Identification with an object that is renounced or lost, as a substitute for that object—introjection of it into the ego—is indeed no longer a novelty to us. In "Mourning and Melancholia" Freud (1917e) wonders about the hypercritical voice of the melancholic and tries to resolve the question of why this is a response to object loss. In a moving passage quoted below he sees this as an incorporation of the abandoning object who now resides in the melancholic, as the latter is unable to let go of his object entirely:

> An object-choice, an attachment of the libido to a particular per-son, had at one time existed; then, owing to a real slight or disap-pointment coming from this loved person, the object-relationship was shattered. The result was not the normal one of a withdrawal of the libido from this object and a displacement of it on to a new one, but something different, for whose coming-about various condi-tions seem to be necessary. The object-cathexis proved to have little power of resistance and was brought to an end. But the free libido was not displaced on to another object; it was withdrawn into the ego. There, however, it was not employed in any unspeci-fied way, but served to establish an identification of the ego with the abandoned object. Thus the shadow of the object fell upon the ego, and the latter could henceforth be judged by a special agency, as though it were an object, the forsaken object. (pp. 247–248)

In the unquiet mind reside shadows, blurry presences of introjected and lost objects, which make the idea of being autonomous rather fuzzy. Does releasing the stranglehold of the harsh superego alone constitute autonomy? Can there be an autonomy from internal objects? Or do we mean the nature of internal objects changes? We may extend this to argue that the assertion of a separate mind is enabled by an internal world peopled by happy residents. Freud looks at the darker side of such presences in the mind. He feels the melancholic is crushed by his lost object's tyrannical voice. We see that the ideas of introjection and incor-poration complicate the question of an autonomous self.

The doubles in many gothic stories likewise take on a variety of functions—from being like a harsh superego in Dorian Gray's portrait to being a benign reassurance against dying as in "The Duchess at Prayer"

(Wharton, 1900) where the likeness or statue of the murdered duchess crouches in the garden as an emblem of resistance.

If we take such splitting as a fundamental psychoanalytic paradigm (and how it is extended by Klein and Bion), then we see the psyche pervaded by powerful and more disorganised dissidence. The psyche is imagined more like an anarchic state than one that is ordinarily conflicted.

So if one strand in Freud leads us towards a striving towards an autonomy, another accepts the impossibility of such a tangible goal, for the sheer unknowability of the unconscious. This latter voice questions ideas of mastery, integration, and autonomy. If we are in the thrall of a daemonic force (death instinct in particular or the unconscious in general), and if our psyche is forever dissonant, wherein lies autonomy and what would it be from? Also autonomy has an implicit linearity, which is belied by the haphazardness of the unconscious if not the circularity of repetition compulsion:

> Given the ordinary unbearableness of this complexity [of having a mind] … we regress in order to survive, but this retreat … has become an un-analysed convention, part of the religion of everyday life … To go forward in life, we go back … back to the places of the mother and father, where we can evoke these figures as inevitably comforting … (Bollas, 1992, p. 245)

We may say that *Oedipus Rex* is the prime instance of how the oedipal aim is messed up, and every change carries in it traces of sameness; that circularity and repetition are never fully exorcised. We may also therefore conclude that the unconscious is in principle a dissenter and a malcontent. In that sense it is independent of the demands for autonomy, linearity, progress, and so even as the analyst seeks to free the ego, it is found to be haunted in new ways. In fact there are in Freud spectres everywhere that haunt autonomy.

In transference, there is the meeting of the analyst's internal objects with those of the analysand's. The room is crowded with these ghosts. The interpretation becomes like a translation of this spectral encounter. No wonder we find ourselves reaching out to see who we have become in the moment, surprised by our own stranger-ness.

For Laplanche (1997), psychoanalysis is located in the enigmatic emotional encounter. The encounter at birth that the infant has is with the mother's unconscious/sexuality. But it is really enigma that is at the heart of the encounter. The baby is all too powerfully struck by this stormy encounter. He is instantly embarked on a mystifying journey of translating m/other's desires. This comes to shape his own unconscious/sexuality. Laplanche is putting us in touch with the idea of unknowability and the ineffable at the core of the unconscious.

In this elusive and ephemeral absent-presence is embedded the metaphysics of psychoanalysis. The notion of autonomy would be anchored in the rational exchange between two people who mean the same thing when they speak. Here psychoanalysis departs by becoming more of a ghost story than a realist narrative. It is again what Freud calls the "beam of intense darkness" that must be cast on the most obscure regions. It is dreams, slips, and the errata that Freud turns his gaze to. These residues of the mind point us towards fragments rather than coherence.

The shifting away from autonomy is evident in Klein. Kleinian and post-Kleinian ideas of primitive states and post-structuralist politics all offer a critique of the idea of the psyche/subject as a unified being—from very different, even antagonistic vertices. Klein (1946) writes of disintegration and splitting as inevitable and even essential primitive states which lead to integration, but the oscillation from one state to another is recognised as ongoing and unconscious.

The need to mourn and repair and feel pain and gratitude foreground the emotionality of the Freudian narrative. By slowly piecing together Freud's object traces, Klein builds an astonishing picture that replaces incest with omnipotence as the chief threat to the psyche. As she vividly paints the internal object world as intense, shifting, and fluid, this is a world always peopled by kaleidoscopic internal objects. So autonomy is not really the goal in the way it is for ego psychology.

Yet the writing remains embedded in a teleological narrative. This telos is located in her almost theological adherence to the capacity to mourn. Here is a concluding passage from her *Narrative of a Child Analysis* (1961):

> This situation altered as the analysis progressed. I have already
> said that his envy, jealousy, and greed, which in my view are

expressions of the death instinct, diminished because he became gradually able to face and integrate his destructive impulses. This was bound up with his capacity for love coming more fully into play, which made it possible for hate to be mitigated by love. As a result, greater tolerance towards other people as well as towards his own shortcomings developed. His sense of guilt, which had existed side by side with his persecutory anxieties, had diminished and this implied a greater capacity to make reparation. He had, in fact, become able to some extent to work through the depressive position.

Another sign of the increasing predominance of the life instinct, and with it of the capacity for love, was that he no longer felt impelled to turn away from destroyed objects but could experience compassion for them. ... This hopefulness, and his ability to maintain a good relation to the analyst as an internal and external object, in spite of resentment, feeling of loss, and great anxiety, confirm my view that as the result of his analysis the good internal object was much more securely established in Richard; and this greater inner security reflected the ascendancy of the life instinct. It is my impression that the changes produced by this incomplete analysis were to some extent lasting. (p. 465)

Implicit in this passage is a child as individual, moving towards desirable and somewhat tangible goals—hope, life, good relations, compassion. The notion of such an individual is one bequeathed to us by humanist ideas which is very much the inheritance of a certain Enlightenment vision. It can be very difficult not to want our patients to grow and yet abjure developmental models.

The idea of autonomy is very close to that of authenticity. The latter implies a lack of self-deception. The philosopher Heidegger "plays on the etymology of the German 'eigen' meaning to 'own' or 'one's own'. Hence to be authentic is to assume 'ownership' of oneself by taking responsibility for one's actions and states of being, as when owning one's feelings" (Skelton, 2016). Sartre (1943) speaks of "bad faith" when he describes not taking responsibility for one's choices. The key to finding authenticity lies in the ability to disengage from externally imposed notions of obligation and moribund ideas of duty. Yet it must be distinguished from the moral relativism as well as individualism, as it carries the weight of Kant's moral philosophy and a self-governance, rather than an abdication of morality. The internalisation of such a moral law is what seems to be at the heart of Kantian ethics.

Seen from the vertex of psychoanalysis, this sounds very much like Freud's superego (1930a):

> The commandment, "Love thy neighbour as thyself", is the strongest defence against human aggressiveness and an excellent example of the unpsychological [expectations] of the cultural super-ego. The commandment is impossible to fulfil; such an enormous inflation of love can only lower its value, not get rid of the difficulty. (p. 109)

Freud's dry-eyed unsentimentality here leaves no room for Augustine's dilemma about the possibility of intrinsic ethical codes. In the light of Freud, Kant's idea of self-imposed governance is autonomy but where the "shadow of the other" has fallen. The idea of authenticity takes centre stage especially within Existential writing and we see the vocabulary of true and false selves contributing richly towards an implicit idea of autonomy. There is a resonance here in psychoanalysis which is linked with its emphasis on avowing what has been disavowed or owning the disowned. If the self is dominated by primitive terrors in its internal world, it may stitch together an alibi for itself which Winnicott (1956) calls the "false self"—a bluff version of, and for, the terrorised creature within us. Winnicott is describing the lack of unity in terms of true and false selves.

In Tustin's writing (1984b), which overlaps with Mahler in many ways, there is an early recognition of the "bipersonal field" (Baranger & Baranger, 2008) created by mother and baby. In one of the most moving passages that turns the gaze to mother and baby, she says:

> The mother, who has probably experienced the child in her womb as an auto-sensuous comfort for the loneliness and despair at the centre of her being, cannot help her baby with this agonising experience which is too much like her own … This description

could be that of an autistic child, the "still, unresponsive face" could be that of a depressed mother who feels herself to be a "non-person", which is the way in which some of the mothers have described their depression. (pp. 142–143)

Tustin connects us to a mother who can barely see or feel herself, and so clings to the infant to create an illusion of oneness. She is in danger of falling back into a depression at the re-emergence of the hole that the foetus had filled for nine months. The baby and mother are experienced as one. The clinging to the skin—which Meltzer (1975a) calls "adhesive identification"—is a response to the dread of that primal emptiness, a void. This may be manifest in the transference as a clinging to the skin of the analyst. The idea of adhesive identification or clinging to the surface of things can make for a certain kind of thinness in the link between patient and analyst. Here we are in the thrall of a potent force that wants to keep the world one-dimensional. These and other forms of mimetic being remain mostly unnamed and camouflaged, as they often blend into the pattern of the fabric.

> Radhika constantly dreams of a home for herself. "It will be in the hills, it will have a balcony, two chairs for us, with a swing and a Kashmiri embroidered tea cosy," she tells me one day. She mails me an image of the painting. It is green and maroon, the colours of my consulting room. She constantly "steals" my skin. She tells me she often listens to see if something unintentional slips out: like do I sound surprised when she mentions she hates pasta or that I sound incredulous when she says she has no time to pack lunch for herself. These she picks up and incorporates in her life. While there is a perverse transferential field, she also evokes a premature separateness. This too early separate-ness throws the baby to its own devices. Radhika substitutes the unreliable environment through stealing my skin and making it her "tea-cosy".

In this we may see the need for sameness, repetitive shapes, order, and various such reassurances of presence in the terrifying void of mother's thinness or vaporousness. Such an infant may posit in an inanimate object or even a form or ritual, what Tustin (1994) calls the "rhythm of safety". This is substitution of another order. The autistic baby cannot tolerate the vagaries of waiting and hoping; instead he replaces the object irrevocably with an inanimate form. He evades mourning, through the creation of a precocious psychic autonomy. Bychowski (1960) defines this as a part of the regressed ego which

> is opposed to the full cathexis of new objects. Instead of full object relations, this ego engages in pseudo-relations with pseudo-objects. A favourable background for such a regression is provided by the inadequate object relations achieved by these individuals. Pre-genital libidinal quanta play here a predominant role. Consequently affects are blurred and every actual emotional involvement appears to be veiled, reminiscent of what one sees in depersonalisation. The formation of new introjects is seriously impeded, so that true acquisition of new knowledge may be no less hampered than the growth of love. This resistance helps the ego to maintain a kind of autarky, a form of pseudo self-sufficiency: in reality, it reflects an attitude of deep dependence on archaic objects (introjects) and their substitutes. (p. 505)

Bion (1955) imagines the psyche splitting violently into fragmented particles to evade pain. All these notions assume the "institution of the reality principle" and a "capacity to grasp whole objects". However, as Bion points out, these may not at all be assumptions we can make universally. Modernist writing captures the sense of fragmentation he describes. The opening page of Woolf's *The Waves* (2015) visually displays this fragmented vision by having a narrator splayed into different voices:

> "I see a ring," said Bernard, "hanging above me. It quivers and hangs in a loop of light."
>
> "I see a slab of pale yellow," said Susan, "spreading away until it meets a purple stripe."
>
> "I hear a sound," said Rhoda, "cheep, chirp; cheep chirp; going up and down."
>
> "I see a globe," said Neville, "hanging down in a drop against the enormous flanks of some hill."

"I see a crimson tassel," said Jinny, "twisted with gold threads."
"I hear something stamping," said Louis. "A great beast's foot
is chained. It stamps, and stamps, and stamps."

We may read the pervasive hallucinatory quality in this excerpt as a kind of "sensorial splitting"—where the senses are no longer in tandem. This creates an internal scape where the object (external stimulus) is experienced as "bizarre" (bits and pieces stuck together not gathered into a coherent shape). This chaos is like the primitive unconscious where all bearers of form—character, plot, narrative—dissolve, mimicking dreams, and psychosis, where the vectors of certitude (time and space) are suspended. The psychotic experience which is actually a dream experience has spilled out into the waking world which has no linearity or even circularity. It has not been made unconscious but is a bizarre explosion of meaning itself.

Bion (1967) takes psychoanalysis to its origins of what he calls the "ineffable" and for this he dispenses with the grammar of the linear world of developmental and ego psychology. This fragmentation we see in Eliot, Beckett, Woolf, and Joyce amongst others is reflected in the "inscaped" texture of Bion's clinical writing. When Bion distinguishes between the Language of Achievement and the Language of Substitution, he is addressing the gap between the language of the ineffable experience and the verbal representations.

In Chapter 7 I have suggested that Bion's form of writing may be like an analytic session. Through all of this we see Bion's tireless and at times even exuberant search for a form that could communicate the impenetrability of the experiences we struggle to describe.

With this in mind, in the next section we will look at how psychoanalytic writing is searching for a form. The form of writing is not always consonant with the grammar of the unconscious. And while Freud is himself searching through his generic indiscipline, psychoanalytic case writing tends to impose order on its unruly subject.

Listening to the syntax

The need for a coherent narrative and with that a "sense of ending" (Kermode, 1966) is so strong that invariably it structures our responses in the session as well as the analysand's. I have found that if we listen to the syntax, rather than the words, we may find in that the transferential link.

Jamuna tells me how she went for a dinner and people commented on her new haircut and how it made her happy. She details their comments peppering it with short, amusing vignettes of these people. I say something about how many interesting observations she has but wondering what to select. She then talks of what she misses about the sessions. She says she feels the pressure of too many thoughts and if she were not to come to me, they would remain stillborn. Away from me, they don't get a chance to live. At the very next moment she is saying, "No, earlier I would be scared or compliant, now I have overcome that."

Then I begin to hear the syntax. She begins with what appear as free associations. These can be quite engaging. It often makes me concentrate too hard and I get lost in the maze of words. But then there is a kind of caesura. After this halt, she turns her attention to me, like she is throwing me a bone. "But since our conversations ..." She has this powerful need to hold the attention of narcissistic internal objects who don't seem very interested in her. This makes for a kind of pseudo-gratitude. It is not arrived at through a recognition of dependence, but has the impatience of wanting to "learn" my "technique" and move away. This communicates her link to me. I say playfully to her that she reminds me of those advertisements of weight loss programmes with "Before" and "After". It reminds me of how this need for a linear narrative is compellingly tied in with a need (hers and mine) to believe in her progress and growth and to constantly shush the sentient voice that reminds her of her "madness".

Case history as technique

"How is the communication between the psycho-analyst reading and the psycho-analyst writing to be made at least as effective as the communication between analyst and analysand?" Bion asks (1967, p. 122), and then undertakes a rewriting of psychoanalysis which is evident everywhere, not least in his case writing. I will look at a passage below to examine his style of clinical presentation:

> When the patient was manoeuvring on the couch I was watching something with which I was familiar. Five years earlier he had

explained that his doctor advised an operation for hernia and it was to be assumed … I continued over the weeks and years, to watch his movements. A handkerchief was disposed near his right pocket … A lighter fell out of his pocket. Should he pick it up? Yes. No, perhaps not. Well, yes … He waited cautiously, furtively … It reminded me of his descriptions, not given in any one session but produced over many months, of the tortuous manoeuvres through which he had to go before he went to the lavatory, or went down to breakfast … (p. 53)

He also writes, "… the real problem arises in the lack of apparatus for recording the only part of a psycho-analytic session that is worthy of record" (1967, p. 129). And thus it is the minutiae of the field that garners his interest—the *Bildungsroman* gives way to a form here that resembles that of a dream fragment. If the dominant unconscious form embedded in us is a *Bildungsroman* it is unlikely that we can look at the moment as it happens because the past and the future invade the present. The short dream fragment offers a space where the microscopic observations of movements in the field create a new syntax of recording and thinking about the aim of psychoanalysis. As Bergstein (2013) writes movingly, "The mere movement and transition are what matters, and not its direction, hence there is no notion of moving forward towards a goal or cure. The movement itself is what expands the mind and facilitates psychic life" (p. 625). It is this movement that Bion's form of case writing seems to capture. This will be looked at a little more closely in the next chapter.

CHAPTER 3

Sentiment and emotion

In a conversation with the psychoanalyst Arabella Kurtz, Coetzee speaks of the impossibility of writing a story which ends,

> "And his secret was forgotten and he lived happily ever after" …
> you cannot have such a story, at least not in its straightforward
> unironic version. In other words, not only the moral-religious
> tradition, but … perhaps even the very form of the story, refuse
> to concede that the past can be buried … there is a sense in which
> the great plot-shapes submit to, or evoke the notion of justice.
> That is to say, the story that can be told—the story of the man who
> tries but fails to bury the past—tells us something about cosmic
> justice; whereas the story that cannot be told—the story of the
> man who buries the past and lives happily ever after—cannot be
> told because it lacks justness. (Coetzee & Kurtz, 2015, pp. 32–33)

It is not so much that the past must be unearthed; in fact it often is not. But more profoundly perhaps, moral-ethical questions and in particular remorse seem to be embedded in the very form of a story. As argued in the previous chapter, we see how unconscious templates shape thinking.

Coetzee here speaks of one particular strand of the Judaeo-Christian preoccupation with guilt. This is a dominant strand within psychoanalysis. Freud's oedipal guilt is elaborated and expanded into infancy by Klein, who builds her body of thought on guilt and reparation. Where then does the word "regret" fit in? The emotional tautness of the word "regret" distinguishes it from its kinship with remorse, compunction, sorrow—all of which have greater intensity.

In this chapter, I look at the etymological history of the word "regret"— from "bewailing" to its modern use as a highly formal expression with little affective weight. This atrophying of affect tells us both a historical story as well as a psychoanalytic one. I read it here as a way in which sentimentality (in its modern usage as exaggerated, self-indulgent feelings with some connotation of falsity) takes the place of emotionality. I want to examine different narratives to see how sentimentality is an embodiment of a negative link (-L) and its syntax is often a nostalgic "if only" (Akhtar, 1996).

The reading of these stories makes a case for analytic listening: the cadences, tense, omissions, exaggerations bring us closer to the emotional truth. Many of these are a part of verbal communication, but read the meaning in the non-lexical elements. We looked briefly at syntax in the previous chapter. Here we look at how communication resides sometimes in the gap between mood and content (repressed content), sometimes in the use of tenses (when the present tense is used for speaking about the past)—it draws attention to the whimsical music of memory. Omissions are either obfuscatory (Cather) or elliptical (Munro). Truth is either arrogant (earlier tone of David Lurie) or reparative (Lurie's later tone). These are instances where emotional listening allows us to tease out the communication. This is perhaps how we listen unconsciously when we are with our patients.

On regret

Etymologically, the route can be traced to the Middle English *regretten*, the Anglo-French *regreter*, from re- + -greter (perhaps of Germanic origin; akin to Old Norse *grāta* to weep), and "to bewail the dead" (*Webster's New World Dictionary*, 1987, p. 1196).

There are different possible ways of using it. It is used to prefix sorrow, repentance, distress. It is also used formally to speak of "failure to comply" (*Oxford English Reference Dictionary*, 1995, p. 1215).

Sometimes, however, regret conveys not one's own loss but an assurance of sincerity in contexts that appear ambivalent or culpable— "I regret having to lay you off" sounds valid while "I regret having cancer" is not. In the latter case, there is no doubt over either the enormity or the significance of the news. In this last sense, the antithesis to "regret" with its clipped restraint is "excessive".

Regret implies moderation, a tempered emotion, not a coming undone. This use would find no place in melodrama or in tragedy. It seems to stop short of deep emotion, tragedy, waste. There seems to be, in its sonorous, consonant-ridden sound, an attempt at containing the profusion of "too-muchness". So it seems the word has travelled a long way from bewailing, to a formal expression of something unfortunate.

The uses of the word tell a story about how the intensity, or the "temperature and distance" has fluctuated (Meltzer & Williams, 2010). Its etymological lineage also embodies how far the word has travelled from its origins: as if it had shed its weight. Is that really so? Is it possible for us to read a story here? Do we see this as a historical-cultural journey? Or as an intrapsychic one?

If only: nostalgia and obfuscation

Fantasies by their nature, Akhtar (1996) observes, deny reality, often following either an "if only" or "someday …" structure.

> "If only" looks back at the past, while "someday …" may have an untenable Micawberian optimism about the future. Such a person is not only looking for the lost object but for an idealised object, and even more importantly, for the time before the object was lost. This covert element of search in the nostalgic hand-wringing is a clue to the psychodynamic kinship between the "if only" and "someday" fantasies … (p. 735)

What is common to these two sets of fantasies is that they seek to evade the inevitability of turns already taken. Willa Cather's (1911) relatively obscure and arguably queer story, "The Joy of Nelly Deane" (referred to as "Nelly Deane" hereafter) illuminates the way these ubiquitous fantasies structure narrative forms. This story lays out the terrain of "if only" and this is compared later with a story by Alice Munro (2001) that follows an antithetical syntax of "what then", which I suggest is a counterpoint to "if only" from the opposite end of the spectrum. In the case of Munro's story, I read it as the former.

"Nelly Deane" is told by a woman who loved the eponymous heroine, Nelly, who is married off to a miser and dies during childbirth. The narrator who has moved away from the hometown (Riverbend) hears of this years later:

> It was ten years before I again visited Riverbend. I had been in Rome for a long time, and had fallen into bitter homesickness … Ah, that was what I wanted, to see Nelly's children! The wish came aching from my heart along with bitter homesick tears; along with a quick, torturing recollection … chattering girl beside me … It felt even then, when we sat together, it was all arranged, written out like a story, that at this moment I should be sitting among the crumbling bricks and drying grass and she should be lying in the place I knew so well, on that green hill far away. (p. 216)

The "homesickness" ("nostalgia" comes from the Greek *nostos*—to return home, and *algia*—pain) has turned "bitter", as the narrator has tried to escape while she "roams" (Rome) away from her "natural" course ("Riverbend"/queerness?). When she finds out the circumstances of Nelly's death—the mishandling by the obstinate husband who calls in the wrong doctor—she cries out: "Oh, Mrs Dow, then it needn't have been?" To which Mrs Dow responds: "We mustn't look at it that way, dear … we mustn't let ourselves" (p. 218).

The unmistakable subtext suggests that the narrator fled from desires that seemed to "bend" away from the course. This is also the moment she regrets her anger and disappointment. The "if only" syntax works as a smokescreen which conceals psychic truths that are embedded. Nelly, as the forbidden object of desire, is the denied truth of the story, where this very denial becomes the font for the story. Nostalgia for lost time becomes a displaced affective ruse for the "love that dare not speak its name". This "lost time" is idealised for being lost. It is not so much a mis-remembering that we associate with nostalgia, but a sense of lost opportunities, of having perhaps never been the time it could have been.

Regret here becomes an attempt to contain the unutterable tenor of the real loss; ruling out any possibility of mourning. The mean-spirited husband becomes the fall guy upon whom blame must be projected rather than shameful love acknowledged. Nostalgia with its bittersweet yearning leans towards melancholia which the voice of Mrs Dow prohibits. She encourages the contact between Nelly's baby and the narrator, which is seen as reparative but is also secretly a compensation.

The poignancy here is in the unnameable nature of the loss: when the desire/object is unnameable, how can the loss be mourned? Regret screens the truth, but reveals the loss. We can see melodrama with its excessive sentiment and its persecutory structure of villains and scoundrels and the sacred figure of Nelly as helpless victim. This clearly obfuscates the true nub of suffering. Perhaps the appeal of melodrama itself can be understood here as allowing some release of pain, but somehow deflected, diverted, and located away from the wound. It fosters melancholia by avoiding mourning. Pain intercedes on behalf of the psyche and avoids the naming of the lost object. The syntax of "if only" is haunted by what Adam Phillips (2012) calls the spectre of "unlived lives"—all those multitudinous possible routes we could have taken. "Our lives become an elegy", he writes, "to needs unmet and desires sacrificed, to possibilities refused, to roads not taken … the myth of potential makes mourning and complaining feel like the realest things we ever do; and makes of our frustration a secret life of grudges" (p. xiii). The quantum of regret by the narrator in Nelly Deane's story is unrestrained. But the story is an elaborate alibi for the real loss. The melodramatic plot and excessiveness of regret indicate the heaviness of what is silenced: it may be that queer love is like the corpse in the attic of this story and the regret "if only" an attempt to contain this ineffable secret.

This story like many such evades the truth in words but hints at it enough for us to be able to reconstruct it, given our historical privilege. The modern reader is struck by the gaps and silences after dropped hints, and these invite the reader to read retrospectively. This is a good instance of the trinity of repression, forbidden desire, and symbolisation. This trinity engenders the syntax of regret, "If only …" The ellipses cannot be filled in. This tone is reminiscent of Jameson's observation on Benjamin's nostalgia as always in a "search for an adequate object" (1970, p. 52). My own pinning it on queer desire is itself a way of giving shape to this melancholia, even though there is something in the odd silences and obfuscatory narrative that lends itself to this reading. We may say that sentimentality (here the "if only" version of nostalgia) offers a cover story for the emotional encounter.

"What then?" cried Plato's ghost

However, contemporary writing is not located in this trinity. In fact there is not just a singular absence of prohibition in the content, there is an insouciance. Often it is the form that communicates the emotions that are evaded. By way of contrast with the earlier story by Cather, I will look at a passage from Alice Munro's story, "What is Remembered" (2001), which marks a break from exaggerated sentiment. The reason I draw upon Munro's chiselled writing is to see how emotionality is embedded in the form, in the margins of the story, in the use of tense, in the pile-up of inconsequential details that suggest the weight of emotion through form rather than words. "Fear is just memory in the future tense," Winnicott (1974, p. 104) wrote in his beguilingly simple way. We are afraid of what has already happened. And perhaps by the same logic, when we desire what we have lost, we have not been able to digest that loss.

I will now look at the opening passage of the story to highlight the creation of an idiom of an emotional experience:

> In a hotel room in Vancouver, Meriel as a young woman is putting on her short white summer gloves. She wears a beige linen dress and a flimsy white scarf over her hair. Dark hair, at that time. She smiles because she has remembered something that Queen Sirikit of Thailand said, or was quoted as saying, in a magazine. A quote within a quote—something Queen Sirikit said that Balmain said.
>
> "Balmain taught me everything. He said, 'Always wear white gloves. It's best.'"
>
> It's best. Why is she smiling at that? It seems so soft a whisper of advice, such absurd and final wisdom. Her gloved hands are formal, but tender-looking as a kitten's paws. Pierre asks why she's smiling and she says, "Nothing," then tells him.
>
> He says, "Who is Balmain?"
>
> They were getting ready to go to a funeral. (p. 219)

I quote this at some length so we can pay close attention to some of its formal features which recur in her writing. The title of the story has already informed us about the idiosyncrasy of memory. I would like to reflect on the use of tense in Munro's work and its hauntingness. The telling of the past is done "elliptically", conflating the past, present, and future (Benjamin, 2003).

We know this time is long gone, because Meriel is a young woman at the time. But written in the present continuous, it juxtaposes the present we inhabit in clock time (external reality) alongside psychic time (internal reality). The use of the present continuous for a long ago time corresponds to the presence of the past in the present and creates an uncanny mood where one is inhabiting different time zones simultaneously. The compression of time itself has a powerfully painful resonance.

This is reiterated in the third line again. "Dark hair, at that time." Now no longer so. It is so lightly slipped in, like sepia colours—the time, youth, and, perhaps, the vicinity of death. There is an uncanny effect from "In a hotel room in Vancouver, Meriel as a young woman is putting on her short white summer gloves." The use of the present continuous rather than the simple past captures psychic rhythm, where past is continuously flowing and filling up the present. Adrienne Harris writes of how the term

> "Nachträglichkeit" evokes the paradox in temporal experience, the sense of being in more than one time zone, in being haunted and often at the same [time], living in the strange near future zone that Loewald reserved by transference. That subjective experience, the sense of being on the edge of something about to occur, is also very powerfully the experience in trauma. Traumatic states are lived in double time—it is as if the bad thing is about to happen, something ominous is pending and yet the past dominates everything. The trauma is simultaneously in the past and about to happen. (2009, p. 12)

So in the story, "Dark hair" is unspecific, but "at that time" wedges in time long gone by. The narrator has Meriel remembering something said by Queen Sirikit, who remembers Balmain. This visual frame of narrator looking back at Meriel who's looking back at Queen Sirikit who's looking back at Balmain is framed like a quote within a quote within a quote. It brings to mind Balter's (2005) ideas on "nested ideation":

Studies of nested ideation in dreams and in art both explore and elaborate two kinds of denial through representations of nonreality ("It is only a dream!" and "It is only a work of art!"). Therefore, this is a very circumscribed investigation. (p. 440)

These nested frames here look back yearningly at a past looking back at another past. Different eras of time are evoked and multiple temporalities reveal psychic time as intricately inlaid textures within textures. We lose a sense of "now", and as time is denied, so is the painful reality. In these nested frames, there is a recursive rhythm of evading the present. It is in this "looking away" structure that we feel the pain of something ineffable.

The "soft whisper of advice" brings in the tenderness of a bygone time and "absurd and final wisdom" gently undercuts the poignancy with irony. Pierre's matter-of-fact question which cuts into the dreamy reminiscence, the non sequitur quality of memory are voices lost but whose traces remain. From here, the tense shifts to a simple past, "They were getting ready to go to a funeral ..." Suddenly the ephemeral quality of memory is intercut with the straightforward third person, simple past. But the mood has been set, the frame and theme established. Meriel reminisces about an adventure she had with a guest who drops her after the funeral. This liaison is like a secret patch of memory which she embroiders, stitching, unstitching, but always holding it as a parallel life which runs alongside her real life. In her secret life, she unpacks and edits it:

> Take me, was what she had said. Take me somewhere else, not Let's go somewhere else. That is important to her. The risk, the transfer of power ... in all her reliving of this moment—of the erotic slide ... He took her to the apartment ... She would have preferred another scene, and that was the one she substituted in her memory ... for years to come. She would keep picking up things she'd missed, and these would still jolt her ... (pp. 235–236)
>
> The fact that he was dead did not seem to have much effect on her daydreams—if that was what you call them. The ones in which she imagined chance meetings or even desperately arranged reunions, had never a foothold in reality ... (p. 236)
>
> When she was on her way home that night it started to rain, not very hard ... So she stayed looking at the froth stirred up in

the wake of the boat, and the thought occurred to her that in a
certain kind of story—not the kind anybody wrote anymore—the
thing for her to do would be to throw herself into the water …
Was she tempted? She was probably just imagining herself being
tempted … (p. 241)

Writing about the non-lexical aspects of analytic communication,
Meltzer and Williams (2010) note the musicality "tone, rhythm, key,
volume, timbre" (p. 25) as enabling a tuning in with unconscious communication. Transposing this onto a written text, we might see, for
instance, the shifting tense from one passage to another is like the choir
of instruments that allow the music to follow the shifting moods: excited,
overwhelmed, lustful, remorseful, and finally ironic. The irony is important, lest the wistfulness, the evanescence, the nuances descend into
sentimentality—which would be a travesty of the emotional experience.

Perhaps what we denigrate as sentimentality is just such a false set
of displaced affects which evades the core of the suffering and relocates
it elsewhere; and "romanticising" would then be a symptom of this.
This story is woven with the skeins of regret but it is not about wrong
choices or mistakes. She regrets neither her unfaithfulness nor her marriage, but the inevitability and the irrevocability of choices which beto-
ken ultimately the finitude of life. The act of looking back seems to have
the sepia colours of nostalgia which it denies: it is so much water under
the bridge now. However, it is the simultaneity of two vertices that give
it poignancy: the present and presumably the future from where it is
utterly insignificant and the past when it was portentous. This juxtaposi-
tion itself creates the lyric of regret.

The nostalgic regret in Cather's story for a dead beloved is more
bearable than to mourn a life with her that could never have been.
Her love was never reciprocated and was not even acknowledged. In
Nelly Deane's story, the ostensible regret is that Nelly's death is avoid-
able, but this appears to cloak and obfuscate the truth. The narrative
remains pregnant with the repressed wish that Nelly need not have
married, and therefore could have remained the beloved of the narrator and alive. When this truth is obfuscated, pain is retained as a
shadow of the real loss and takes on the syntax of regret, which we may
refer to as "if only".

Munro's story, in the same section, rejects "if only". Here regret is in the idiom and form, not in the content. The narrator may have remembered more accurately and if she had, she could have had another life, not better, just different. In the first story of Munro's, memories are woven into the present. The story muses on the nature of memory as fantasy, as memories are tweaked and fiddled with constantly to compensate for the dreariness of quotidian life. Our memories as they dwell in fantasies sustain our lives, not escape them here. This notion of memory does not take on the dimension of regret. The malleability of memory is used to contain the discontentment. Paradoxically, even as the escapade remains the stuff of lifelong fantasy, it helps reinforce reality, rather than deny it. Had she remembered differently, she muses, her life may have been quite different, but she is quick to add, "not better"; nostalgic rhythms jostle against the questionable fantasy of regret.

The narcissistic fantasy embedded in "if only" gives way to a more depressive position, which one might term, following Yeats' (1936) poem, "What then?" If the paranoid-schizoid can be seen in Cather where there is an external agent of badness (husband), here the narrator strenuously steers the memory boat away from nostalgic "if only" ruminations towards a more depressive reminder that "even if things had worked the way she had desired, her life would have been only different and not better" (p. 242). There is only the internal machinery that has to be navigated and she does it while steering memories. She can hold in her mind different possibilities, but they do not carry with them unfulfilled promises. This constant conversation between different shapes life could have taken is a turbulent place to live, but it is an inevitable price paid for emotional aliveness. Describing a highly sensitive patient of his, Meltzer (Meltzer et al., 1986) says,

> It is in exactly this way that Henri demonstrates as a pathological state of mind the peculiarly heightened sensitivity to self and world that characterises the artist and, in particular, the poet. While Henri has not learned to master and employ this heightened sensitivity most of us, on the other hand, have, in Wordsworth's words, "given our hearts away" for the sake of "constancy". (p. 181)

Despair and the gravel pit

Personally of course I regret everything. / Not a word, not a deed, not a thought, not a need, / not a grief, not a joy, not a girl, not a boy, / not a doubt, not a trust, not a scorn, not a lust, / not a hope, not a fear, not a smile, not a tear, / not a name, not a face, no time, no place … that I do not regret, exceedingly. / An ordure, from beginning to end.

—Beckett, 1953, p. 37

Unsurprisingly, these mordant lines from Beckett rip open the seams which encase the word "regret" and explode the walls of regret to reveal failed containment, taking us closer to the etymological origins of the word. The short story by Munro, "Gravel" (2011) deals with a terrible tragedy but the circuitousness of its narration resembles the path of sidestepped grief. This "pit" of grief has been filled with the gravel of life. But gravel can only try to fill, it cannot remove the pit. It is this throbbing presence of a wound that can never go which reverberates through the story. "At that time," the narrator tells us, "we were living beside a gravel pit" (p. 91). Once again, memory allows the muting of light and affect:

> My mother was the one who insisted on calling attention to it. "We live by the gravel pit out the service-station road," she'd tell people and laugh … I barely remember that life. That is, I remember some parts of it clearly, but without the links you need to form a proper picture. (p. 91)

Some sense of impending disaster is ushered in by the choppiness of the narrative, its back and forth rhythm of tenses. The mother's memory feels remote with time; the tone also indicates an estrangement between the mother with her brittle laughter and the daughter/narrator. She seems to be encircling an event that is not shared till much later, something which the gravel pit seems to represent. Slowly the pieces coalesce. The mother who was pregnant with her lover's child had walked away from her old life taking along her two daughters and dog. The narrator says,

> I do know, though I don't remember it, that my father wept and for
> a whole day followed my mother around the house, not letting her
> out of his sight and refusing to believe her … and instead of tell-
> ing him anything to make him feel better, she told him something
> that made him feel worse … She told him the baby was Neal's …
> My father gave up weeping. He had to get back to work. (p. 94)

The catastrophic beginning is captured in these brief lines, where mourning is amputated and regret is startlingly absent. That "He had to get back
to work" forecloses mourning. The grief is in the foreclosed sentence.
The rupturing of the family which has torn them apart is treated with
breezy casualness: "… my father wept and for a whole day followed my
mother …" She stays distant from the moment, "does not remember, but
has been told," to paraphrase. But the shadow of the catastrophe hangs
over us from the beginning. And this despite the repeated disavowals:

> Sometimes I wondered about our other house. I didn't exactly
> miss it or want to live there again—I just wondered where it had
> gone. (p. 96)
>   What did he think of all this? Neal. His philosophy, as he put
> it later was to welcome whatever happened. Everything is a gift.
> We give and we take. (p. 94)

She wonders what her mother's lover might have to say. Here the word
"later" is again ominous, reminding us of the treachery of the gravel pit.
Caro, the elder of the two girls, drowns in a peculiar accident which
remains unclear in the narrator's rendition. Out on a walk, that fateful
day, Caro had instructed her sister to go back to the trailer van and tell
the mother and her lover, Neal, that:

> … the dog had fallen into the water … Caro instructed me to
> do as I was told. Why? I may have just said that, or I may have
> just stood there not obeying … [but] When I dream of this,
> I am always running … All I have to do is watch and be happy—
> nothing required of me, after all. (p. 103)

She dips her toes into the moment when she says, she may have just
stood there not obeying, but then the voice returns to the present:

Josie is the only person who ever talks about Caro, and even she doesn't do it often. She does say that my father doesn't hold my mother responsible. My mother cannot be made to recall any of those times, and I don't bother her with them. I know that she has driven down the lane we lived on, and found it quite changed … I went down the lane myself but did not tell anyone. All the eviscerating that is done in families strikes me as a mistake. (p. 107)

Both mother and daughter drive down memory lane. But they go separately, each wrapped in her peculiar anguish and shame. The darkness of an internal world can never be shared, lest the emotional encounter explodes the fragile link they have held onto. An emotional fork seems to shape the story—a voice that decries excessiveness, muffled grief, but which is quickly followed by the refusal:

Accept everything and then tragedy disappears. Or tragedy lightens … I see what he [Neal] meant. It really is the right thing to do. But in my mind, Caro keeps running at the water and throwing herself in, as if in triumph, and I'm still caught, waiting for her to explain to me, waiting for the splash. (p. 109)

This recurrent dream betrays the presence of the past, which the words shrug off. She still awaits an explanation, the paralysis of that moment carries on. She's still awaiting understanding, because that involves letting go of Caro and her own guilt and disappearing into the pit of despair. Both mother and daughter drive around the lane separately, each one unable to relinquish the pain and the subsequent omnipotence latent in "if only …" This inability to relinquish the object, with all its concomitant pain and the crushing loss of omnipotence is shared by the narrator of this story as well as Cather's. But here we see painful reality as modified by the narration. The details of the past event are punctuated by age and distance, indicating the uncontainability of the loss; whereas in Cather's story it dwells in the hushed silences, reality is evaded.

"Such a manoeuvre", Bion writes, "is intended not to affirm but to deny reality, not to represent an emotional experience but to mis-represent it to make it appear to be a fulfilment rather than a striving for fulfilment" (1962, p. 49). Cather's story misrepresents the emotional truth and the melancholic strand of regret which provides the background strumming is woven out of just such a painful evasion of the truth; in "Gravel" the remorse is almost too great, it is in fact uncontainable. The mother and the daughter can drive back to the old lane, but never have it back. Nor avow the culpability. But this is not to obfuscate, because the magnitude of remorse demands private suffering, there is no reprieve, no shared suffering that alleviates the pain.

The narrative attempts to contain this as do the different voices in the story. Not saying it directly is here not denial, but acknowledgement that to put it down in words is to try to seek comfort and to seek reprieve which would be wrong. The gravel pit which stands for the pit of despair and remorse is about the attempt to symbolise. But while it endeavours to contain, it is more like a burial ground that holds in the dead remains, rather than a container that metabolises grief.

"Gravel" can be read as a story about the limits of containment. It may be read to represent the twin aspects of the word "regret" which is the impulse to contain (evident in writing the story, finding a metaphor) but also the immutable aspect of the remorse which refuses containment and collapses into a pit. Nelly's death, unlike Caro's, is metonymic, it lends itself to the expression of loss, it is associated to her unnameable loss, but it is not the loss itself. She cannot mourn what she lost, because the object of love is yet to be recognised.

From shame to remorse

David Lurie in *Disgrace* (Coatzee, 2000) is a middle-aged professor of English in Cape Town, twice divorced, has only the occasional comfort of prostitutes, teaches romantic poetry to desultory students, and is trying to write an opera based on the lurid life of Byron. His ecstasies seem all out of place, his life irrelevant. Life itself is puttering out, when in walks this student who stirs him. He allows himself to be swept away by Melanie Isaacs, with whom he has an affair after the briefest pursuit. For some moments, his moribund life is lifted out of its dreariness and there's a flicker of hope. It all ends badly. A complaint is filed against him by her, there is a scandal, and he becomes a pariah. When he consults his lawyer, the latter asks him, "Was it serious?" And he responds, "Would seriousness have made it better or worse? After a certain age, all affairs are serious. Like heart attacks" (p. 42). His truth here is that for him it was a matter of life and death. His life is empty from the moment the novel opens and it is an irredeemable deadness, till the girl crosses his path.

His ex-wife, Rosalind, tells him off at dinner. He reflects later upon her brutal words and admits, "Perhaps it is the right of the young to be protected from the sight of their elders in the throes of passion. That is what whores are for, after all: to put up with the ecstasies of the unlovely" (p. 44). When called in by the committee after his resignation, he is charged, "Ms. Isaacs did not attend … or submit all the written work … for which you have given her credit." He responds, "I plead guilty to both charges." He confesses, but there is a bloodthirsty clamour for "abasement". He has a choice: he can express his regret and return to his job, or lose his job. The media turns up hungrily:

> "Do you regret what you did?"
> "No," he says. "I was enriched by the experience." (p. 56)

He appears stony and, one is tempted to add, heroically so. He says to a well-meaning colleague:

> "Manas, we went through the repentance business yesterday. I told you what I thought. I won't do it … I pleaded guilty, secular plea. That plea should suffice. Repentance is neither here nor there. Repentance belongs to another world, to another universe of discourse." (p. 58)

Lurie here waves off guilt and remorse as out of place in a secular world. He is being tried and the register ought to be secular, legal. He does not submit to the clamour for public avowals. Does he sincerely feel remorse? He says he doesn't, not on the charges he's facing. He does not consider it in the metallic light of "abuse". Honesty must be brutal and towards that all sentiments must be cast aside that soften the edges of truth, and political correctness which is the contemporary version of sanctimony must be dispensed with. "He has never been afraid to follow a thought down its winding track, and he is not afraid now" (p. 76).

Lurie feels antiquated. He is writing on Byron's period in Italy, where he went to escape a scandal; where he also had his last big affair. This dovetails Lurie's own life. It seems as if his refusal to express regret is not so much a lack of reparative guilt, as it is a defiance of a sanctimonious culture that seeks ritual expressions of guilt. Public confessions seem to be more about shaming than reparation. Whatever he is, Lurie remains authentic to his feelings, to his emotional truth. But it is a partial truth, we learn along with him. For him to regret possibly his last great affair feels false and the emptiness of his life is palpably intense.

The closest to family he can claim is his daughter Lucy, who lives a peasant life on a smallholding. She has clearly turned her back on her parental legacy of bourgeois white intelligentsia. These two solitary figures cohabit for much of the novel. She asks him why he's so unbending, he could have offered to have done counselling, after all, it's an admission to being imperfect. He says he's too old-fashioned for public apology, that he would rather be shot. What he does not say is that reparation must emerge from guilt—or more accurately remorse, not shame and disgrace.

> No appeal. I am not complaining. One can't plead guilty to charges of turpitude and expect a flood of sympathy in return. Not after a certain age. After a certain age one is simply no longer appealing, and that's that. One just has to buckle down and live out the rest of one's life. Serve one's time. (p. 67)

His "disgrace" comes from the world that demands superficial gestures and rituals; it is a culture of shame, located very far from the world of remorse. During the trial Lurie says:

> "Our paths crossed. Words passed between us ... Suffice it to say that Eros entered. After that I was not the same ... It is not a defence. You want a confession, I give you confession. As for the impulse it was far from ungovernable. I have denied similar impulses many times in the past, I am ashamed to say." (p. 52)

He is "ashamed". That is also why the register of remorse is out of place. His fatal flaw is narcissism in that there is no other in his world; which has an obvious resonance as a white man in South Africa. The breach of code does not require remorse, but symbolic contrition, ritual abjection.

He refuses hypocrisy which substitutes for contrition in a post-remorse culture. Adrienne Harris writes, "Shame is a curious shadow state, attendant on grieving" (2009, p. 7). Interestingly, Harris makes shame not the superfluous cousin of guilt, but a handmaiden, waiting in the shadows, an accomplice to grief. She gives shame a depth that is not usual in psychoanalysis. So when Lurie leaves and goes to live with Lucy, is this his willingness to bear his grief?

Living with Lucy is in fact his encounter with otherness that he had evaded. It is where he sees her living so far from his academic life in which he finds meaninglessness and boredom; here in the wild regions, he sees hate in visceral ways; Lucy is raped. They survive it. Towards the end he has been able to make connections with the odd circle. He helps bury castaway dogs:

> The dogs are brought to the clinic because they are unwanted: because we are too menny … He may not be their saviour … he has become a dog-man: a dog undertaker; a dog psychopomp; a harijan … Curious that a man as selfish as he should be offering himself to the service of dead dogs. There must be other, more productive ways of giving himself … But there are other people to do these things—the animal welfare thing, the social rehabilitation thing, even the Byron thing. He saves the honour of corpses because there is no one else stupid enough to do it. That is what he is becoming: stupid, daft, wrongheaded. (p. 146)

The punishment is complete in one sense of the term: from teaching poetry, he is now helping to lovingly kill unwanted dogs. The reparation is embedded in the actions, even as the ironic tone dismisses an old-fashioned language of reparation and remorse; what it is actually turning away from are the gestures that have come to replace this. In the world he inhabits, shame substitutes guilt, regret replaces remorse, counselling sessions act as confession boxes, and so on. Lurie has to encounter otherness; the painfulness of this encounter is the price he pays for his selfishness. This had to come from within him and hence he had to turn away from its cynical substitute. To express a formal regret there would have saved him from the utter alienation he actually undergoes, but it would never have allowed him to refind a meaningful contact with another, as he does with Lucy and her cohorts.

The first part of the novel set in Cape Town and a shallow academic world is not so much a cause of his moral turpitude, but a symptom of it. He has been unable to forge a real communication and contact with anybody. He has to make do with occasional bouts of empty sex. Going to Lucy's world with all its alienating otherness, its lack of sophistication, its bareness and frugality, he is forced to look within; and the brutal rape of Lucy, the attack on her dogs and belongings bring in him tenderness, fear, and concern. The relentlessly ironic stripping of meaning gives way to deeper, more painful underlying parts. He drives back to George and tracks down Melanie's father. Mr Isaacs invites him home for dinner. The meal is awkward and full of prevarications. Then it is time to go and he says:

> "One word more, then I am finished. It could have turned out differently, I believe between the two of us, despite our ages. But there was something I failed to supply, something"—he hunts for the word—"lyrical. I lack the lyrical. I manage love too well. Even when I burn I don't sing, if you understand me. For which I am sorry. I am sorry for what I took your daughter through … I apologise for the grief I caused you and Mrs. Isaacs. I ask for your pardon." (p. 171)

So, where at the beginning he refuses to comply with expressing regret, by the end he feels contrition. Not for the situation, but for a failing in his character. His failure is in fact his blindness to the other. Irony represents here, as it sometimes does, the denial or even denudation of meaning. In fact it may not be too much of a stretch to argue that if regret as an affect attempts to contain intensity, irony as a mode attempts to contain through denial and disavowal. The story takes a deeply ethical turn towards reparation, and through that suffering, meaning emerges; meaning is not in writing Byron librettos but in being able to feel and "sing". The novel carries almost through it a tension between an ironic stance and an ethical one. And yet in a world where sincerity is always suspect, for the regret to be believable, there must be the prior establishment of Lurie's amoral irony.

When he comes to Lucy, he is totally bereft of honour and money. She suggests that he helps Bev Shaw who helps dogs die. He says he will help as long as he is not "expected to become a better person". But as if belying his cynicism, while talking to Lucy he also admits that every woman he has encountered has taught him something about himself. We can also see the formal and structural cleavage in the novel as two different worlds that Lurie inhabits. There are two different responses to a morally emptied universe: the collusion by his colleagues or a cynical, grandiose amorality. But when he journeys away from this world to his daughter's, the story takes an ethical turn. Pitted against the elements, stripped of the grandiose cover of brilliant wit, he is reduced to ordinariness, and confronted by the starkness of his narcissism.

Disgrace captures the journey of the word "regret". It travels from a narcissistic plane where it is a byword for hypocrisy: where there is an absence of remorse or concern, regret is an empty shell. But eventually the protagonist in exile learns to bear remorse, and mourns, and the original meaning of the word is restored. The loneliness is relentless but he finds shreds of meaning in helping dying dogs to die: there is an identification with the lowliest and most unwanted. When he is able to bear his pain, he also restores the original meaning of the word. This is also conveyed tonally by a whittling down of his relentlessly ironic voice. He learns to bear the suffering which was buried under his narcissistic relation to the world.

Coetzee believes that this painful encounter seems to be demanded by the very form of the story. Is it even possible for there to be a story that does not carry within it a lattice of morality, however hidden? In the story of Lurie is also the story of the word's journey from an empty shell back to its original meaning of bewailing and pain. This journey of Lurie's from the narcissistic city into a remorse-bearing wilderness feels analogous to the psychoanalytic quest. The breakdown of all internal objects brings a catastrophe which is at the centre of the novel, but the journey does not end with the catastrophe; by contrast in Munro's second story, the messiness remains unresolved as the dream keeps recurring and the catastrophe occupies both centre stage and the immutability of grief. Here the suturing of the wound is not a possibility.

To end with a discussion on *Disgrace* is to return to Coetzee's point about the inextricability of morality and narrative. If this novel is read politically, which it seems to invite, it seems to suggest that the white man's "turning a blind eye" (Steiner, 1985) from the truth, creating a libretto to turn a deaf ear to the atrocities must lead to a moral bankruptcy. In that sense, David Lurie is a fiercely honest admission to such moral failure. His inability to feel for the other is admirable because he exposes the smugness with which "regret" is bandied about. In order to restore emotionality, there has to be the recognition of otherness and the journey to this deeply painful truth is what "regret" was meant to be. To him and his ilk, this turning away comes at the cost of complete alienation from the self. The savage violence brings on a catastrophe that allows for the working-through at the end.

We might find here a primitive notion of equalising, injustice for injustice (an eye for an eye, a tooth for a tooth), which seems to structure the book and illuminate Coetzee's point about the inextricable tie of narrative with morality. There are also echoes here of the Truth and Reconciliation Commission. The story can be read intrapsychically and politically, and depending on which vertex we read it from, the journey can be read as internal as well as allegorical.

Tempting as it might be to read it only as a political allegory or a cultural commentary, however, takes away from the poignancy of the internal journey which is at the heart of the subjectivity of both narrative and psychoanalysis. It would also denude the peculiarity of Lurie's choices and his own distance from the cynical world he is a part of. The return of the repressed is not just a function of the harsh superego, but what we seem to need to create in order to keep our disorderly selves in check. Narrative, it seems, is shaped by the Scylla of transgression and the Charybdis of reparation.

Conclusion

"Nothing will come from nothing, speak again ..." (Act 1, Scene 1). In this line from *King Lear* (1606), which, in many ways, is the quintessential play about regret, Lear asks Cordelia famously to revise her words, or regret the consequences. Blow after cruel blow, it is he who must learn to regret the consequences: "I have no way and therefore want no eyes, I stumbled when I saw" (Act 4, Scene 1). Lear mourns that he could not see the truth when he had eyes, and therefore Oedipus-like, he deserves blindness.

Having looked passingly at a few stories, what we might cull from here is that there is a lability in the word which can be seen by comparing its etymological origin to its more common usage. The word allows a gathering in of the emotion it refers to, representing an attempt at containment while its more prevalent usage betrays the terror of its intense potential. Harking back to Beckett's tragicomic lines from *Watt*, it might be possible to conjecture from this that culture frowns upon what is excessive, ushered it seems by the fears of catastrophic breakdown. We can also see the terror of excessiveness embodied in the consecration of work of which the Protestant work ethic is just one instance; while the underside reveals a demonisation of dysfunctionality as pathology.

What it does sanction often is a displacement of this excess (Chapter 1) onto false theatres which spawn melodrama, sentimentality, and exaggerated affect pinned onto mismatched contexts. It is no coincidence that the central psychoanalytic paradigm moved from repression to containment; where repression suggests prohibition, while containment recognises unbearability. While both have validity, as we see in the stories discussed, the shift appears to be from what cannot be acknowledged to what cannot be experienced. Lurie's deadness is also a cultural defence against emotionality.

The shrinking of the emotion linked to the word "regret" tells a story that embodies the psychic terror of catastrophic collapse which is then marshalled into a collusive culture of avoidance. So instead of asking the question which we are often carrying in our heads constantly—is it the psychic or the cultural or is it the inside or the outside?—here, for a moment we can tarry and say, in the journey of this word and its "penumbra of associations" (Bion, 1967, p. 138), lies a pause where the outside, the cultural, the collective, come together with the psychic, the solitary terrors. Eventually, what is at the heart of the matter is the terror of being overwhelmed by our helplessness. "It is a mark of our own resistance to our helplessness," Phillips (2010) writes, "that we deem the ineluctable to be catastrophic; as though anything we don't make for ourselves is bad for us" (p. 148).

CHAPTER 4

Pride and arrogance

"The meaning with which I wish to invest the term 'arrogance,'" Bion (1958a) writes, "may be indicated by supposing that in the personality where life instincts predominate pride becomes self-respect, where death instincts predominate, pride becomes arrogance" (p. 144). It is unusual to come across references to life and death instincts in Bion's writings, but what is interesting here is the ordinariness of pride and the perversion of it into arrogance. Pride allows us to link creatively with ourselves and our objects, while arrogance creates minus links. Having said that, it is still difficult to get away from the syntax of arrogance.

The analyst is seen by the patient as omniscient and often omnipotent and is invited to participate in this powerful fantasy. As the words spoken by the analyst are imbued with great magnitude by the analysand, it is a constant temptation that has to be resisted. Bion suggests this is a constant danger. Can we perhaps locate a narrative that is structured by anti-arrogance? How can we be with our patients without participating in our mutual fantasy?

Etymologically "arrogance" (*OED*, 2009: Latin, late Middle English: from Latin *arrogantia* "taking too much upon oneself as one's right") suggests an undue sense of one's entitlement; and implicit in this is a rejection of the other's claim. Like the figure of Narcissus, arrogance only sees a mirror, while otherness remains a feeble, foreign language. It needs must deny mortality, finitude, incertitude, and so sweeps away the truth of human existence, making an exaggerated claim for itself. The Greek word "hubris" appears to be an equivalent term.

Psychoanalytically there emerges an intertwined nature of omnipotence and arrogance. In order to sustain itself, the ego calls upon arrogance to aid and uphold its omnipotence. This omnipotence which may be linked with survival (and hence life) appears linked to the primitive part of the personality.

In *Poetics* Aristotle (c. 330 BC) observes that the tragic hero must have a flaw (*hamartia*—fault, failure, guilt) that undoes his fate. It is remarkable that he specifically isolates hubris as central to tragedy and a sense of waste, despite the immediate sense of distaste that the word itself evokes, in all its manifold translations. "Aristotle argued that hubris is what destroys a city. One can not destroy the other without destroying the self" (Willett, 2001, p. 184). In his more political writing, Aristotle will proclaim it a crime to be banished, but "privately"—in his poetic theory—he laments how it destroys the best of men. This bifurcation is very much the heart of the matter here and Bion's own Platonic duality about poetry in psychoanalysis is inflected by it. And I will refer to these two responses as tragic and moral; perhaps suggesting that narratives are born out of a skirmish with arrogance. But in itself this will not suffice. Are there narratives that elude arrogance—its grammar and its idiom?

Greek gods like their counterparts in many mythologies may be read as omnipotent versions of their earthly equivalents—bestowing benedictions or destroying at will. Most stories emerge from the confrontation between wishes for magic and the dread of such an arbitrary world. What divides men from gods in these mythologies is power, and mortals aspire to divine omnipotence, immortality, and other versions of infinitude. One such myth is that of Aphrodite, where this beautiful goddess falls in love with the all-too-mortal shepherd, Anchises. Dazzled and awed, he is deceived by her momentarily into believing she is mortal too. Aeneas—the invincible one—is born from this union of man and god, which embodies this tragic quest for perfect coupling. Before bidding Anchises the inexorable farewell, Aphrodite says:

> If you could only stay the way you are, in looks and constitution,
> staying alive as my lawfully-wedded husband,
> then akhos would not have to envelop me and my sturdy phrenes.
> But now wretched old age will envelop you,
> pitilessly, just as it catches up with every man.
> It is baneful, it wears you down, and even the gods shrink back
> from it. (Homer, c. 500 BC)

In Aphrodite's haunting words we can read the disappointment at being merely human. In an interesting intertextual moment, Aphrodite cites the story of Tithonus (in which the goddess Aurora or Dawn fell in love with Tithonus, the beautiful shepherd). Aurora had pleaded with other gods to have him immortalised but failed; Aphrodite knows better than to ask! In Tennyson's (1859) languidly melancholy rendition, Tithonus now haunted by immortality looks at his once beloved Aurora and the pain underlying his envy of her eternal youth allows the sadness to wash over envious longing:

> How can my nature longer mix with thine?
> Coldly thy rosy shadows bathe me, cold
> Are all thy lights, and cold my wrinkled feet
> Upon thy glimmering thresholds, when the steam
> Floats up from those dim fields about the homes
> Of happy men that have the power to die,
> … Thou seëst all things, thou wilt see my grave:
> Thou wilt renew thy beauty morn by morn;
> I earth in earth forget these empty courts,
> And thee returning on thy silver wheels. (ll. 65–76)

Myths are often haunted by this shadow-line that is crossed and then either betrayed by tragedy or proved illusory. And yet one could well say that without what Aristotle calls "hubris", there is not just no tragedy; there may well be no narrative. Hubris seems the closest Greek equivalent to arrogance. It is often seen in a gesture of defiance of gods, followed by nemesis. The core of hubris or arrogance seems to point to the inability to accept the constraints of being human and to surrender to suffering the pain.

The tragic response: arrogance as fatal flaw

Writing about the tragic, Arvanitakis (1998) observes, "Aristotle's belief ... was that tragedy was born when a member (*exarchon*) of the choral fusional mass broke off and started acting independently and speaking in his own voice, thereby becoming the first actor" (pp. 957–958). There appears to be a paradoxical link that connects the act of individuating with arrogance, ergo tragedy. The roll-call is pretty formidable: Odysseus, Oedipus, Antigone, Prometheus, Sisyphus, Adam and Eve ... Aristotle's masterly stroke really is to see that hubris is innately tragic.

There is an unspoken imaginative sympathy implicit in this. He imagines the audience moved by the spectacle of the hero's fall on account of his hubris. The hero has to be good enough and the structure must be one of a fall of fortune. And somehow this fall must be caused by his moral flaw and this *hamartia* or flaw (usually identified as "hubris" or pride). This brings us to the proximity between arrogance and omnipotence which I will discuss in the third part of this chapter. It is tragic because the choice Oedipus actually has is between submitting to his destiny or trying to fight it. Hubris is in fact everywhere: what was Laius thinking when he got rid of his child? Or Jocasta when she remarried? How did they dare to think they could defy fate?

Aristotle's master Plato saw it too, but his response, as we know, was more terrified: poets (bearers of emotional truth) ought to be banished from the ideal state, because they did not organise narrative to ensure that good would be rewarded and evil punished (Plato, c. 380 BC). Plato intuitively felt that poetry ran counter to the ordered structure he sought. Poetry (narrative) seems to be born out of the knowledge of this inevitability of this fatal flaw. What is profoundly interesting is how pervasively it is dreaded. So much narrative seems to be infected with a fear of arrogance. And even as different voices endeavour to disengage themselves from it, "mnemic traces" of it may be found everywhere. So what would be its other? And where would it be? Can it sustain narrative? The Plato–Aristotle fork corresponds to the moral–tragic one. And the analyst often finds herself at these crossroads in the session. We may find ourselves condemning the arrogance, the narcissism, the omnipotence, probably because we dread our reflection.

Oedipus and arrogance: inability to renounce omnipotence?

Every generation, as we know—not from Oedipus alone, but from Antigone locked in war with Creon, from Prometheus who tried to steal fire, and Satan who tried to defy God, from the challenge by Oedipus to Laius, by Krishna to Kansa, and by Christ to Herod—represents a threat to the previous generation. So is Oedipus about this threat or is it about trying to undo fate? Is Oedipus actually about the arrogance of youth or is it about arrogance itself? And who is being arrogant? The one who thinks he can question established wisdom (Antigone, Oedipus, Prometheus, Faustus) or the one who feels nobody can question his omnipotent hold (Herod, Cronos, Laius)? Perhaps it is in the field and the link itself is one of arrogance. (And it is this field that we will return to later in the chapter.) In fact, *Lear* is tragic because the perspective changes: Lear's blindness to his daughter's love has a counterpart in Cordelia's cussed refusal to humour an old man in his dotage.

An interesting variant on the oedipal theme is Yayati's story in *The Mahabharata*—an ancient tale with dubious ethical codes is discussed at length by both Goldman (1978) and Ramanujan (1999). Ramanujan referred to it as the reversal of the Oedipus myth. It tells the story of yet another ambiguous hero, King Yayati who consorts with a beautiful princess, Devayani. Some years later, he encounters her waiting woman of noble birth in the woods. This woman is "in her season" and in urgent need of a man who can inseminate her. She argues and equivocates with him till he succumbs to her persuasive beauty. When Devayani discovers this, she is livid and complains to celestial powers who curse Yayati to premature decrepitude. He asks for it to be reversed, which is not possible, but if he can get one of his five sons to agree to swap his decrepitude for their youth, that can mitigate the curse. The four refuse, but the youngest Puru agrees. And for a thousand years, Yayati is able to feast on a prolonged and borrowed youth. Puru is then rewarded with the gigantic kingdom. The cultural twist it brings to the oedipal tale quite apart, what we can also take away is that Yayati is unable to accept the consequences of his choice. He tries to hold onto his omnipotence (here embodied in powerful kingdom, abundant beauty, plenitude) and by a thread—by what Ramanujan calls "reversing the charges" (pp. 385–387) onto his son—he is able to.

The myth can be read as dealing with a denial of reality, or a fantasised postponing of death, a promise of plenitude in one form or another. So does the inevitable clash between generations give birth to tragedy, or is it more profoundly a trigger for the intrapsychic wrestling between the quest for omnipotence and a dread of just such a fate? Is the intergenerational rivalry contained by its oedipal dynamic or is it a part of an overall hatred of temporality? Perhaps oedipal rivalry provides a framework within which we can play out the war against our mortality. This latter possibility is one that Bion (1958a) seems to suggest when he writes about Oedipus who has the temerity to think he can reverse his destiny:

> I shall rehearse the Oedipus myth from a point of view which makes the sexual crime a peripheral element of a story in which the central crime is the arrogance of Oedipus in vowing to lay bare the truth at no matter what cost. This shift of emphasis brings the following elements into the centre of the story: the Sphinx, who asks a riddle and destroys herself when it is answered, the blind Teiresias, who possesses knowledge and deplores the resolve of the king to search for it, the oracle that provokes the search which the prophet deplores, and again the king who, his search concluded, suffers blindness and exile. (pp. 144–145)

Instead of paying much attention to the content of the play, Bion actually de-centres the Freudian reading. As we know from the paper alluded to above, he begins by saying that when the session is strewn with references to curiosity, arrogance, and stupidity, we should be forewarned that we are in the face of a psychological catastrophe.

In my interpretation of Bion's reading, the characters in *Oedipus Rex* become Curiosity, Arrogance, and Stupidity. These take turns and speak variously through Oedipus, Jocasta, Sphinx, Teiresias, the Chorus. By stupidity, Bion implies an obstructive presence that refuses projective identifications, and the subsequent absence of thinking. The model he has in mind is of a mother who is unable to take in her baby's terrors. The internal objects have a shallowness, a no-space for receiving messages or projections. This corresponds to an inability to think. By curiosity, I think Bion means an intrusive interest; a mind that seeks to invade another's insides, but is looking for excitement rather than knowledge.

Oedipus sets out to find the answers (curiosity), is arrogant about finding out the truth, and fails to see it (stupidity—blinded by arrogance) when the audience can see it from the first scene itself. Even before the play, the act of Laius and Jocasta in order to save themselves from their son is an arrogant and "stupid" act. The suicide of the Sphinx at having the riddle solved is linked to arrogance, as her omniscience is lost. Curiosity leads to a search for knowledge and while that is the analytic goal, curiosity (intrusive) can also be a perverse diversion from the truth, as Steiner's (1985) remarkable reading of Oedipus points out. In his reading Oedipus' entire quest is a cover from the truth. The search for truth and knowledge is all too easily corrupted into a shallow curiosity that can divert the analytic couple away from the truth. Bion seems to demand constant vigilance from the analyst to pay heed to what force is driving the session and be on guard against the characters—Curiosity, Stupidity, and Arrogance—which enter as a psychotic trinity that derail the analysis. Bion unapologetically confronts us with a storm that we participate in unwittingly. As opposed to this vertex is the one that comes from a dread of this in ourselves.

The moral response: dread of arrogance

Christ

> Every one [that is] proud in heart [is] an abomination to the LORD: [though] hand [join] in hand, he shall not be unpunished. Pride goeth before destruction, and an haughty spirit before a fall.
>
> Better it is to be of an humble spirit with the lowly, than to divide the spoil with the proud. (Proverbs 16:5, 18–19, *The Bible*, King James Version)

While narrative as we discussed in the section above arises from ambiguity, Christianity warns consistently against the deadly sin of pride and through this it wishes to dispense with ambiguity. The quotations above are instances of how it warns of pride in no uncertain terms, as something that will be punished. The Bible and its commentators repeatedly warn against pride and vanity, but one finds these dire warnings belied by actions. Like a hydra-headed monster, arrogance returns in changed forms. So while the New Testament asks us to renounce our pride, it upholds itself as the "true faith", condemning all others to being heathens who chase "after strange gods".

We can perhaps safely assume that no story endorses arrogance. So even though "pride goeth before a fall" in every narrative, the location of the narrative can fall broadly either into the phobic (paranoid-schizoid) or into the tragic (depressive) pattern. Paganism allows tragedy, while Christianity inhibits it. This can be traced from the myths to Christianity and even to psychoanalytic narratives. Christ—as the son of man—gives a strange new twist to the idea of divinity by embodying his mortality. Compassion replaces omnipotence and cuts away radically at earlier more anthropomorphic, wilful notions of gods. Christ disarms with humility. But when we look closer, he triumphs, and not just morally, he also performs miracles. He makes water into wine, he cures the lepers. This contravenes the spirit of the lamb, the son of man, the redoubtable ally of beggars and thieves. The incredulity of this is immortalised by Blake (1794) when he addresses "the fearful symmetry" of the "Tyger burning bright": "Did he who made the Lamb make thee?" (p. 23).

If God creates both lamb and tiger, he must indeed be a very split figure.

But finally it is the story of resurrection that actually put paid to this endeavour of an all-too-human Christ. That this mere mortal can return to earth after he is crucified, is a telling drama in itself: while the story of Christ can be seen to represent the wish to renounce omnipotent strivings through immortal legions of gods, it seems as if the psyche finds it too hard to sustain such renunciation. Philip Pullman's *The Good Man Jesus and the Scoundrel Christ* (2010) actually is a story born from the incompatibility inherent in the story of the messiah: that in fact, the humility and passivity seem to run counter to the miracles and mysteries.

The gravitas of its theme notwithstanding, this novel cheekily unpicks the two impulses embedded in Christ's story by splitting. This fork is represented by making it about a pair of "un-identical" twins. The passionate, charismatic, and radical Jesus, and his rather diminutive twin, Christ— the shadow of the big man. Weak in flesh and spirit, he follows the rather potent Jesus around surreptitiously, scribbling down his words. Finally, he is commissioned to write the story of Jesus' life. And here is the really clever twist: in order to ensure posthumous influence, the crafty plan is to incorporate the register of miracles. When Christ demurs, the stranger who is allegorically the Church or institutionalised religion, says:

> The Spirit is inward and invisible. Men and women need a sign that is outward and visible, and then they will believe. You have been scornful lately when I have spoken of truth, dear Christ; you should not be. It will be truth that strikes into their minds and hearts in the ages to come, the truth of God, that comes from beyond time. But it needs a window to be opened so it can shine through into the world of time, and you are that window. (p. 227)

And a little later we watch as

> Christ sat … he couldn't help thinking of the story of Jesus and how he could improve it. For example, there could be some miraculous sign to welcome the birth: a star, an angel. And the childhood of Jesus might be studded with charming little won-der-tales of boyish mischief leavened by magic, which could nevertheless be interpreted as signs of greater miracles to come … if the child born in the stable had been not just a human child, but the very incarnation of God himself, how much more memorable and moving the story would be! And how much more profound the death that crowned it! (p. 243)

Its irreverential tone notwithstanding, the book captures the impossibility of renouncing omnipotence in any absolute way. So even as Christianity attempts to reinvent the spirit by anthropomorphising God, this impulse is overridden with the desire to be in the presence of something awesome, reverential, infinite. The paradox between man's desire to know the truth and his terror of finding it unbearable is embodied in the way the Christian hero is man and yet, son of God.

In the next section, I look briefly at a particular refrain in Gandhi—another prototype of Christ—who eschews omnipotence, who represents humility and attempts to redefine heroism and courage by stripping down, rather than arming; defying through surrender rather than fight, by emasculating rather than muscularity. But rather than comment on his corpus (which is beyond my scope), I want to look at a particular moment that through its reiteration itself dismantles the avowed humility.

Gandhi

In *My Experiments with Truth*, Gandhi (1925) "retells" a particular "story" three times. Each of these episodes that "retell" can be clustered together in Gandhi's term as "faith on its trial"—where there is a life-threatening illness, and he is faced with the predicament of dying or allowing a contamination of purity, that is, vegetarianism. The first time it is son Manilal whose life is endangered, the next time it is wife Kasturba, and finally it is Gandhi himself. I would like to speculate on the repetitious nature of these "trials of faith" and what is being established:

> Though I had hired chambers in the Fort and a house in Girgaum, God would not let me settle down. Scarcely had I moved into my new house when my second son Manilal, who had already been through an acute attack of small-pox some years back, had a severe attack of typhoid, combined with pneumonia and signs of delirium at night ... The doctor was called in. He said medicine would have little effect, but eggs and chicken broth might be given with profit ... Manilal was only ten years old. To consult his wishes was out of the question. Being his guardian, I had to decide. The doctor was a very good Parsi. I told him that we were all vegetarians, and that I could not possibly give either of the two things to my son. Would he therefore recommend something else? ... (pp. 298–300)

He goes on to narrate his obdurate refusal of the doctor's advice and persistence with hydropathy. The fever remains unabated. We see here the "if this, but then …" obsessive syntax of defiance followed by guilt and finally a recourse to God's will. Gandhi's voice skims past the logical lacunae: what would people say of me? Do parents (father) determine right of life? God is invoked here as the arbiter, but this apparent "surrender" is in fact a very active choice:

> I knew Kuhne's treatment, and had tried it too. I knew as well that fasting also could be tried with profit. So I began to give Manilal hip baths according to Kuhne, never keeping him in the tub for more than three minutes, and kept him on orange juice mixed with water for three days … But the temperature persisted, going up to 104 degrees. At night he would be delirious. I began to get anxious. What would people say of me? What would my elder brother think of me? Could we not call in another doctor? Why not have an Ayurvedic physician? What right had the parents to inflict their fads on their children?
>
> I was haunted by thoughts like these. Then a contrary current would start. God would surely be pleased to see that I was giving the same treatment to my son as I would give myself. I had faith in hydropathy, and little faith in allopathy. The doctors could not guarantee recovery. At best they could experiment. The thread of life was in the hands of God. Why not trust it to Him, and in His name go on with what I thought was the right treatment? (p. 300)

The justificatory tone, the sliding quickly past his own preferences, foreclosure of "God's will" point towards an attempt to invisibilise his active, even insistent choices. The certitude of his beliefs seems to be at complete variance with the professed passivity (and humility) in submitting to God's will. He writes that God will be pleased with what he decides, but the assumption itself, that it is possible to know God's mind does not trouble him. Needless to say, he elides over what he raises earlier: "My mind was torn between these conflicting thoughts" (p. 300). Fortunately for him there is a happy ending and the ruminations end with a recovery. Renunciation and hard decisions are rewarded. This is again

the language of miracles. We see this particular anxiety in his language—
the fear of his belief in omnipotence:

> Today Manilal is the healthiest of my boys. Who can say whether
> his recovery was due to God's grace, or to hydropathy, or to care-
> ful dietary and nursing? Let everyone decide according to his
> own faith. For my part I was sure that God had saved my honour,
> and that belief remains unaltered to this day. (p. 301)

This is an especially interesting construction. Manilal's recovery may be
attributed to "hydropathy" or "careful dietary and nursing" or "God's
will"—the offhand tone underplays the dilemma for a professed believer.
If God's will is supreme, why is this in question? More to the point, we
see that "God had saved my honour". Subtly the concern slides from
gratitude about Manilal's recovery, to relief over his defiant choices not
being punished.

A similar episode towards the end of the book in a chapter called
"At Death's Door" describes him following a diet of "groundnut butter
and lemons". He contracts violent dysentery and lies dying. But he writes,
"All interest in living had ceased, as I have never liked to live for the sake
of living" (p. 549). This appears to be the kernel of Gandhian courage.
It is what makes him voraciously seek causes. His life can well be read as
a fervent pursuit of causes followed with over-scrupulous zeal, the tenacity of which becomes the source of gratification. Here as he lies nearly
dying, refusing all sources of nourishment for the sake of his dearly
beloved (vegetarianism is the overvalued ideal object that is picked over
real human relationships). The "doctor too took up the strain: 'If you will
take goat's milk, it will be enough for me,' he said" (p. 552).

We see how lightly he holds an attachment to life and how hungry
he is for a cause that can tempt him to live. The entire narrative can be
organised as his fight against temptations—whether it is sex, alcohol,
or meat—in fact all symptoms of life itself. Being over-attached to life
seems to make for a lack of courage:

> I succumbed. My intense eagerness to take up the Satyagraha
> fight had created in me a strong desire to live, and so I contented
> myself with adhering to the letter of my vow only, and sacrificed

its spirit. For although I had only the milk of the cow and the she buffalo in mind when I took the vow, by natural implication it covered the milk of all animals. Nor could it be right for me to use milk at all, so long as I held that milk is not the natural diet of man. Yet knowing all this I agreed to take goat's milk. The will to live proved stronger than the devotion to truth, and for once the votary of truth compromised his sacred ideal by his eagerness to take up the Satyagraha fight. The memory of this action even now rankles in my breast and fills me with remorse … (p. 552)

Truth—the idealised object in this passage, as often in Gandhi—is a rigid, morbidly absolute, almost persecutory object, which is pitted against life. It is truth but used as a weapon of destruction at moments. Heroism is about renouncing everything to its absolute command and all desires for life are seen as temptations that steer away from the path of righteousness. Conquering desires (linked with pleasures of living) forms an omnipotent armour against the uncertain rhythms of life. We also see the gap between the professed humility and an embedded arrogance in the syntax.

Omnipotence: flight to arrogance

"It is like a blowfish—if I don't believe I am the god Apollo, then I just collapse and am annihilated." (A patient once described his manic armour thus.)

In this part of the chapter I am going to argue that the pervasive fear of arrogance is an acknowledgement not just on account of its ubiquity, but also because it is linked with the fear of madness within us, it feels unmanageable, and as my patient put it, like a blowfish that cannot help inflating when it senses danger, the flight to grandiosity on the wings of arrogance hurtling into omnipotence, then crash landing! Altogether a flight into madness and a return to sanity that feels cataclysmic.

Freud hears echoes of childish omnipotence almost everywhere. *Totem and Taboo* (1912–13), written in the form of speculative history or anthropology, may also be read as an allegory of the psyche, if we replace "primitive man" with "primitive parts of our mind". Freud imagines the primal experience of helplessness, that needs must be countered first by a flight into omnipotence. When this seems to flounder, animism is born: if I cannot do this, someone else can—the renouncing of the wish is harder than the transferring of power. So when I am disappointed in myself, I look towards my objects, and when they disappoint, god is summoned and religions created. In our impotence, we desperately imbue spirits and inanimate objects with power.

Sorcery, Freud implies, is the handmaiden of animism—it creates rituals by which to appease, mitigate, or vanquish these omnipotent spirits created by the disappointed ego. By contrast, magic ignores these animated presences and looks to create its own treasury of rituals by which it can manoeuvre its fate. Writing here of the difference between animism and magic, Freud says, animism imputes attributes of life to inanimate objects (projection) to then seek some degree of control, while magic is more directly assuming an omnipotence of thoughts (if I think this, it is bound to be—or not). The contrast as Freud builds it here between magic and animism is analogous to that between narcissism and love: it is either an overvaluation of the self (narcissism) or the other (anaclitic). Fundamentally both postures deny the surrender to what the ego experiences as the essentially unbearable experience of helplessness (pp. 78–92).

Let us briefly consider how closely the syntax of arrogance resembles that of omnipotence. The mythical figures we know embody attributes that bypass human frailty in one way or another. It seems that the narrative impulse arises from a search to bypass the constraints of being human and it is countered by a recognition of not just the futility but also the inevitable danger of such flights. So even as Achilles represents invincibility he is belied by his heel, Tithonus' desire for immortality is foiled by omitting to ask for youth, Orpheus is unable to exercise restraint on his longing to see and so he loses Eurydice forever, Tiresias' omniscience is rendered useless by his equivocating, Narcissus is destroyed by his inability to see anybody else. The Three Fates (allegorical in themselves but figuratively speaking here) loom large over the whole canvas of drama—destiny can be translated as unwanted reality that the characters fight—an act at once futile (Sisyphus), foolhardy (Icarus), and tragic (Oedipus).

In and through our patients we often catch glimpses of our own "bastions"—our little fortresses that hide pouches of primitive omnipotence. I am thinking of a patient who was always late, who would be shocked that the clock had moved. Time ought to have stood still for her: it always shook her that it hadn't. My grey hair was something that shamed her—she coloured her own assiduously. Time should have stood still for me too. Time is the great antagonist, most powerful warrior in the enemy camp. She collects models of old watches and had about 360 at the time.

The underlying refrains in her talk vary from: I can fix everything, I am not going to die, life and time stand still for me, I can wrestle like a man and give birth like a woman, I am both man and woman. I can heal everyone. I can renounce anything. Death will not come to me. I am immune. She taught me a great deal; chiefly that I could not help her. But she appeared to learn nothing from me—at least, as she emphatically put it, nothing of what I wanted her to learn; instead she perverted the analysis into a seduction, a pursuit of me, and adhesively identified with what was not meant to be a part of the analysis (such as the colour scheme of my room, the brand of my laptop, etc.). Her arrogance suggested narcissistic internal objects with whom she was engaged in a manic assertion of her superior power/knowledge.

These rather fragile attempts at establishing some degree of control hum faintly of arrogance. In them we may hear a poignant plea to be spared harsh reality. Narcissus haunted by absence, and mocked by echoes of himself. Lear uses this syntax of narcissism. His affections are trampled by his injuries which he cannot distinguish from insults. And such insults destroy all relationships. In the lonely rantings of patients, there's often a longing to be autonomous, to be freed of the inevitably disappointing vagaries of relationships; to rise from their own debris, if not ashes. And that echoes the Phoenix myth—the unconscious fantasy of giving birth to oneself. Grotstein (1997a) refers to something similar as "autochthony"—(literally native or indigenous)—for those who unconsciously feel they sprang out of earth all on their own. Thoreau's *Walden* (1908) is a more secular, contemporary version of the same. And we see these not just in psychotic states but in the syntax of primitivism. I don't need anybody's help. I do not depend on anyone. Touchingly, it is an ode to survival. This becomes clearer in the next section where I write of a peculiarly autistic version of arrogance. Unlike a more violent, psychotic syntax, this one appears more "given up" than proclaiming superiority. Yet they are on a continuum, as it is often a kind of pseudo-humility.

The effaced self: the other to arrogance?

From here we just need to retrace our footsteps, and look again at all the heroes mentioned in the first section: what emerges as one common attribute is being intrepid, courageous, willing to die. So is Beckett the other side of a hubristic coin? In the final leg of this chapter, I would like to examine the syntax of Samuel Beckett with whom perhaps high modernism reaches a kind of apotheosis. Beckettian protagonists are indistinguishable from each other, which is already symptomatic of the effacement that may be read as the other to arrogance. The tone is an unvarying insouciance about life, and an affectless waiting in a land-scape of death, and perhaps most remarkable in creating an idiom that evacuates life and meaning from existence.

Cheated into impoverishment and rendered homeless, the narrator of *The End* (1946) wanders around aimlessly:

> I unbuttoned my trousers discreetly to scratch myself ... It passed the time, time flew when I scratched myself ... It was in the arse I had the most pleasure, I stuck in my forefinger up to the knuckle. Later, if I had to shit, the pain was atrocious. But I hardly shat any more ... Normally I didn't see a great deal. I didn't hear a great deal. Strictly speaking I believe I've never been anywhere ... You become unsociable, it's inevitable. It's enough to make you wonder sometimes if you are on the right planet. Even the words desert you, it's as bad as that ... (pp. 25–29)

Relentlessly, there emerges a bleak, objectless landscape—unforgiving, ruthlessly empty. These anti-narratives usually end without conclusion, for to give closure suggests sequence and implies meaning. This is the syntax I hear in my patient Mohan's autistic musings. (In Chapter 1 we discussed an autistic use of language where words are drained of meaning.)

X lost her parents in quick succession between the ages of eight and ten. Understandably, mourning could not be tolerated. I begin to feel it is not possible now or ever. Day after day, I hear her steady stream of words, like a leaking tap. Unable to feel anything, she mimes other people and denies all connections. There is neither anger nor bitterness directed at anyone. But in the rhythm of a language drained of affect, sometimes, a line may jump out which gives a clue, a flicker of life. It dare not last. In a passage from Beckett's *The End* (1946) the harsh and arid landscape may momentarily flicker with life, an object might appear. It is hard to tell whether it is an oasis or a mirage:

> I knew them well, even as a child … It was evening, I was with my father … I would have liked him to draw me close with a gesture of protective love, but his mind was on other things … the fires turned from gold to red … I knew what it was, … How often had I set a match to it myself, as a child … The sea, the sky, the mountains and the islands closed in … The memory came faint and cold of the story I might have told, a story in the likeness of my life, I mean without the courage to end or the strength to go on. (p. 31)

This line about "father" quietly slips in, in the midst of such consistent disaffection for life, almost as if it needs to go unnoticed, as if such sentiments were beside the point, and the only real point was of being indifferent to life, and yet it is a revelatory slip in a text that obstinately refutes the possibility of meaning. To repose meaning in any object is to relinquish control over it.

Beckett's oeuvre seems to be forged from an indifference to life and it can be seen as the other end of the spectrum of narratives from the myths of omnipotence. The debris-self of his characters is as far as possible from the godlike figures discussed. As if in fact the arrogance of the divine pose concealed the terror of this debris-self within. Can we read this as the other to arrogance? Or is the refusal to attribute meaning the last bid to preserve some control? While this is the furthest we can seemingly travel away from arrogance, it is an attempt to survive the onslaught of an inherently changeable and hence perilous world. And yet, looked at from a clinical point of view, it feeds the autistic clamour for omnipotence, for repetition, for intransigence.

The arrogance is in the link between the subject and the world. The "evening" described in the passage above seems to have strayed in almost against the grain of the omnipotent claim that nothing matters and the pseudo-pathos of nobody cares. The autistic voice as best embodied by Beckettian characters has a kind of mellow cynicism, often an ironic derision of sincerity, meaning, and value. Simultaneously or alternatively, it has a plaintive pathos and a kind of pseudo-sadness. I say "pseudo" because it is more like an intimation of sadness than a lived experience of it. The omnipotence is maintained by a severed link with feelings and this is what is both triumphed over (cynicism) and mourned (pseudo-sadness).

Arrogance as link

Bion's 1958 paper on arrogance radically shifts the vertex by examining the link between the analyst and analysand. Arrogance seems to be the negative of knowledge (-K). There is a constant force in the field which demands the analyst turn the gaze back on her own arrogance; thus locating both the inevitable presence and its blinding impact in the field.

As mentioned previously, Bion reads the Sophoclean play as one where most characters take turns at being curious, stupid, and arrogant. This triad grows together and spreads out in the session, as these personified characters do in the Sophoclean play—speaking through different personae. In his brief clinical study, Bion, as mentioned previously, looks closely at the link and finds it one where the patient and analyst can also take turns at being curious, arrogant, and stupid. For instance, if the patient is "stupid" (shows curiosity by asking questions but unable to take in what the analyst says), the analyst may feel arrogant and partake in the stupidity. When unable to communicate through verbal means, Bion writes, "[T]his obstructive force was sometimes in him, sometimes in me, and sometimes occupied an unknown location" (p. 145). This "unknown location" is the analytic field which has got charged with a kind of collaboration between the oedipal characters (curiosity, arrogance, stupidity) to which both analyst and patient contribute interchangeably. Bion, by turning his attention from the patient's arrogance, turns to the analytic field where a powerful link (colluding and/or breaking down) is always present and the couple is ineluctably drawn into the triad of curiosity, arrogance, stupidity.

An interesting sidelight of this paper of Bion's is the invention of a form that resembles an analytic session. In the beginning is an observation of patients from a distance, but by the end, it has pulled the analyst into the fray. The form of writing seems to suggest: if you thought you could be paring your fingernails at a distance, how arrogant you were. Unless you are pulled in, there is no vitality in the link, ergo there is no change.

For instance, the "stupidity" of the patient who is adhesively mimicking her analyst and enviously "stealing her skin", may stir up her arrogance. As it did with my patient G. He is somewhat older than me and delusionally believes he will be an analyst someday. He wants to get on with his analysis and is always bragging about his conferences and workshops. He is aware of the occasional public presentations I make; he even attends some of them. But rarely has an opinion on any of them. I have on occasion responded with hostility that feels projected into me and the combination of his arrogance with this inability to put his thoughts together with coherence makes me bristle with arrogance. For instance, he will come with a very arrogant attitude to the session and rail against some colleague of mine. Sometimes the intent is to flatter me, and at other times to provoke:

G: What does Y think of himself? He has published nothing. Have you seen his WhatsApp DP? I mean …

Me: [*G and I are in danger of colluding in an envious attack*] We analysts seem so ill-deserving. And you could do so much better …

G: I am only talking about Y … I had this complete argument ready at night, while sleeping …

Me: What was it?

G: [*evasively*] Something about masculinity complex … haven't heard about too much of it in our context …

Me: [*my arrogance in the chagrin I felt*] Our …?

G: Indian masculinity is very different …

I could carry on with this session, but I think this much will suffice to show how a certain arrogant stupidity is in the field and how I have become a character in this theatre. No longer able to hold on to my analytic position, I am reduced into a caricature who is arrogantly trying to trip my opponent. To carry on would be both redundant and embarrassing.

The Kleinian model may read this as projective identification—as the patient projecting perhaps the arrogance of his internal objects into the analyst. But the nature of this projection would vary if there were another analyst. A more bipersonal model would perhaps say that we look to place our unwanted parts depending on the shape of our container. An ambitious young analyst may excite a lot more envious attacks than an older, reticent one.

I do want to say that while analysis should ideally take us towards a truthful sense of our tentative knowledge as we are hourly faced with a deepening realisation of our blindness, ironically an incorporation and mimetic use of psychoanalytic ideas all too often takes us to arrogance, and what may well emerge is a triad of complacency, omniscience, and deadness. This is especially true where there is a great mismatch between the shallowness of the analysis had by the analyst and the acquisition of deeper concepts much later. Often these new concepts become weapons in the armoury of some practitioners, as they are learned not through experience but through what Meltzer (Meltzer et al., 1986) calls "scavenging" or "mimicry".

Conclusion

In this chapter I began by looking at how arrogance or "hubris" seems to bind myths and narratives. Aristotle recognises hubris as a fatal flaw that precipitates tragedy. This "tragic" response is indicative of its inevitability. By contrast, Plato's response to tragedy is a "moral" one, which corresponds with Christianity. Freud in *Totem and Taboo* writes about how the primitive mind is linked to magical thinking and omnipotence.

From here, it is argued that it is our inability to bear omnipotence that underlies arrogance. Unable to tolerate our disappointments and failures, so that we take a flight to mania, grandiosity, and arrogance. The morality against arrogance in Christianity runs counter to its own claim as a supreme faith. Philip Pullman's contemporary take on the story of Christ is seen to undo the tragic-moral binary, by revealing the need for the register of omnipotence.

Gandhi's autobiographical account *My Experiments with Truth* offers another kind of self, like Christ's, that fashions itself as embodying the antithesis to the scintillating heroes—he is humble, flawed, passive. But on a closer look, this also reveals its fissures. So the distinction I make at the beginning between two responses to arrogance as tragic and moral seem to sag in the middle, if not snap completely.

We then look at an anti-hero in a quintessential Beckettian anti-narrative, *The End*. Surely this abject figure, standing at the last outpost of civilisation, must mark the furthest distance from the language of arrogance. And Beckett does indeed create an idiom where the self is effaced. In doing so, he turns the tables on life. The evacuation of all meaning from life forges an insouciance to life and apparently disavows all possibility of attaching value. This resembles the patient who is in the grip of a death wish, who elects objectlessness over mourning and in doing so, replaces life with death.

Unlike "heroism" where courage demands that death is not feared, here in Beckett death is awaited as the only certitude, while the uncertain pleasures of life are seen as pointless. This indifference to life forges its own form of vocabulary of anti-heroic but hubristic rejection of life. Yet, every now and then, something slips in almost against the grain of this fabric, which reveals the unbearableness of disappointment and it is in such breaches that we may hear faintly the terrors against which we arm ourselves with arrogance.

Finally, I have ended (as also begun) with Bion: in his discussion of a case in "On Arrogance" where he speaks not of the patient's arrogance, but the arrogance in the field between patient and analyst; thereby turning the tables on analytic omniscience. A small vignette from my own work illustrates my becoming a character in the field—precisely what Bion cautions against.

Part II

Vertices

CHAPTER 5

Womb and foetus

t a restaurant I see a family walk in and take the table next to me. They smile apologetically. The parents look weighed down, prematurely old. One of the two daughters looks sadly overweight and seems autistic. She makes loud, babbling, incoherent noises when the waiter brings in a bread basket. She asks him repeatedly if it has something sweet in it: "Candy? Cake? Cookies?" The father looks pale and withdrawn and looks blankly at his daughter eating through the bread basket without a pause. The mother looks thin with worry and talks rapidly about mounting debts, failing health, and her husband's depression to her other daughter who has thick glasses and vacant eyes. I see the poignantly parasitic relationship of this hapless, overgrown girl with her family. Later it occurs to me that the family is unable to imagine this child in any other way but as a liability. It strikes me that it is not inevitable for this to be a parasitic network, but that the hopelessness and defeat of the parents, the power of the death wish that had to be warded off rendered all other possibilities remote; parasitism here is not only inherent in the situation but also fostered by an imagination denuded of hope.

So far as we can see parasitism is used as a derogatory term. But this could well be a paranoid way of understanding the phenomenon: one where psychic parasitism is smeared with malevolence and intentionality. By contrast, the life sciences see this as an evolutionary achievement, as ubiquitous and as extremely dynamic. Blomfield (1985) made a similar point where he expanded Klein's (1955) view of placental parasitism as a form of projective identification. Is it time to revise the term in order to open the sessions up where we feel leeched upon? Does the limitation of our vocabulary impede our work? And is this semantic roadblock related to an autistic island created by the moment of encounter of two autistic parts?

Parasitism in the natural sciences

> Symbiosis: "Any of several living arrangements between members of two different species, including mutualism, commensalism, and parasitism. Both positive (beneficial) and negative (unfavourable to harmful) associations are therefore included, and the members are called symbionts. Any association between two species populations that live together is symbiotic, whether the species benefit, harm, or have no effect on one another." (*Encyclopedia Britannica*, 2020)

> Parasitism: "All varieties of inter-specific associations in a gradient of inter-dependence. Therefore, associations defined as commensalism, mutualism and symbiosis are distinct features of a same phenomenon—parasitism. Moreover the classical definitions of mutualism, commensalism and symbiosis do not establish clear cut-offs that distinguish them from parasitism." (Araújo et al., 2003)

The two definitions from the natural sciences above disagree on the nomenclature of the umbrella term. But in a more fundamental way, they are markedly similar. They each define the umbrella term as including all living arrangements between two species. The degree of dependence varies, as does the nature of the relationship. The second definition also draws attention to the dynamic quality of such association.

In common parlance parasites (literally *para*—besides, and *sitos*—food) "receive bad press" (Matthews, 1998, p. 16). The *OED* (2009) defines a parasite as

> One who eats at the table or at the expense of another; always with opprobrious application: "One that frequents rich tables and earns his welcome by flattery" ...; one who obtains the hospitality, patronage, or favour of the wealthy or powerful by obsequiousness and flattery; a hanger-on from interested motives; a "toady".

But natural scientists observe that predators that kill are often admired while the parasite is a figure of revulsion for us. This is indeed ironic. Yet something inhibits us from sharing this generous vision of parasites with their human counterparts; what is fascinating is the number of permutations that can exist between hosts and parasites. In psychoanalysis, as in Shakespeare's use of the term, a parasite is a scrounger—repugnant and insidious—in some ways the antithesis of the mother–child relationship, or so we imagine. But I am going to look at this from another vertex:

> To see this spirit of maternal generosity carried to its logical extreme, consider Diaea ergandros, a species of Australian spider. All summer long, the mother fattens herself on insects so that when winter comes her little ones may suckle the blood from her leg joints. As they drink, she weakens, until the babies swarm over her, inject her with venom and devour her like any other prey. You might suppose such ruthlessness to be unheard-of among mammalian children. You would be wrong. It isn't that our babies are less ruthless than Diaea ergandros, but that our mothers are less generous. The mammal mother works hard to stop her children from taking more than she is willing to give. The children fight back with manipulation, blackmail and violence. Their ferocity is nowhere more evident than in the womb. (Sadedin, 2014)

I have quoted at some length the above passage to provocatively extend the idea of parasitism as a more pervasive phenomenon. The foetus embodies a parasitic relationship to the maternal body (Blomfield, 1985;

Giard, 1913). In fact, the foetus will not remain so and, throughout life, equations change and even reverse—old parents often being experienced as a "burden" by their children. How can we give shape to the internal world of a parasite? I suggest that the womb–foetus link can be read paradigmatically to imagine the birth of parasitism. The womb may be seen to correspond with an enclosed chamber of the mind in the transference, and the ferocious response engendered in the foetus which is desperate to survive may be what we experience as parasitism in the field. The enclosed chamber is like an enclosed part of the analyst's mind that confronts the patient and creates an autistic island in the field.

Parasitism in psychoanalysis

You knot of mouth-friends! ... Most smiling, smooth, detested parasites
—Shakespeare, *Timon of Athens*, Act 3, Scene 6

Psychoanalysis, like Shakespeare above, tends to use "parasitic" derogatorily. Envy—which is a pervasive emotion—can be responded to by throwing out everything (devaluing the goods), the interventions of the analyst (throwing baby out with bathwater), or it can be responded to by stealing something. This is a very interesting difference. When envy is unbearable, it often leads to projection or vomiting: everything that is given is stripped of its value and expelled with fury. But it may take another route. The envious gaze may actually see the value and decide to steal what is good but appear to reject it. One way of looking at it is that the parasite is more hopeful, in that he does not expel everything. Stealing shows a potent need for survival as compared to evacuating. It may also point to an internal object world that stimulates a desire to rob—it could be figures who are withholding or castrating. The possibilities are endless.

Here it might be helpful to recall Klein's distinction between greed and envy.

> Greed is an impetuous and insatiable craving, exceeding what the subject needs and what the object is able and willing to give. At the unconscious level, greed aims primarily at completely scooping out, sucking dry, and devouring the breast: that is to say, its aim is destructive introjection; whereas envy not only seeks to rob in this way, but also to put badness, primarily bad excrements

and bad parts of the self, into the mother, and first of all into her breast, in order to spoil and destroy her. (1977, p. 180)

Extrapolating from this, envy disables splitting, and nothing good can be introjected. This is not so with parasitism where hunger overcomes envy. The parasite does not just survive, s/he thrives. Unlike with some forms of envy, the good news with parasitism is that the spirit is alive to beauty. However, if the beauty can be quietly imitated or plagiarised, we don't need to feel obliged. We don't need to repay or feel inferior or beholden. The object who possesses the beauty is experienced internally not as a generous one but in fact mean-spirited.

Blomfield's (1985) is among the first fully fledged investigations of parasitism from different psychoanalytic vertices. He recognises Klein's idea of the foetus discharging its waste into the host as a parasitic link between the womb and the foetus. When Klein (1946) writes about the "infantile phantasies" that "attack the mother's body in many ways, including the projection of excrements and parts of the self into her" (1952, p. 311), Blomfield observes rightly that this again suggests a "parasitic derivation" (1985, p. 303). He adds that the

> biologist Giard (1913) considered that mammalian evolution incorporated a stage of endoparasitism—the foetus being a true "placental parasite". Giard's (1898) concept of metamorphosis permits a hypothesis which escapes the fantasy of current views, still influenced by a "homunculus" attitude involving the projection of infancy into the womb. (p. 308)

Taking this forward, we can link this with Bion (1977) who characterises a dyadic relation as being between a container and a contained; on the model of either a nipple-mouth or penis-vagina. This link can be either commensal, symbiotic, or parasitic.

> By "commensal" I mean a relationship in which two objects share a third to the advantage of all three. By "symbiotic" I understand a relationship in which one depends on another to mutual advantage. By "parasitic" I mean to represent a relationship in which one depends on another to produce a third, which is destructive of all three. (p. 95)

He sees parasitic as destructive to "all three", that is, the parasite, the host, and the link between them. In the transference, the link between the patient and the analyst and the link between their thoughts may be seen to take on any of these shapes.

Meltzer and Harris (1976) identified six dimensions of mental life—one of which was the geographical notion of mental life (p. 1). This dimension helps us to identify the psychic link in parasitism between objects as being more reliant on intrusions rather than projections. This suggests the foetus did not find room in the womb and had to nestle, even camouflage itself elsewhere—somewhat like in an ectopic pregnancy. This is akin to what Meltzer (Meltzer et al., 1982) terms the claustrum which describes the "inside of the object penetrated by intrusive identification" (p. 202).

> Having perversely entered the object, the subject becomes prone to identity confusion, "geographical confusions" and claustrophobic states within what he terms the claustrum. Inherent in this geography is the notion of a multi-dimensional space, which may be containing or confining, entered intrusively, by consent or invitation, and by concrete or imaginative means. (Skelton, 2016)

It is when this entry into the mind and/or body is through violence and stealth that it feels parasitic. It would not be untrue to say that such violent entry evades separateness through mourning, and that such relationships perversely intrude into a territory and deny this invasion, so as to obfuscate debt, gratitude, dependency.

But this register suggests semantically an intentionality to what may well be minutely fragmented bits of ego that cannot reside without taking residence inside another. Sandy particles require a shelter, but can only be sheltered by entering the body and mind, because outside every breeze is a storm. My point then is of a continuity between an autistic part of the personality that seeks refuge parasitically in another (Ogden, 1989). This is not unrelated to the idea of a continuity between the intra-uterine life and the "caesura of birth" that Freud (1926d) writes of. This is the transitional stage between the foetus and the baby; where the baby still needs sheltering from the overwhelming stimuli, he can only tolerate modulated contact with reality. The baby's need for a warm shelter, his helplessness at the overwhelming stimuli may be experienced as parasitic, viewed from a scientific perspective. Bion's idea of a "binocular vision" may be seen in the two distinct vertices from where to view parasitism (intrapsychic or bipersonal/scientific or emotional). This chapter tries to embody this binocular vision in its form as well as content.

How do we know parasitism in the field?

Unlike encounters that are demanding or challenging or exhausting, here there is a peculiar sense of being drained and squeezed. The parasitic encounter is marked by depletion. It can be either the analyst's or the patient's. It can be common or alternating or fluctuating. There may be other tell-tale signs. By stealing the skin of the analyst: sounding like her, dressing like her, buying the same car or jewellery. By hiding changes from the analyst. By telling stories of how s/he spoke to someone in which one hears echoes of oneself, but it is never acknowledged. But all this can be misleading unless it is echoed in the feelings the patient evokes in us.

For instance, the patient may look unresponsive when we say something that may be important, but use it in a subsequent session, where he or she may be saying something similar to a third person. It may stir in us a fantasy that something is being stolen and reused, passed off as the other's: the fear of plagiarism. When we offer analysis, the patient either takes what we have or rejects it. But s/he may also take while not letting on. Do such patients let on changes in some way? And if not, is it because they can't bear that you have anything to give or do they secret away what they get because they can't bear for you to know? It is this last response that is experienced as parasitic.

The above passage is written as it is experienced in the mind of the host who is unable to think about it or shift his vertex. This experience in analysis is marred by what is often our inability to locate this—terming an incapacity as resistance, envy, or ingratitude makes this an unapproachable island in the work, akin to a "bastion" (Baranger & Baranger, 2008). But while the "bastion" is a turning away from something unbearably painful, I suggest the island is a collision of two rocks that do not know how to communicate with each other.

The case vignettes have been written in the way my own understanding developed. The initial understanding of each of these people was superficial on my part—histrionic, narcissistic, perverse, and of course the link felt parasitic (as I felt like a paralysed and reluctant host).

But it is only over time that I am beginning to see a pervasive underlying pattern—of coming upon that object in the transference—finding myself too shallow to be able to think about them. I thus gave them no choice but to cling to the surface of my mind. I was then collaborating on an autistic link by the limits of my mind—my thinness, opacity, and "stupidity" (Bion, 1957).

Case 1: When the womb goes rogue

Most extreme form of togetherness in the bladder of a rodent—the male lives in the uterus of the female.

—Matthews, 1998, p. 4

J's utterances are always dotted by the word "depleted" and "drained". I hear her talk of the work she does and I feel enchanted by her description—she for her part speaks only of how depleted she feels. In her mind there appears no difference between exhaustion and depletion. Reserves are always being drained, because there is no experience of nourishment. When I say this to her, she is startled. She had never thought there was a difference. Perhaps the entire colony of internal objects were experienced like termites eating into the woodwork. And yet my experience of her is not parasitic. I have felt hopeless, but not leeched off. This allows us to imagine the possibility of the presence of parasitism in an internal world, to which the psychic response need not be to join in. But to survive with a measure of helplessness. This survival feels like an act of courage.

J has often spoken of being bisexual, even though she is mostly single. One lonely day J decided to invite one of the men who she met in a virtual chat-room. The man came two hours late. She led him inside and offered him tea. The man seemed preoccupied with his phone and she went into the kitchen to make tea. I might add here that J lives a hermit-like existence in a very desolate part of the city and works from her home. In short, she has barely any company other than me.

She wanted to ignore the bell, but it rang again aggressively. She felt gripped by terror and went slowly to the door. On opening it, she saw "a haggard-looking man" who demanded to know what kind of prostitution racket she ran. She denied this. He pushed her roughly aside and entered. After two harrowing hours, the two men left, but only after they had humiliated and molested her, stealing everything she had: cash, camera, iPad, and also innocuous things—bed sheets and towels. They took pictures of her lying on the bed and threatened to expose her. Paralysed for hours with terror and shame, J finally fell asleep. In a session later, she speaks of preferring her own corner to everywhere and everyone: "I would rather be in my duvet than anywhere else in the world. Just order in food, finish my duties online on my laptop. Never to stir …"

I imagine a jealous womb suffocating in its grip. She tells me about the experience of being preserved in a jar. "Sterile," I say, "with both its meanings—safe and lifeless." J's internal world seems infested by parasites. They take but are never sated. Every time she manages to save some money, she buys expensive gifts for her widowed mother. This robbery leaves her depleted. J remains tied to this parasite, unable to travel, go to another city for a job. Even though she lives on her own, it is in the same district as her mother. She spends her last reserves trying to buy love. She buys her jewellery for every occasion, every new gadget for the home. But she comes full of tears—mother did not like the colour of the ruby—it was more pink than red, she never wore the gold chain, she never looked at the camera.

I feel myself swell up in anger—"Why would you keep on trying? Just give up on that parasite"—comes to my mind. J is abundantly grateful. Nevertheless she brings in a parasite. She seems to be swallowed up by this bloodsucking object. It feels as if the session sometimes takes the form of trying to deliver the baby from a womb that has gone rogue. The mother is experienced as a leech who needs to suck everything J has. When J complains these are often pseudo-complaints and do not usually indicate a wish to separate, but are more masochistic in nature: where complaining has a masturbatory pleasure. Sometimes it feels she is offering chunks of her flesh to others, so they may do the same. In the exaggerated adhesive attachment to me, I see an intensely furious attempt to swallow me in. In those moments I feel suffocated by her as she does by mother. But it takes me a lot longer to figure out that this is how she is experiencing me.

When she is unable to give me what I seek (words, logic, proportion), she is enraged and screaming back at me: "What do you want? I give you what I can and you are never happy!"

When I begin to decipher this, our space together becomes the "autistic envelope" she describes as the bunker that can be seen to emerge as a momentary respite from an otherwise relentlessly parasitic link (McClelland, 1993). Parasitism here is born from the "confusion of tongues" (Ferenczi, 1988)—the mismatch between the analyst/mother who cannot recognise the infantile needs of her baby and recedes as she is overwhelmed by his growing neediness.

Case 2: The opaque object

> *Antagonism: In ecology, an association between organisms in which one benefits at the expense of the other. As life has evolved, natural selection has favoured organisms that are able to efficiently extract energy and nutrients from their environment. Because organisms are concentrated packages of energy and nutrients in themselves, they can become the objects of antagonistic interactions. Although antagonism is commonly thought of as an association between different species, it may also occur between members of the same species through competition and cannibalism.*
>
> —Encyclopedia Britannica, 2020

Many people strike us as adolescents through their lives: bored, restless, unable to stay for long anywhere, hanging out in groups. The group dynamic is one of extreme rivalry with each other and in which members often have perverse entanglements with each other. The popular American high school comedy *Mean Girls* made me realise there was a thriving adolescent sub-genre catering to a narrative of bullying among girls. The heroines are disingenuous in their naivety, while they are pitted against wily and vain antagonists. Catfights erupt over delectable but rather pointless boys and gang wars that trivialise to the point of ludicrousness. These gangs are different from the mafia-type gangs Rosenfeld (1983) describes, for instance in the following passage:

> The destructive omnipotent way of living of patients like Simon often appears highly organised, as if one were dealing with a powerful gang dominated by a leader, who controls all the members

of the gang to see that they support one another in making the criminal destructive work more effective and powerful. However, the narcissistic organisation not only increases the strength of the destructive narcissism and the deadly force related to it, but it has a defensive purpose to keep itself in power and so maintain the status quo. The main aim seems to be to prevent the weakening of the organisation and to control the members of the gang so that they will not desert the destructive organisation and join the positive parts of the self or betray the secrets of the gang to the police, the protecting super-ego, standing for the helpful analyst, who might be able to save the patient. (pp. 10–11)

Girl gangs are different in that while boy gangs attack reality by grandiosity, these live on the surface of reality and are more trivialising than grandiose. If boy gangs brutalise and dare their members into risk-taking behaviour—drugs, speeding, drunken brawls—girl gangs have catfights, boyfriend poaching, and bitching. While destructive narcissism may still be the force that pervades such a group, here it is the shallowness that is striking, reminiscent of what Meltzer calls "empty-headedness" (Meltzer, 1975b).

Such a member I will call Q—a young divorcee. A very attractive beautician who married her high school sweetheart, but whose marriage broke up within six months. They were only twenty-two. When she first came I recall feeling enchanted by her prettiness. Even deeply sorry. She could not understand what made her husband "drop" her. He seemed to want to get back his bachelor life. "Poor Q," I would think. "One who tries so hard and gets envied by everyone. How badly everyone treats her."

To the innumerable times I tried to get her to process her grievances and injury, she would always respond by saying she had done nothing to deserve this treatment. I was reminded of how initially I kept making excuses for her maltreatment by thinking it was the envy of her peers. It was almost as if she wanted me to say how they envied her. While dating, it seemed she would be pursued forcefully and then suddenly dropped after a few weeks. Initially she could not understand what she was doing wrong. Later we could not see what she was doing at all.

She would just lie down on the couch with her eyes closed, tell me the events in-between and then wait for me to "feed" her. Her manner began to remind me of how Martha Harris (2007) describes a patient: "that wanted to go on existing as a sort of parasite baby that was excused all difficult things, that could just go on dreaming and being comfortable" (p. 107). She always agreed and left after telling me how I had nailed it this time. And yet, nothing ever budged.

Eventually these feelings gave way to seeing the aridity of the desert that she felt. This then was the pattern of her relationships. A show of adoration masked the deadness, docility posed as thoughtful listening, eager movements suggested attentiveness, mimicry looked liked synchrony, disingenuousness passed itself off as innocence. The disenchantment I felt had elements of not just disappointment, but anger. As if she had wilfully deceived me. But of course the hollowness of the posture had to reveal itself.

I felt each session become a repetition of the last and the gang of high school friends seemed never to leave the room. She was falling off the map. It seemed all the men had fancied her and the women were envious of her sexiness. They all accused her of "stringing along" men. Naturally Q has no idea of intimacy. She has no idea of who or how to pick: "If someone asks me whether I prefer vanilla or chocolate, I don't know what to say. I look around and see what others are choosing ..."

Tustin (1980) writes about how autistic objects are a response to

> unbearable frustration, but they prevent the development of thoughts, memories and imaginations which, in normal development, in some measure, compensate for the inevitable lack of complete satisfaction which being a human being entails. Another result is that the children themselves are vulnerable to being manipulated as autistic objects instead of being treated as human beings (p. 31).

For Q, her girl gang functioned—amongst other things—as a substitute for a mind. She would keep returning for decisions. No matter how pernicious the values, gangs are extremely decisive. In the transference I often felt like one of the mean girls.

I wondered if some coquettes (derisively named molls, dolls, airheads) were made of this indecisiveness which comes from an enclosed rather than a repressed part of the unconscious. When the psyche encounters "opacity" (Bion, 1977) in the object, the words mostly bounce back. The communication has the quality of deadness, the voice sounding an indistinct echo of itself; akin to echolalia (Tustin, 1969, 1980, 1984a, 1988). There can be either an embracing of this deadness or else, as in the case of Q, a despairing quest for a host. Searching for a mind that can think for her.

For Q, the gang had been her mind. She would return to different members who spoke in different voices, creating discord. This "anti-mind" only exacerbated dependency, which was antagonistic to the mind the analysis sought to create. Helpless without judgement, she sought instructions. She was drawn to people who exuded power and authority. Symbols of power were located in prom queens and older men with BMW cars. Here we see another variant of parasitic organisation— where the host body is a part of a perverse organisation and the parasite leeches on in order to cling for survival. This then is clinginess—latching onto a breast that does not want you.

The link between us felt parasitic—as if there were no real communion or intercourse, but just a stowing away of my gestures and sounds. Words could be repeated, but the meaning could never be, without an echo of hollowness. And yet it seemed to be needed as a gesture and posture. Till such time as the plant's stem becomes a bark, it feels like a protecting cylinder is needed. And the analysis is just that encasing for Q. The inability to think, Bion (1959) realised, makes thoughts themselves antagonistic presences.

In Q's recognition of her need, there was a hope. Her coming to me, noticing the externalia, was a space of waiting for the bark to grow. So what felt like parasitism and in fact was so, in one manner of speaking, was also about locating a womb outside the mother's body. Where the foetus experiences the mother's abortive wishes, and feels blocked, he may develop a tenacity that feels parasitic to the womb that has drawn up the walls. It requires me to observe my walls rather than to feel frustrated by Q's inability to climb them. For now she can only stick to the walls, in what Tustin (1984a) calls "adhesive equation" because there is no interior to introject into.

Case 3: Living in his penis

Castrator pea crabs live up to their name. They live inside the sex organs of marine molluscs and prevent them from reproducing. But it turns out the pea crab's parasitic ways also make it terribly tricky for them to find a mate. Castrator pea crabs (Calyptraeotheres garthi) are tiny parasitic crustaceans found off the east coast of South America, from southern Brazil down to Argentina's Valdez Peninsula. They spend most of their adult lives in the sex organs of various slipper limpets.

—Joshua Rapp Learn, 2017

F runs a PR company and is fairly successful. She has long known her partner's yen for pornography. It feels as if he does little else. In my fantasy, he lives off pornography and she leeches off his addiction. This arrangement seemed to have provided a scaffold for them till she found he was cheating on her virtually with her closest friend. This brought about a complete breakdown and she turned to therapy. But it often appears like we are stuck inside a revolving door. She seems to want to restore her omnipotent fantasy of being inside him and little else. She only speaks of betrayal, dwelling on the details of their sex chats and little else. Rage and bitterness enter me and paralyse my thinking. This voyeuristic and perverse obsession formed a loop or "chuntering" (Joseph, 1982) which she used to avoid a breakdown.

I would try not joining in the loop of pseudo-thinking: "So does this mean I should leave him? But why should I? But I can't bear being with him." As a true connection between thoughts forces reality, and brings unbearable pain in its wake, this was aggressively expelled. As the agent of that, I would be subsequently attacked:

"So are you saying I should leave him? I have no self-respect because I carry on … Are you trying to say I should carry on staying with him. That means I have accepted what he did …" This pseudo-thinking carries on even now after four years, but is a bit reduced. Yet it comes back especially after there has been a pause, a breather. As if the winds of change presage pain, she returns to the loop. "Again he was looking at porn last night. I told him to leave the house, so he left."

"It's been a week now. He is in a different hotel every night and keeps sending me texts, photos, porn … I saw it … I am so afraid."

Again I feel very exhausted, unable to think. Then I think of castrator pea crabs and I wonder aloud: "Do you live in his genitals?" The nauseating rhythm of her "yo-yoing" grinds to a halt. She quietens down. "Yes," she says after a pause. I tell her, "You will be dropped from there if he ejaculates." What has also been a refrain is the exclusion from the primal scene, F's way of dealing with being excluded is to force her way in. Somehow I think being inside the penis ensures that she sleep right inside the most intimate point of contact and ensures she is not ejaculated. This brought us a brief reprieve.

In the early sessions, I recall the bottomless nature of her neediness. If I ever did answer a question directly and simply, as opposed to interpreting it, she would ask another before taking in the first. This could carry on till I felt completely emptied. It felt like I was seeing her gulp down whatever I gave, without biting, chewing, or swallowing. I did not realise how little her digestive system could process. Very soon she would begin burping and even on occasion, farting.

How is this related to her experience of her internal objects? Over time I have come to see a misalignment—the mother who overfeeds her baby to compensate for her not wanting a baby in the first place. Much of this is based on our work together. But it was quite concretely evident in her habit of burping in almost every session, especially when I was finding her unbearable, even repugnant. This makes her cling to me more tenaciously, with a biting fury. But pleading helplessly her inability to digest what she gets. She also recognises that is all I can give—words. Something from me is preferable to nothing. She can't digest words but she can use the sound of them as pacifiers.

It seems she seeks to return to the claustrum-like space she was in, where in fact she has been conceived and born. This would seal her together and stop her from falling apart. Her objects typically suffocate and engulf her, but they are also experienced as having a perverse interest in her. With the discovery of her partner's virtual affair, she has been rudely expelled from there. She has to claw her way back in through any portal that is left open through violence, intruding through virtual history, phone texts, through the penis, the vagina, the anus. This is evident even in her perversion; unlike her partner who is addicted to pornography, she is addicted to him and seeks to enter him through all his orifices. It is not surprising that he can never ejaculate during intercourse.

We see perverse relationships emerge in the transference where I would find myself wrestling with the desire to expel her. This has been dealt with by entering through another portal and the analysis begins to feel as suffocating. Meltzer (1990) identifies the different zones where residence may be taken. In our work, we can say, the patient finds it hard to leave the genitals/anus which have encapsulated them and they are as yet unfamiliar with being in the mind of their objects. I find myself unwilling to give more, somewhat repulsed by the primitive quality of her neediness and her lack of responsiveness when I give. I would feel myself swell with irritation when she would turn to look at me, a strong urge to screen myself.

But while Q would float giddily on the surface of my mind, F tends to pierce me. She peeps in to my house, the enclosed space behind my table, sniffs the air, comments on each tiny sound I make, buys the same car as I have. I thought of this as intrusive and perverse, but it is a psychic stance around objects that are so thin that they stare back hungrily rather than contain as vessels do. This misalignment between us is telling. I was unable to think beyond the obvious—"Whenever mother sees me, she tries to feed me. I hate food, I hate eating ..." This complaint of hers echoed her experience of me. Her analyst seemed to have solid meals for her, while she wanted soft mush. My rigidity of sticking to age-appropriate food and a disapproval of her immature digestion was in fact, again, an encapsulated area of darkness for me. Looking back now, I can see how my autistic retreats in childhood were ridiculed and chastised. Are we witnessing a repetition of the same frustration with "primitivism"?

Conclusion

The impetus to write this chapter came from the feelings stirred in what appears to be an experience of parasitism in the clinic. The door of the mind seems to close itself against the seeming stealthiness. Scientifically, however, parasitism may be seen as a form of relating that is not dissimilar to symbiosis. Does that allow us to reconsider the lens through which we view parasitism? As mentioned, the foetus is a parasite to his mother. This role is reversed when older parents may become parasitic on their children. Can we use a "binocular" lens—looking at both our emotional responses and the scientific approach simultaneously? And if we do, where might it take us?

Can the link be a dynamic one like the kea parrot of Australia that starts out in a commensal link by cleaning the sheep's skin by eating the ectoparasites, but in winter turns parasitic? Often it seems we have a meaningful link with our patient, and speak the same words, but then we come upon winter and an "impasse" (Rosenfeld, 1987) arrives. We are no longer able to see our way out. Is this perhaps the limit of our imagination? The as-yet "encapsulated" part (Bergstein, 2009).

I have suggested through my epilogue that if the mother/analyst is unable to see what s/he receives from the baby/patient, a parasitic link may be forged. This may be seen in our inability to re-imagine the patient, to be able to expand our spectrum into imagining areas outside the ones we know in ourselves. Parasitism has been related to envy, but differs in the way that it steals to survive. Or when something is offered, it may be stowed away, but the giver does not know; there is a convoluted relationship with both what is given and the giver.

This overlaps with perversion, in that the relationship between giving and taking, mother and baby, or analyst and analysand is "perverted"— "to turn round or about, turn the wrong way, overturn, turn to error or ruin, undo, corrupt" (*OED*, 2009). And yet at times this may be our inability to dream that is experienced as opacity. If we shift the lens from reluctant host, to bewildered, to thin and despairing host, it reveals a variety and complexity that is closer to a sterile link between two hard castle walls.

When the foetus finds a closed-off womb, it takes residence wherever it can find space. I have suggested the priority of this link to the nipple–mouth link in Kleinian writing. This link may provide a paradigmatic space for understanding the primacy of survival in parasitism. The womb has been either parasitic on it, suffocating it like with J. Or the walls have been like those of old castles—opaque and sticky, and the foetus has had to cling tenaciously to the surface—as we saw with Q. Or very thin glass that can only stare back, a travesty of the containing mother. The inaccessible part of the mind can feel attacking but it can also feel asphyxiating or suffocating. This may be experienced as what Meltzer (1990) evocatively calls the claustrum. I have tried to see the claustrum-like space in the bipersonal field as possibly emerging from a stalling of analysis because of an "autistic barrier" (Tustin, 1986) in the analyst. Or the moment of encounter where both patient and analyst seem to be in what Ogden calls the "autistic-contiguous position" (1989).

Often the way to survive is to try to cling to the skin ("adhesive identification" or "adhesive equation"), akin to the clinging of the ectoparasite or to claw a way into the genitals or the anus (perversion). This "claustrum-like" space we could experience in the transference in the feelings of revulsion, suffocation, engulfment, feeling hoodwinked, and even feeling robbed. However, I have tried to suggest that this is a paranoid reading that comes from the roadblocks in our mind. Perhaps tolerating the adhesiveness and the thinness of the parasitic patient is made possible when we see it related to our own opacity, thinness, and rigidity; seeing the "autistic barrier" in ourselves. Parasitic links may be seen to emerge from autistic uncoupling (sterile proximity) when there is a collision between the encapsulated parts of the analytic dyad and an island is formed.

Epilogue

When this was first written one could not possibly have imagined the extent to which a virus, which is considered closest to an "obligate intra-cellular parasite" (as it cannot reproduce outside a host cell) was going to change the world for us. Yet other vertices—environmentalists argue—remind us that it is human encroachment above and beyond all reasonable limits that has ricocheted on us. Different epidemics have reminded us repeatedly of how the hostility of our relationship with nature creates parasitic links. The inability to look beyond a paranoid way still stands in the way of being able to think of this unimaginable assault on human lives. Parasitism may well be the link we form with the other (nature or human being) and not the creature itself.

CHAPTER 6

Mind and body

Prologue

Soul: O who shall, from this dungeon, raise
A soul enslav'd so many ways?
Body: Joy's cheerful madness does perplex,
Or sorrow's other madness vex;
Which knowledge forces me to know,
And memory will not forego.
What but a soul could have the wit
To build me up for sin so fit?
  —Andrew Marvell, "Dialogue between Soul and Body" (1681)

In the lines above, the soul and body have a dialogue where tellingly, the body is granted the last word. The body accuses the soul for ridding it with its own torments. Only the soul (mind/unconscious?) has the wit to inflict such suffering on the body.

Here we see the body as feeling saddled with the mind's torments—an instance of the idea of permeability, a crossing over the schism of mind and body. However, if Western thought is seen as traditionally

117

assuming a body/soul schism, there has been a counter-tradition of seeing a continuity. According to the *Oxford English Reference Dictionary* (1996), Hippocrates (c. 460–370 BC) thought the humours in the body determined temperaments. This idea was the basis of medical treatment and remained popular through the ages. Robert Burton's *The Anatomy of Melancholy* (1628) picked up on the same ideas and created a compendium on an excess fluid in the body (melancholia coming from the condition of having black bile (*OED*, 2009)—an idea harvested by playwrights, doctors, and scholars. Freud's ideas on the mind and body link are a part of this counter-tradition where he brings together a body of knowledge based on ideas of continuum. This continuum reaches its apotheosis in Bion's idea of the protomental system. I suggest the immune system corresponds to his idea of the protomental system.

Introduction

This chapter arises from the repeated and frequent mention patients make of autoimmune conditions. It began to seem like a silent accomplice to what brought them. Sometimes they make causal links: "I visited mother over the weekend and we had this bitter exchange … my ankles and knees have swollen up …" Sometimes the symptoms are an end in themselves: "The fever is back … my stomach hurts … there's bleeding and constipation … then loose motions. I called my gastro … He said there was nothing wrong." And often they are never mentioned but we observe allergic responses, ephemeral pains, and swellings. The chronicling of this became very urgent for me. I will trace here some of the history of ideas on the mind–body link before I conclude with Bion's idea of the protomental apparatus. I suggest that autoimmune conditions appear to belie the mind/body binary. Interpretations in the here and now, however, enable mental functioning and allow it to emerge from a protomental functioning.

In order to explain his theory of thinking, Bion often refers to the digestive system (1962, p. 62), the respiratory system (1965, p. 131), the synaptic system (1962), and musculature. In this chapter it is the immune system (autoimmunity) that I look at to map the primitive ways of the mind, or rather, what Bion refers to as the protomental system, where the mind can only transmit and experience somatic sensations. Perhaps this protomental system exists in the body and the tiniest bits of matter in the body carry particles of what has not become a part of the mind.

Symptoms in autoimmune conditions are often liminal—mysteriously appearing and disappearing. They defy causality and symbolic meaning. Like Bion's (1962) description of minute particles, the relation to internal objects seems to have splintered and scattered all over. Like beta particles (unbearable sensations/stimuli), it is as though cells, tissues, and organs have their own minds.

Autoimmunity is seen briefly from different vertices, including psychoanalysis. It is argued that a "quantum theory of the mind" corresponds to the vagaries of the immune system. It seems that in autoimmunity, the model of the mind follows the logic of Bion's "quantum" theory and not classical Newtonian physics.

This chapter works heuristically, keeping at least three vertices—the immune system, beta particles, and quantum theory—in mind. Finally, it also reflects on its own heuristic devices—the clinical vignettes and the use of analogy and "multiocular vertices" as a way of expanding thinking (Bergstein, 2015, p. 167).

Continuum model: review of literature

When Heisenberg (1971) writes, "The same organising forces that have created nature in all its forms, are responsible for the structure of our soul, and likewise for our capacity to think", he is in fact writing about what I have here called the continuum model. From another vertex, Civitarese writes of how the "continuity between conscious and unconscious experience lies in the fact that 'everything can be transposed'" (2016, p. 118).

Freud decisively moved the deity from Plato (the priority of the mind over body) to Proteus, in Greek mythology, "a minor sea god who had the power of prophecy but who would assume different shapes to avoid answering questions. His name is sometimes used to mean a changing, varying, or inconstant person or thing" (*Oxford English Reference Dictionary*, 1995, 1996). Freud observes how symptoms and feelings constantly change form—slipping, disguising, and morphing. Freud saw hysteria as a variable symptom which attempted to build a bridge (ego) over troubling psychic conflicts (superego and id). It was a condition not defined by its symptoms (which were protean), but by a unique link between body and mind. These ideas central to hysteria are pivotal to the psychoanalytic understanding of a dynamic unconscious, and the psychic capacity to change forms.

When he says "hysterics suffer from reminiscences" (1937d), he effectively bypasses the distinction between body and mind. The bodily symptoms uncannily emerge from unplumbed caverns of the mind. He then extends this to obsessional neuroses. About this he observes,

> There is only one thing he [the obsessional] can do: he can make displacements, and exchanges, he can replace one foolish idea by another somewhat milder, he can proceed from one precaution or prohibition to another, instead of one ceremonial he can perform another ... The ability to displace any symptom into something far removed from its original conformation is a main characteristic of his illness. (Freud, 1916–17, p. 43)

Thus while psychoanalysis travelled in different directions after Freud, one of the common strands has been the assumption of such protean shapes. "If, for Freud, the body was first and foremost sexual, now the emphasis is on protean; versatile rather than sexual," Dimen (2000) writes. "Instead of a contradiction to be resolved," she says, "perhaps the mind-body problem is a paradox to be explored" (pp. 13–14). Most early work maintained an emphasis on the symbolic meaning of bodily symptoms. This "translation" of conflicts into symptoms remains our dominant legacy. Except that what preoccupies psychoanalysis more now is the absence of mentalization in primitive states. These terrors remain sequestered as unmentalized drawbridges in the mind that have closed off excessive psychic pain.

The work of the Paris School of Psychosomatics led to a greater interest in areas where there appeared to be an absence of psychic meaning. This in turn, questioned the paradigm of causality. Unlike in hysteria where there has been a magical leap from the mind to the body, in psychosomatic illnesses, "[T]he body does its own thinking" (McDougall, 1974). Slowly the shift (Marty, 1967; McDougall, 1974, 1989) takes place from psychic conflict to somatisation. "On a similar note, Rosenfeld (2001) mentions an apparent absence of anxiety in psychosomatic illnesses as the split between mental and psychic spheres is complete" (Bronstein, 2011, pp. 184–185).

In her comprehensive paper, Bronstein (2011) observes that while the

> distinction between psychosomatic illness, hysteria and hypo-
> chondria is one that is still generally maintained ... it is not easy
> to discriminate between the three entities and there are many
> analysts who question the validity of making a big difference
> between them. Valabrega ... sees a continuum of a spectrum
> between hysteria and psychosomatic phenomena and he
> proposes a theory of a more general psychosomatic conversion
> where every symptom has a meaning and within which hysterical
> conversion has a place (Valabrega, 1954). Within the Kleinian
> tradition, Herbert Rosenfeld (1964, 2001) described a similar
> mechanism underlying both hypochondriacal and psychoso-
> matic states. (pp. 175–176)

Her point here is that there is a difficulty in distinguishing between symbolised and unsymbolised forms of illness. But she again suggests a continuum between source and content when she writes that the "body is not only a source of unconscious phantasies but can also become an important part of the content of unconscious phantasies". A patient mentioned how she saw her son eating a lot of seeds, "because he wants to grow a baby inside, just like Mummy". Mother's body (and his own) were a source of his phantasy as well as the content of it. Tustin's (1972) "autistic objects" can comprise both parts of the child's own body as well as parts of the outside world experienced as though extensions of the baby's body (p. 64). The self–other distinction does not exist here.

While maintaining a distinction between hysterical and psychoso-matic illnesses, Bronstein suggests that the body

> can function as the arena onto which unconscious phantasies can
> be projected and unconsciously enacted. I think that psychoso-
> matic phenomena are linked to more primitive phantasies and
> to a more concrete form of symbolic functioning than the one
> found in hysterical symptoms but that, however rudimentary and

primitive the patient's capacity to function symbolically might
be, there is always a possibility of establishing some meaningful
contact with his internal world. (p. 163)

The symbolised and unsymbolised coexist in a patient, and the area that
distinguishes them is a bit fuzzy. Bronstein argues for what we may call
a "continuum model". Here the distinction between self and other is
elastic. Bronstein quotes Valabrega (1954) here who argues for a symbolic meaning to psychosomatic illnesses. In this "continuum model"
distinctions are hard to sustain.

On a related note, in his paper on "autistoid" states in non-autistic
patients, Nissen (2008) traces continuities between autistoid and various
other states—narcissism, as-if, obsessional behaviour, eating disorders,
and so on. He traces this idea of the autistic continuum back to Klein
(1980), Bick (1968), Tustin (1986), Ogden (1989), Meltzer (1975c), and
Mitrani (1992), among others. Psychoanalytic theory seems to have
been expanding aspects of the continuum: between the mind and
body; between neurosis and psychosis; between hysteria and psychosomatic illness. In fact, Grotstein (1997b), with his usual felicitousness,
condenses the "bodymind" as a "thinker" of unthinkable thoughts and
"feeler" of disavowed feelings. In other words, "the bodymind seems to
be forced to become the mindbody's keeper" when the latter fails to process what is "on its mind", so to speak … that is, the "body" becomes the
"mind's" "toilet object" (Grotstein, 1997b). This echoes Body's complaint
in Marvell's poem mentioned above. Bion's "momentous turning point
resonates in his concept of the protomental system, something that, like
the drives, stands between the body and the psyche, and that is a part of
the broader protomental group matrix" (Civitarese, 2016, p. 34).

Meltzer (Meltzer et al., 1986) elaborates this connection between what
Bion calls the "basic assumption group mentality" and this "protomental
apparatus". This former has its origins in a deeply unconscious level, the
"protomental apparatus" whose operations correspond closely to Freud's
description of primary process and the prescription that first the ego
is a skin ego. "This seems to mean that at this primitive level the ego does
not make mental representations of emotional experiences but both
construes them as bodily states and reacts to them with bodily states
and actions" (p. 35). Meltzer's expansion here of Bion and his correlation

between basic assumption groups and the protomental apparatus is crucial to understanding the structure of autoimmune disorders and the minus links between groups (bodymind as a whole) and their individual (specific parts of the body) members.

History, culture, symptom: change and continuity

So are we always plagued by the same conflicts and do the same symptoms masquerade differently? Or are we indeed changing as a culture and society and hence manifesting different illnesses? Historically speaking, it appears that the environment is propitious to some illnesses, and less so to others. Within the analytic world, we know that hysteria opened the doors to a vestibular relationship between the body and mind. Many have tried to argue that hysteria is still very much alive, that it has always been protean (Bollas, 2000) but it just has new manifestations such as anorexia nervosa and chronic fatigue—an autoimmune condition (Showalter, 1997). Susan Burke (1992) has argued that chronic fatigue is really a latter-day neurasthenia.

Mitchell (1996) sees hysteria as continuing, but sees a change in Freud's interpretation of it:

> The early psychoanalytic interpretation of hysteria emphasised repression (the pushing into unconscious of illicit ideas). What is emphasised in this middle period by Freud is the importance not of repression in hysteria, … but the importance of regression, that hysteria is in fact a regression to a very early state. In other words, in this period when Freud is not publishing much about hysteria, what he might have been beginning to question is an oedipal theory of it. (p. 474)

Mitchell's idea of continuity (Burke, 1992; Showalter 1987, 1997; Mitchell, 1996; Bollas, 2000) seems to take into account the historical materiality of illnesses. Hysteria and the neuroses took on a political dimension which has over the century exploded into a sexual revolution. Looking back, we see that hysteria had its heyday: associated variously with misogyny, shame, repressed sexuality, creativity, and dissent. But despite attempts to resurrect it, it has gone out of favour.

It was preceded and succeeded by melancholia. Melancholia too has had changing fortunes. As Frosh (2014) observes, the term "melancholia" metamorphoses through history. From being a malady, to a cult (Burton, 1628), to a pathologised diagnosis, to now being "resurrected" evocatively as a response to a divided world—for instance, in the way it is used in post-colonial thought. In two different contexts its use by Kristeva (1992) and Pamuk (2005) harks back nostalgically to its own history.

Narcissism, bipolarity, and ADHD became the more frequent diagnoses through the decades that followed. The diagnosis seems to replace the problem. This often gives the incoherence in primitive states a shape and a form. Following others like Lasch (1979) who make a connection between capitalism and narcissism, D. G. Butler (2015) makes a link between neoliberalism and the precarity/precocity of the autistic spectrum. He speculates when:

> ... the environment is "cracked," the infant's psyche is rendered precocious, threatened with falling or leakage, and forced to compromise with the formation of a precarious second skin (Bick, 1968) or autistic shell (Tustin, 1980). Precarious defenses are often seen in obsessive-compulsive processes such as addiction, or even in quotidian phenomena such as incessant talking, unwavering eye contact, compulsory procrastination, and so on. All create a psyche-somatic boundedness that arrests any sense of falling, leakage, or disintegration ... Time and the sensorium can become autistic objects (Tustin, as cited in Ogden, 1989) against which an amorphous psyche coheres. (p. 35)

He then argues that in a neoliberal environment "working against" or "around" the clock evokes the autistic quality of time as object (p. 35).

While I am more than a little circumspect in asserting this particular link between neoliberalism and autism, it is difficult to deny the number of us who use work as an "autistic sensorium" and the frequency with which we have begun to see autistic mechanisms in neurotic patients (Bick, 1968; Meltzer et al., 1975; Tustin, 1986). Here the suggestion is that historical and material conditions provide a kind of fertile soil and the symptoms get shaped by the soil and the environment. For instance, D. G. Butler suggests, the neoliberal pressure to "make it" forces a kind of "hyper-entrepreneurialism" (p. 36) which brings in its wake fears of falling and leaking—fears we now associate with the autistic spectrum.

In this vein, Ahumada (2016) points out,

> Relevantly, Freud did not grant epistemic priority to theories: "They are not the bottom but the top of the whole structure and they can be replaced or discarded without damaging it" (Freud, 1914c, p. 77).
>
> Moreover, changing as they do across different epochs, human beings are historical, and so is the psyche and its pathologies: therefore psychoanalytic thinking, stemming from the study of neuroses, must change as its object of study changes. (Ahumada, p. 839)

Two lines of argument emerge with somewhat differing emphases. Some might insist on the sameness (protean shapes of old conflicts), while others might emphasise change (psyche changes like everything else).

Having said that, one must guard against binary thinking that always lures the mind, I would like to invoke Heisenberg's idea yet again that Bion (1965) evokes. "The facts to be observed are distorted by the very act of observation" (p. 45). We know this from our experience of analysis where something quite imperceptibly starts to shift, just by our observing it. The either/or between history and psyche is perhaps to be tolerated (even encouraged) and not resolved.

Further still, about limitations in Einstein, Heisenberg says there remains a distinction between observer and the observed, subject and object. However, with quantum particles, this is no longer possible. Being under observation changes the nature in ways that are not measurable or knowable because of "discontinuous changes characteristic of atomic processes" (1971, pp. 2–3). Analogously, these quanta (smallest quantities of energy) are the equivalent of Bion's beta elements or the debris of undigested experiences.

It is this track of thinking that seems to suggest a way of looking at the mind–body link in autoimmune conditions. Bion compares the mind with digestive processes as well as the respiratory system—the "mind is an expelling organ like a gun" (1965, p. 131). It is suggested here that the hypervigilant immune system in many ways follows the strange and uncanny indeterminacy that drew Bion to quantum physics for mapping unmentalized areas of the mind.

Bion asks, "Is it possible to talk to the soma in such a way that the psychosis is able to understand, or vice versa?" (1976, p. 319). I suggest that autoimmunity is one such language in which psychosis speaks through soma. Autoimmune conditions are mostly idiopathic—in that there is no known cause, and hence we are no longer looking for causes, though our writing carries that in its structure and syntax. I think autoimmunity pushes to the brink our thinking of the relationship between the mind and body, in the way the function of the mind (to discern between self/other, me/not-me, friend/enemy) is no longer localised but scattered through the body in different cells, tissues, nerves, and muscles. These different units of the body each "have their own mind" and act with host/ility towards the (host) body which they do not recognise as such. There may or may not be apparent triggers but the symptoms cluster together in what are now recognised as discernible patterns. Hypervigilance acts as an autistic shield that fends off attacks at any sign of psychic unbearability. It wages war and different clusters get militarised. The insurgency is located dynamically—someone with psoriasis could easily get rheumatoid arthritis. This will be discussed later in the case of Pam, whose case I narrativise as a metanarrative on somatopsychic disorders.

Historically and culturally, there has been a startling increase of this diagnosis. About eighty autoimmune diseases have been identified and these include one variant of diabetes, chronic fatigue, fibromyalgia, ankylosing spondylitis, rheumatoid arthritis, lupus, eczema, psoriasis, and multiple sclerosis. These are the better known ones.

There has been growing evidence of the increased frequency of autoimmune diseases across the globe in the last decades. Researchers feel the rise in autoimmune diseases parallels the surge in allergic and cancer conditions while infections are less frequent in the Western societies (Lerner et al., 2015). Does this mean these are on the rise or that we know about them as a related set of conditions and does that shape this perception? However, that is beyond the scope of this chapter which seeks to reflect on how autoimmunity stretches our understanding of the mind–body link and, in order to do so, it proceeds through analogy with quantum physics which seems to have influenced Bion's theory of thinking.

Autoimmunity and monadism

Immunity [ad. L. immūnitās freedom from public services or charges, in med.L. privileged place, sanctuary ... [In] Law. Exemption from a service, obligation, or duty; freedom from liability to taxation, jurisdiction, etc.; privilege granted to an individual or a corporation conferring exemption from certain taxes, burdens, or duties.

—*OED*, 2009

Medical science has skirted around the connection between autoimmune disorders and mental illness. The connection between autoimmunity and neuropsychiatric symptoms has long been acknowledged, and William Osler provided a description of psychosis in systemic lupus erythematosus in 1895. The myasthenic syndromes are good examples of how autoantibodies can cause neurological symptoms.

In one such study (Kayser & Dalmau, 2011) it is noted:

> A role for autoimmune dysfunction in psychiatric illness has been actively investigated since at least the 1930s, when autoantibodies were first reported in a schizophrenia patient. Since that time, there have been myriad reports of specific autoimmune responses to self-antigens in psychosis, affective dysregulation, and other behavioural abnormalities. (p. 90)

Interestingly, in one of the studies on chronic fatigue, it is mentioned that "The authors excluded patients with psychotic illness, organic brain syndrome, or substance dependency; those with concurrent physical problems that the doctor felt could have caused fatigue symptoms; and those obtaining mental health care" (Darbishire et al., 2003).

I quote this passage to note the waiving off of psychotic disorders here. Biomedical discourse arrives at a dead end as it is examining the body as a logically unified entity whose boundaries are marked off by skin. While environmental factors are an obvious and ready factor, medical discourses flounder after making vague hypotheses. The non-causal nature of these illnesses remains mystifying for medical science that tends to be intolerant of incertitude and indeterminacy. The hypotheses may vary from certain environmental factors (Hood, 2003; Smith & Germolec, 1999), to gender (Angum et al., 2020).

The 1948 Nobel Laureate Frank Macfarlane Burnet had begun to wonder about allergies. The usual "scavenging" (Anderson, 2014) process of the body is to get rid of the unwanted cells, but when the immunological system behaves inappropriately, it starts attacking something in it, like nerve endings as in multiple sclerosis. The condition is caused not by an external enemy (bacteria, virus, fungus) but by an attack from within. The muddled up immune system can no longer tell the difference between enemy and friend. Analogously it resembles the psyche under siege which tries to immunise itself from pain that threatens to dissolve it. Neuroses are like civil (in both senses of the word) war; psychoses are like multiple insurgent groups who lose sight of the whole picture.

Derrida's (2003) use of the autoimmune is mostly as a metaphor for the state. His use of the metaphor has at its heart the idea of the self-destructive instinct, or the death drive. Biomedically defined as the state where the immune system destroys the body's cells and tissues, Derrida sees autoimmune conditions as the protective system destroying itself. "As we know, an autoimmunitary process is that strange behaviour where a living being, in quasi-suicidal fashion, 'itself' works to destroy its own protection, to immunise itself against its 'own' immunity" (p. 94).

Lowental (1986) distinguishes two mythological kinds of death: Ker, the violent painful death of the Greeks, and Thanatos, the natural easy one (p. 358). Eigen (1997) sees autoimmune as a form of self-hatred and thus an extension of the death drive. He describes a patient whose "system recoiled and developed an autoimmune illness, signalling she could not take too much of herself" (p. 38).

Teitelbaum (2008) describes one of her patients,

> She suffers as one who dearly loves cats but whose hyper-vigilant auto immune system makes contact with her pets life-threatening. She is allergic to people … hopes in opposition to herself. Her starved psychic-soma, cataclysmically split, is at war with itself, a ghastly self civil war. Neither army is strong enough to carry out the sadistic super-ego's marching orders fight to the death. The psychic haemorrhage, a material experience of floods of violent feelings (Freud, 1950a; Bion, 1953) is an affect with a physical double she knows well. (p. 177)

Once again we see here autoimmunity being seen as a civil war.

Brody (1995) however sees an autoimmune response as corresponding to psychic hypersensitivity. Hatred seems to be at the heart of Brody's observations here as he sees these patients recover from near fatal illnesses and slipping into psychoses. She felt the "autoimmune reaction was related to the psychic hypersensitivity stimulating the patients' inner hates. For such individuals, psychosis served as a survival function" (p. 67). Brody mentions that the medical reports "continue to show a lower incidence of cancer in schizophrenics than in non-schizophrenics" (p. 67).

Brody seems to suggest a distinction between hatred expelled and hatred incorporated. The former is linked with psychoses and the latter with threatening illnesses. If we extend the monadism of classical psychoanalysis, hatred is the most primitive but also indivisible unit. But perhaps hatred itself is constituted by quasi-particles such as dread of pain, thinness, and the unbearability of an unwilling/unavailable container.

While most psychoanalytic theory starting from Freud, as well as post-Derridean theory, seem to use the idea of the autoimmune as linked with the death drive, a form of aggression against the self, I would suggest that both analogical thinking (Derrida) and death drive theory have as their basis a monadic view of the self—that the self is one enclosed unit but which is afflicted by conflict. Akhtar (2015) makes a distinction between "malignant" and "benign" death instincts:

> The malignant variety might be responsible for attacks on linking (i.e., destruction of relatedness, either of thoughts themselves, or of interpersonal bonds in general), black holes in the mind, autoimmune disorders, and intense sadomasochism. The benign variety might be responsible for positive emptiness, dreamless sleep, fallow states of mind, and the psychic pause that often precedes a creative act. (p. 878)

Here Akhtar makes a direct link between autoimmune disorders and a malignant death drive, but parenthetically he mentions "holes in the mind" and "autoimmune disorders" that gesture towards the resemblance between the psychotic part of the mind which like the immune system, is a bustling universe with minute specks of matter, reacting haphazardly to random movements. This has implications for both metapsychology and technique. When we observe the peculiar pattern of hate perhaps it shifts the focus of the technique from interpreting (distance) to experiencing (in the field). The second case discussed later attempts to map the process of building the capacity to think.

Autommunity and quanta

We can say that the idea of self as a unified entity is a monadic view that psychoanalysis questions with its idea of alterity. But otherness is also a coherent formulation that may be within the confines of an integrity of a self. These ideas are still within the realm of classical physics. Britton (2013) makes the point that Freud's idea of the self driven to pleasure is derived from the hydraulic model which is a legacy of Newtonian physics. These ideas had already begun to lose their centrality when Freud was writing—becoming replaced by ideas from quantum physics, but these had not yet permeated widely. Britton writes that Bion's break from classical psychoanalysis is analogous to that of Newtonian physics from quantum mechanics:

> … classical physics is a scientific extension of our natural, perception-based belief systems about the world that shape the structure of our language, whereas quantum mechanics runs counter to these belief systems and can only be expressed in mathematics. We see Bion in his writings of the '60s trying to emancipate psychoanalytic discourse from common-sense language, while simultaneously acknowledging that this language is all we have. (2013, p. 311)

Godwin (1991) suggests an "isomorphism" between the ideas of Bion and those of the physicist Bohm. To him, Bion's work reveals a relationship between the order of the mind and the order of the universe. Quantum theory locates discrete quanta—subatomic particles as primary units. This makes the basic unit unseeable and unverifiable by human perception. This dislocates the principle of causality that Newtonian physics emphasised. We can say that with Bion, the understanding of the psyche moves away from such verifiable ideas of causality and psychic determinism.

Godwin notes that psychoanalysis keeps slipping into the cause and effect language of mechanics. Bion tried to move towards the "implicate" model of matter, where verifiability is seen to be limited to what is "explicate". The underlying field that holds matter together remains hidden. These invisible subatomic particles are held together by the forces of the field but their relationship is not causal; rather it is multidimensional and ultimately unknowable. Only the "explicate", the manifest can be observed and this can constitute provisional knowledge. Bion distinguishes between truth (which is unknowable) and knowledge (what we may feel as the moment's truth).

For now, I will follow the "isomorphism" between the immune system, the life of quanta, and the behaviour of beta elements. If we use the paradigm of quantum physics for our understanding of human workings, we can see that the psychotic part of the personality comprises exploded matter. In Bion's version, a catastrophe underlies the psychotic part of our mind and results in spewed particles of the ego and the object forming bizarre constellations. This to me suggests an ambience of wariness, a mistrust of everything, and a breathing in and out of hostile gases. In such an environment, hyper-vigilance and suspicion form security protocols that are unable to distinguish between friends and enemies. These spewed particles form constellations which act like rogue armies; the symptoms formed by these attacking armies defy causality. These do not have the coherence to discriminate between me and not-me as they are driven by the forces in the field, and too splintered to have a sense of "national" boundaries.

This kind of scattering which Bion traces back to psychotic events, Nissen (2013) sees as a part of what he calls the "autistoid state" in which he locates two features:

> Firstly, the absence of projective identification because hope of containing objects has been abandoned, and, secondly, psychic quality is not sufficiently installed in the elements … Thus, the unmentalized elements that have not found a container are left to roam in a spatio-temporal nowhere. (p. 239)

Either way, these unmentalized elements roaming freely seem to gather together into unstable little militant knots in battle mode as they are not bounded (abandoned hope of containment) and free to attack any other particles.

According to quantum theory, an electron can behave both as a wave and as a particle. In the quantum realm, the particles do not behave consistently or coherently. Here then lies one way of looking at autoimmunity—the cells and tissues, analogously, can behave as parts of the same body (as they do most of the time), but they can also behave autonomously.

Clinical vignettes

In much of the material patients bring, there are passing references to autoimmune symptoms and conditions. However, the autoimmune condition is not what brings them, and the proliferation of symptoms made it difficult to choose the material to discuss here. Should I be using them to "illustrate" some predetermined theory? Or can I write them and see what emerged? I had hoped to do the latter; however, it is hard to banish narrative as it binds the material. I will address these preoccupations in the next chapter. Eventually what emerged were the idiosyncratic nature of these attacks and the thinness of the sessions. I would suggest no causal link but a co-incidence (constant conjunction) of these.

Which of the many patients would I pick? After a lot of revisions, I decided on two. Pam for the long years I have spent, and the chance I got to see the unfolding of the protean nature. It mirrored my own experience of chronic outbursts of different autoimmune states and I have written it as a metanarrative of such a response. Hopefully it gives structure to a peculiar but rather frequent response of the protomental state.

Events in her life had seemingly triggered responses in her immune system. But these had acquired different forms over the years. They appeared like ephemeral expressions signposting painful psychic events. As though the cells and organs "changed their minds" but seemed to be interrelated in ways that fall beyond my understanding and hence beyond the scope of this chapter. Working with Pam has been an intimate experience for me. Unknown to her, I was often living out similarly incoherent clusters of symptoms.

For the second case, I chose Lina because I wanted to reflect on texture and technique. The diffuse, incoherent beginnings which were hard to tolerate, being often followed by some relief, gave her sessions a very distinct rhythm. Extending the idea of reversible arrows, Bion (1965, pp. 80–81) suggests that the psychic state may often move between the poles of "narcissistic⇌socialistic", that is, we are constantly moving between being self-absorbed and object-related. I have extended this further to suggest that we are always moving between states of mind that move between poles: somatic⇌mentalized, incoherent⇌coherent, diffuse⇌substantial. I have tried to abjure causation mainly because this condition belies causality. It is built around the paradigm of trigger rather than cause. A patient, for instance, can't bear the sun, and there is no "cause" for it. Triggers tend to pose as causes. I have instead tried to weave the illogic of quanta into the two vignettes—the mysterious coming and going, the absence of cause, the diffuse states, the spectral coherence (an uncanny feeling of déjà vu) in various registers.

Case 1: Metanarrative of autoimmunity

Pam was about thirty-five when she came to me, attractive—if you looked carefully. At first sight, she looked small, diffident, sketchy. She had a very sombre, sad manner. Mother had been an invalid ever since she could recall and had a proliferating number of symptoms. As she recalled it mother had a long, complicated menopause (which little Pam imagined as a form of cancer); this was followed by "clamminess", migraines that would last for days, and palpitations.

In her childhood, mother would ask her children to massage her constantly because she was in so much pain. Father took care of mother. Husband took care of Pam. [*Of late she had developed an embarrassing allergy to her husband. Every time he touched her, she broke out into pustules.*] But her main symptom was anxiety—about coming to me, going to work, meeting people, travelling. Everything, in short. And it made her retch—just thinking of coming to see me. All encounters made her nervous. She would speak of all this in a very dead, monotonous voice. Here is an excerpt from a very early session where she speaks about how anxious she was about coming to me:

She: The other day the office internet had broken down, and we were supposed to sit at home and work, and I felt much calmer, was able to work at my own pace, and in the order I wanted to.

Me: I see you as a tortoise trudging along with your house. It weighs you
down, slows you, but it ensures you are never without an armour.
It would be scary to meet me without it.

She had been very angry with her family, especially mother for having
been an invalid all her life. She was very slow to agree to come for
sessions, impersonalising me as she talked, making me feel inanimate. Her marriage was reasonably "happy". She came when mother
was dying. She mostly avoided going to her natal home. As a young
girl, she had been somewhat given to bouts of illnesses. The family
took these seriously. Her childhood had been plagued by what we
now realise was irritable bowel syndrome. However, in a family that
somatised and self-medicated, she had had endless antibiotics and
painkillers.

Being with her felt very lifeless initially, and I could only feel her
obliviousness to me. She would weep silently about how numb she felt.
She felt disconnected from her parents and her husband, and could not
bear to hear their problems. The tears felt evacuative—of pain that she
could not suffer. In her twenties, she developed excruciating pains in
her back and joints. It was diagnosed as fibromyalgia—an autoimmune
disorder where there is a lot of pain in bones and muscles and fatigue.
Her husband decided that children were off the table for them.

After a year or so, however, she did get pregnant and decided to have
the baby. The pregnancy seemed to have gone by without too much anxiety. She did not complain of physical pains. She had a daughter but this
could not bring her back to life. Her husband did the mothering, while
she lay in her bed with a collapsed back.

When her daughter was about one, Pam met her old love who had
moved to another city. This is when she burst into life. She resumed work
and her figure seemed to become womanly all of a sudden. She con-
fessed she had been very guilty of having loved this man, even though
she had married the man her family had arranged. She had kept this a
secret from me till then. This man had also subsequently got married,
and she was relieved when she heard that. "I could not bear to hurt my
husband, you see," she said by way of explanation.

This man, W, a writer, became an obsession for the next six years of
the analysis. She stalked him online—his photos, the articles he wrote;

she collected news of him from an extended circle of acquaintances. But equally she would take great care to avoid bumping into him since he moved back into her town. She was convinced he was very drawn to her, and there would be a great volcanic eruption if they met. This avoidance was carried on with the same obsessive zeal as the obsession itself.

Then one day, despite all her precautions (not going to his neighbourhood, not meeting his friends, not taking that route, not visiting that grocery store), she ran into him. It was at the movies. She was with a friend and he was alone. He spotted her from a distance, and came up to her and they had what sounded like a flirtatious conversation. She said they bonded instantly—as always. She had not slept since then. I was surprised that there was some basis to her fantasy.

But soon after this she had a prolonged breakdown which lasted for about four years and which I watched with complete helplessness. She would find herself writing to him, going to his neighbourhood, drinking the same coffee he drank, eating the same food, reading the books he read.

She also began to smoke weed (like him) and drink. She would lock herself in her bathroom, and hug her knees, and bang her head softly, rhythmically, or just lie on the bathroom floor weeping, slapping her face lightly. After this attempted expulsion of her uncontrollable feelings, she would smoke a joint, wash her face, and resume her routines. The family did not appear to notice these mini-breakdown states, she said. Although her little daughter told a story about a girl whose mother never ever smiled.

Then came summer which was long. Pam was now working in an office close to W. She heard that W and his wife were going to have their second child in the wife's native country. Pam had never been abroad. She took to walking in the hot afternoons around his area, almost tracing his path on blazing summer afternoons. That is when the strange symptoms started. She got a light fever that would come on every single afternoon. She said she could not bear the pain. She could not believe he had a wife and child—no matter how much she tried to imagine it. She would stand in her shower and slap herself hard, trying to make herself believe this, but could not. I would feel her need to get some contact with her pain. Inflicting the body was for her a way of tolerating it and ameliorating what was so unbearable for her mind. This is reminiscent of the Muharram processions where followers of Islam hit themselves in the name of the martyrs Hassan and Hussain.

She then developed a pain in her small joints, stiffness, intense back pain, and spondylitis. The intensity of these symptoms would fluctuate mysteriously. After a month or so, her husband took her for tests. Eventually they said it was a form of auto-immune disorder. They told her she had a rare disorder—ankylosing spondylitis—because her spine was straightening. Rest won't help, sleep won't refresh. She could barely sleep as it was. After summer, this man W returned to town. She met him now, by design. These meetings would still lead to a flaring up of anxiety. She was unable to sleep. She would always wake up at 2 a.m., sweating and palpitating. After six months, she was able to get back to work.

But come next summer, there was a repetition of the same situation. Now she would occasionally call W and they would talk. After each such episode, she would have hives that would look like whiplashes on her back and neck. But next summer, she had terrible palpitations, on occasion having to take an anti-anxiety pill to "steady her heart" she said. "At times I have to rock myself to and fro because otherwise I will burst." "I have to rescue him," she would insist. I would feel helpless in dealing with what sounded delusional. She made no mention of his wife or child/ren. "He will break down." Perhaps with some irritation, I would ask her why she wasn't helping him in that case. "I can't bear to hurt my husband." There was this repetitive rhythm in her speech. She barely noticed her daughter. All this while the fever raged, as did the anxiety. But now the pain had travelled from her fine joints to her body. This was "chronic fatigue", her doctor said. The rashes continued to come and go. But the fever wore off after some months.

Despite her obsessions and delusions, Pam can now talk about her "madness" with ironic amusement, when she is not rocking herself on the couch to soothe herself. But what she continues to go through is not something to do with her hysterical fear of her bursting sexuality. In fact over the years, there has been no real interest in pursuing this man. They are good friends now, and her obsession has abated. But symptoms return every time—and often clustered differently—when there is an emotionally difficult situation like when her husband had to undergo surgery, when she got laid off at work, when she had to pay off some family debts. But she says she has learned to live with the fatigue, and she pushes herself really hard, and when she does she can force herself "against gravity". After getting up, stretching, and walking, she can resume her routine.

Retrospectively I learned that she had experienced throughout her childhood and early teens long stretches of being bedridden. She had been suspected of juvenile heart disease and rheumatic arthritis—both of which her system had "mimicked"—but which she was apparently cleared of having. She had suffered years of irritable bowel syndrome. These bits of information were not connected in her mind. There appeared to me something quite uncanny in the way the immune system "mimics" diseases.

It feels like a language was being forged. In Pam's case, it was a family language. They communicated with each other and with themselves through these strange, uncanny, somatic telegraphs. W was for Pam the threat to her psychic economy. She knew that an encounter with this very beautiful, sensitive man would usher a long awaited encounter with unlived pain and she both courted and evaded this. She did meet him and her breakdown was moving for me—it felt as though she longed to get in touch with her pain. Later, I felt my inability to make sense of her experience drove her to desperation. With Pam I had felt dread and emptiness. I saw Dali's elongated clocks in my mind and the barren desert landscape of my childhood would flood my mind. These images of aridity would not cohere into an experience I could name. I felt I had no thoughts but heaviness which I longed to get away from. This despair began to take shape as an object who dreaded the passage of time as it was filled with irrevocable losses. I had become the object who could not translate sensations into feelings and emotions. Our link was rife with incoherence. Then Pam's mother died and she was visited by her aunt. This aunt told Pam her mother had been left with her grandparents when she was a baby. That she returned to her parents and siblings at a much later age. Yet she never spoke about this and not even her husband ever learned this. Instead she spoke with the deepest affection for her parents and an idealised childhood. The bodily symptoms had become the percussion instruments for these consoling lies. The music Pam inherited was filled with such percussion. And it was this deafened object that I had become in the transference. She had been telling me of time having melted away like the clocks while she awaited meaning. I had remained in a stupor, unable to give meaning to the dreams.

I have written a rather long account of Pam. It seemed difficult to map such a formless landscape without some detail. But I did want to record the peculiarly protean nature of these symptoms that seemed to move like a batch of waves.

During the ankylosing phase, the pain in her joints had an ephemeral quality. It could move from finger joints, to the wrists, to her toes. It took the form of different disorders, but each of these clusters was discrete. There seemed to be a very wide spectrum of symptoms that promiscuously and erratically came together apparently devoid of symbolic meaning. They would group together and then disperse and then regroup in another location. I was able to put together her story as I wrote this, and much of it made sense to me as it mirrored my own peculiar history of ephemeral pains, their abrupt onsets, and their erratic duration.

Perhaps one is always tempted to look for patterns, and so the different clusters of autoimmune illnesses seemed to suggest an "incoherent" pattern. Such a pattern is not spatially or temporally predictable or knowable in advance. But when there is an outbreak, there appears to be some pattern and the break takes the shape of one autoimmune condition or another.

Case 2: Texture and movement

Lina is about thirty-five years old and she got in touch saying she had been diagnosed with multiple sclerosis. She had been my patient almost eight years before and had terminated after what seemed a sufficient analysis at the time. She was one of my earliest analytic patients, and I remember how intimate our experience of closeness was. She had moved to this country from her own troubled country—to seek shelter and employment. She was very fragile then.

This time round, I only notice her diffusion. She seems to respond to the comfort of the room, my silent somewhat unsmiling presence, the hum of the air conditioner. It is early days yet, but there has not been a relapse or hospitalisation since she came in. Much to my chagrin, she only gives credit to the medication. She sounds confused and disconnected, hiding in her enclave. Afraid to emerge from there. She speaks of her repeated hospitalisations, different drugs being used, the randomness of the attacks, and the unpredictability of the fatigue levels. There appears to be very little mentalization. I do not recognise her as the same young girl who came all those years ago. She had been a charming, quite beautiful young woman men fell in love with but went on to discard quickly. But she has aged more than the years allow for. Her waist has thickened and she has acquired a dull, vacant look. She giggles at many things, like language that is not concrete—analogies, metaphors, conceits: all feel absurd to her. Her responses to me are often facetious. This "attack" on thinking does not come from her envy, but is more like a nervousness at her inability to comprehend. It is a confusion that is somewhat shaming. Occasionally she would take recourse in the intellectualising (using rehearsed politically correct ideas) about not having "desire" or about not believing in "biological" families. There was a great deal of what Meltzer describes as an "idealisation of confusion".

Session

She: So I can't decide whether I should take up this offer at work. I spoke to my boss and I said I was quite keen and … then I was quite ambivalent. I said I can go after eight to nine months … nothing is clear [*yawns*] … the rent control act is proving to be a nuisance in [x] case … I am so exhausted … last night I forgot my medication and I felt different … this morning my husband gave me a neck rub and my body felt different … I am feeling very tired today … ate a lot of rice and potato for lunch …

Me: [*confused*] It is difficult to think when there is so much confusion …

She: Yes. Nothing is certain … paperwork, job, medical treatment …

Me: [*I now speak about the effect of her confusion*] When there are so many different thoughts, it creates confusion, if there is no processor. For instance, this air conditioner here needs a voltage stabiliser [*she giggles at this*]. Otherwise the AC will either trip or die.

She: [*suddenly awake*] It is funny. My leg feels like that. May I show this to you? [*I nod—she shows me how her leg can either stay rigid or else swing crazily. It has no "stabiliser"*]

We spoke of the mind as a stabiliser, how it needed to regulate impulses. To be able to distinguish between outside and inside, it needed to regulate the current, so that it can keep the machine whirring. This changed the texture of the session. She became quieter, more thoughtful.

In another session she spoke of the usual. Fatigue. Bad sleep. Inability to complete her work, feeling like a failure. She then got out of bed to google MS.

She: There were all these things people say, bit depressing. Put a lot of pressure on you—you just have to force yourself … etc.

[*I found myself agreeing with her annoyance over a particularly unappealing kind of popular register of mastery.*]

Me: It feels frustrating to hear all this positive thinking …
She: You just have to force yourself and then it happens … Totally.
Me: And it's a bit like retreating into a room, when the world is grey and frustrating.
She: It's the fatigue that makes me like this …
Me: I thought you retreat into this room because you are frustrated and then fatigue overcomes you …

[*She looked suspicious as if I were suggesting the fatigue was unreal. This was always a temptation and I had to guard against the trap of suggesting that her symptoms were fabricated, that I was in any way denying her pain.*]

She: Well, it's funny actually, when I came in I was feeling very fatigued, and I still have the same sensation now. Only now I feel it like an excitement.
Me: Hmm … the mind translates this sensation differently, doesn't it …?

[*I would find myself wanting to argue, to assert the primacy of the mind. Much like the self-help stuff she loathed.*]

Me: When I say that I sound like the self-help books. It seems you can master your symptoms, while you are actually overwhelmed.

She: What am I so overwhelmed by? What do I need to retreat from?

[*There was an irritation in her tone and these felt like pseudo-questions. After a pause, she resumed.*] I don't feel like talking about work. [*She was afraid of being laid off by her company and there wasn't another job on the horizon.*]

Me: Sometimes you wish I could soothe your mind without visiting such unpleasant thoughts …

[*She talked about her fatigue again.*]

She: I feel like an old woman.
Me: Prematurely old. Hmm. [*Must be quite comforting, I think.*] It feels risky to feel things …?
She: [*suddenly roused*] Oh it's risky all right, to listen to music, to watch movies, to read books …
Me: To feel things …?
She: I am so afraid of hurting C … [*her husband*]. It's very nice to be like this old woman, with no desires; he takes care of me. I feel like there is a huge thick wall between the world and me. It's tiring to come out from there … Once I leave here though, I am usually feeling better.
Me: The fatigue is so great, everything else is blurred …
She: But when I am mentally stimulated, I feel less fatigue. The connection with physical activity is erratic. Sometimes it will make it worse, sometimes better. When I wake up, I feel most tired. I don't know why I am coming here. I have done no exercise this last week. My body feels bad. I am scared it's coming back. The fatigue you know … just so much work, could not make it to exercise. [*She presses points in her arms.*] There are currents in my arms. Tingly feelings … I feel I am regressing … probably not. It just feels like it. There are only four weeks left with you. I find it reassuring …
Me: [*I felt the flatlines of our connection and I thought of how intense it was over a decade ago. As though we had been trying to stimulate memory and desire to connect.*] Perhaps you are comparing this

with how you used to be when you first came to me. It was all very intense then. It would be nice to go back to that. But it just doesn't come easy. We are both a lot older now.

She: That's true. Then I had fantasies I liked to speak to you about …
      But this time, it's different.

[*The sessions would come to life if I managed to pull at some thread that felt alive. I could hear her think.*]

In the next session she would return to the same monotonous repetition of fatigue. Many sessions have her yawning and saying she has work on her mind.

Me: It feels like you are coming here for my sake. Somehow it is my
      need to see you and not yours.

She: It does feel like that … You know I am working so hard with the
      refugee crisis. There was this meeting with a minister and I had to
      come here!

Me: Perhaps you have a lot of important assignments and significant
      tasks at hand, and this feels small and unimportant.

She: [*sheepish*] I feel very ashamed of being like that. I dreamt that I was
      having dinner at R's [*an important political figure*] …

By the time the session ended, she was thinking more clearly and feeling grounded. This emergence from a self-absorbed state would enable her to think more clearly.

   This movement is reminiscent of Bion's (1965) aforementioned idea of narcissistic⇋socialistic (pp. 80–81). This would usually coincide with some movement from somatic⇋mentalized. The somatic sensations would give way to mental functioning and this would be apparent in the changes of tone, mood, and alertness. After the eight-year hiatus, Lina is a different person. She had come before because she would fall intensely in love and it would end disastrously. Through the cataclysmic violence of her love affairs, she would flare into life. But this would leave her feeling wrecked. In Lina's first analysis, I think we collaborated in a seductive relationship of great mutual admiration. This may have given her a glossy, confident air. But this link itself was unanalysed as was the underlying debris. When Lina came back, she had understandably a belief in my magical powers. But it had been long and I was incredulous at how differently I felt. This must have been a crushing disappointment for her. The nervous giggles, the flippant comments, the big talk, were her ways of pulling me down, so we could go back to where we had left off; a mutual admiration club of sorts. But this time I felt moral about her childlike seductiveness and dealt her a blow. Giving meaning to the movements in the session was like breaking a spell. This was met with derision as she was hurt and confused by the changed object. The infantile mother and her angelic baby were imperilled by a harsh, thinking object. This was no longer an infantile mother, but a steely, no-nonsense mother. Thinking through some of this in the transference mobilised movement, but was painful for her and felt brutal to me. We were living in the transference of the mother, who on discovering her child's gnawing, pubertal body, suddenly withdraws her love. It seemed Lina had experienced something like that.

Bergstein (2020) suggests that hypochondriacal pain while undoubtedly felt by the patient is "hallucinated in the way Bion uses the term—not organic but induced to contain the rupture that threatens to unravel the psyche with its formless opacity". Accordingly, Bergstein writes: "Hypochondriachal symptoms may therefore be signs of an attempt to establish contact with psychic quality by substituting physical sensation for the missing sense data of psychical quality" (p. 5). Autoimmune symptoms, it seems to me, are an attempt by the body to form a language through which there might be a link with the mind. It is a desperate language with a very unfathomable vocabulary and idiosyncratic syntax. And yet it is quite unmistakably a language. It is just that we don't seem to know how to read it.

When we are able, occasionally, to expand her mind to make connections, to give meaning to sensations, the experience of the symptom will change. Also, from being more self-absorbed, she showed awareness of my presence. The carapace makes room for her to feel in touch with herself and me. She is to leave the country now and we will have to terminate again. Her talk has more flesh, it feels less airy. We are able to speak about our termination this second time, and how she was able to carry our connection over the years.

With both Pam and Lina there is a strong wish to retreat into their shells. The differences are manifold, but it is the similarities that I am keener to focus on. Pam's internal world feels more dead. They are more like a frieze than flesh and blood people. Lina's world is peopled by gauzy objects that are thin, diaphanous, and keep disappearing. Both appear self-absorbed and superficially appear narcissistic. But it is an economy that is aimed at keeping its equilibrium. The outbreak of symptoms seemed to come in discrete wave patterns, and there was no predicting the next one. There remains a kind of probability that is between "possibility and reality" in the way Heisenberg describes it:

> The probability wave … meant a tendency for something. It was a quantitative version of the old concept of "potentia" in Aristotelian philosophy. It introduced something standing in the middle between the idea of an event and the actual event, a strange kind of physical reality just in the middle between possibility and reality. (Heisenberg, 1989, p. 12)

Epilogue

Meltzer (Meltzer et al., 1986) writes,

> … we cannot expect to deal with psycho-somatic phenomena by interpretation of content whether they present as disease entities or as transient events in the course of analysis. We must set ourselves an entirely different task, namely that of discovering the emotional experience which the patient is unable to dream about and to do his dreaming for him. One implication is quite clear, that we cannot perform this function intellectually; it requires an unusual degree of identification with the patient, an unusual depth of reverie in the session, and an unusual degree of tolerance of feeling mad oneself. This also implies at this point of the discussion that we must entertain the hypothesis that it may be a mad theory which finds its appeal within a psychotic part of our own personalities. (p. 37)

It is significant that Meltzer here locates our tolerance of the "psychotic part of our personality" as pivotal in the analysis when dealing with unsymbolised illness.

It is suggested that autoimmunity can provide a new dimension for the relationship between mind and body. Bion often thought analogously and suggested that the mind worked like the digestive system or the respiratory system. Thinking analogously expands our way of thinking about the mind/body. Autoimmune illnesses can be thought of analogously if we allow that minute particles have minds and are full of proto-thoughts and proto-emotions. This paves the way between a mind divided against itself, to the idea of smithereens of the mind dispersed all over the body, that is, minus links between the mind and body.

I have followed what we may term Bion's "quantum theory of the psyche", where he imagines psychoses like a nuclear explosion (catastrophe). Such an explosion releases heat, energy, light, and small often unstable bits of subdivided particles. In the psyche, exploded beta particles (feelings and sensations that have not got shape as they have not been experienced) come together in apparently incoherent ways forming patterns that we may see, but these do not conform to the logic of a nation state. The links appear absent but there appears to be an eloquent if ineffable pattern. There yet remains some kind of communication between these particles and some inexplicable language that autoimmune conditions speak. We are not yet sure how to listen to these communications.

These particles of un-tolerated experiences have sprayed all over but they can also come together. Hence there can be processes equally unknowable that cause fission and fusion, explosions and implosions, assembling and splintering.

This corresponds to the behaviour of symptoms discussed in the two clinical vignettes. The analytic work was mostly about giving form to sensations. This seemed to have a cohering effect and sensations became legible as feelings in the here and now. It was about trying to stay with the experience of being together in a lively way. Perhaps this was more true in the first case where my own history permeated my experience of Pam. Over time, she did become more reachable—both to me, and to herself.

While leaning into other disciplines to elaborate psychoanalysis, Freud warned that even as "provisional ideas [to] assist us in approaching something unknown", it is important "not to mistake the scaffolding for the building" (Freud, 1900a, p. 536). But as I write this, I become aware of how much psychoanalysis relies on other registers to elaborate its rather counter-intuitive speculations of the inchoate unconscious.

Analogy and metaphor are pivotal in this exercise of mentalizing the unmentalized. This "work of figurability" (Botella & Botella, 2005) is always in danger; I write this to reiterate that while I am using Bion's idea of the mind to try to elaborate how the idea of autoimmune extends the mind–body relationship, I am acutely aware that despite professing to extend metaphoric (Derrida) and analogical (Bion) ways of thinking about autoimmunity, I have used it in a literal and clinical way as well.

It proposes an analogy between certain ideas in quantum physics and the unconscious.

This analogy works like an "isomorphism" or a correspondence and hence it exceeds its analogical function and lays itself open to dangers such as allegorising complexity. But perhaps this is the limitation of the mind. Perhaps it is best to think of this chapter as creating a multiocular experience:

> The fact that different disciplines, at different times and from different vertices, describe the same experience gives this experience greater validity … this encounter between different vertices is an emotional experience in itself … of discovering coherence … (Bergstein, 2019, p. 167)

I have given instances of work with patients where I have worked in the way I would any other time. Clinically it was and often is hardest to be in the area of diffusion (where thinking is thin or absent, and the thoughts like a thin spray of particles appear to attack one's thinking). Faced with diffusion, I would either impose my own need for coherence by projecting my experience, or retreat autistically.

But just being and observing my own feelings (when possible without floating away into my autistic corner) would enable a shape and form to the diffusion, which once observed would change. I found that rather than trying to give meaning to the symptoms, being alive to the shift in symptoms during the here and now would embody the functioning of the mind, separating it from the bodymind. I also found that in the transference I became the "stupid" internal object with Pam and the disappointed (and disappointing) internal object with Lina.

Just as a metaphor points to something else, locates the centre of meaning somewhere else, we must remember that ultimately there is not, nor can there be, one definitive centre of meaning. By the very nature of our capacity to use metaphor, we are guaranteed continuous new meanings (Gargiulo, 1998, p. 416).

There is no way I have of "understanding" autoimmune illnesses and yet the hope is that by observing them, one can expand certain ideas we have of the links between the mind and the body. Accordingly, it may be apposite to conclude with a conversation Heisenberg (1971) has with Bohr:

If the inner structure of the atoms is inaccessible to an illustrative [anschauliche] description, as you say, if we basically have no language to speak about this structure, will we ever be able to understand the atoms? Bohr hesitated for a moment, then he replied: "Yes we will. But at the same time we will have to learn what the word 'understanding' means." (p. 64)

CHAPTER 7

Endings and failures

... we keep our watch and wait the final day, count no man happy till he dies, free of pain at last.

—*Oedipus Rex*, Sophocles, 429 BC

Psycho-analytic research is perhaps always to some extent an attempt on the part of an analyst to carry the work of his own analysis further than the point to which his own analyst could get him.

—Winnicott (1949, p. 69)

Prologue: *veritas* and *mendacium*

Phaedrus' fable mentioned in the epigraph to this book is a good reminder that *veritas* and *mendacium* resemble each other far too much for us to be certain of our truths. Here we may read the dissembling impostor as our abundant capacity to evade the truth in our writing.

Ineluctability of failure

Away from the incandescence of truth, the dazzling luminosity of candour, falls the penumbra or the indeterminate area that is neither truth nor deceit. Freud paves the way to a notion of truth that is by its nature in this penumbra. In a letter to Fliess, Freud (1888) quotes Gregory Zilboorg: "In truth, we are potentially or actually hallucinating people during the greater part of our lives" (p. 25). This rich and paradoxical line foregrounds psychoanalysis and its relationship to truth. Perhaps "hallucinating" is the way to reach psychic truth. The pursuit of truth while being crucial to psychoanalysis may also be experienced as hallucinatory.

About falsification, Freud (1937c) writes,

> We know that the first step towards attaining intellectual mastery of our environment is to discover generalisations, rules and laws which bring order into chaos. In doing this we simplify the world of phenomena; but we cannot avoid falsifying it, especially if we are dealing with processes of development and change. (p. 228)

On a related note, for Bion (1967), the analytic encounter is ineffable, always exceeding verbal communication. When we write down our sessions, we can either mechanically reproduce the words, or we can artistically capture the encounter, like a dream. Either way, we have moved away from the lived experience of it. The writing of it then is a falsification, one way or another: "The report of a session ... must be a literal and incomprehensible jumble or it must be an artistic representation ..." (p. 131).

I want to expand on the idea of failure here, and link it with analytic untruth which is not a conscious or moral violation, but marks the limits of analytic thinkability.

In a previous chapter, it is observed that most often, when we write, our narratives move from despair to hope, from darkness to light, from chaos to order, and our narratives often end up reading like *Bildungsromans*—stories of patients who grow, mature, and develop. In this chapter I wonder about other kinds of analytic links which could be destructive—like stillborn foetuses, premature births, abortions, miscarriages. There can also be fruitless unions of sterility and barrenness. These too could be placed on the negative grid.

In this penultimate chapter I reflect on how untruths and un-successes may fall in the backyards of our mind. These could be linked to impasses and failures—evasions of emotional truth. This is similar to the idea of "bastions" (Baranger & Baranger, 2008), except that perhaps a bastion is a very particular structure of collusion between the analyst and analysand who together evade corresponding truths. Instead, what I imagine is something inevitably recalcitrant in the nature of unconscious communication, and something ineluctable in arriving at the limits of our thinkability, or "autistic islands". There may be mistakes we make that prove irreparable. And there are those that go unnoticed by patients and those that go unnoticed by analysts. There are momentous failures as well as ordinary failures.

Among the quotidian failures may be patients who remain erratic, who drop out, who cut down the number of sessions, who insist on termination before we think they are ready, those who "move cities", and the hardest category—usually the trainees (ourselves included)—who may just carry on for years with no apparent change. All these may not announce themselves as dramatic failures, but they do fall on the spectrum. In fact I use the idea of failure to include the invisible forms and shapes of un-success. And many of these may be traced back to a blindness towards neglected areas of transference, but we often find it a rather elusive phenomenon that keeps slipping away and changing in the analytic space—somewhat like a shape-shifter. This brings up questions in my mind about what areas go unexamined in our daily practice. First I will look at some of these in my own practice. Could these be setting the tone for some of what feels like failure?

Questions about some neglected areas in transference

We find many people who are keen to get help and we each of us turn away many of these potential patients. When we have a free slot and find ourselves in a place where we need to choose a patient, what are the ways in which we pick and choose our patients? Do we take the first one who calls? If not, why this one and not that one? And what do we tell ourselves when we agree to X but refuse Y? Do we assess their economic potential? Is this more important when you have a sliding scale?

A patient of mine who is a consultant told me he was having a Zoom meeting with a new client, and all the while he was listening to this man he was also looking at a painting behind his client and assessing how much he could charge him. I recall the intensely uncomfortable feelings this evoked in the transference. Was I the same as him? Did I need him to be rich when I took him on? There may also be other not so noble reasons we have to take on new cases—maybe to have an influential patient who is famous and who may lead us to fame—and even more ordinarily, to take a patient who is "interesting". This is in fact quite common and may disguise other deeper transferential feelings. Who do we find interesting?

In fact, I would like to go out on a limb and suggest we always do have some criteria. And that these often go unnoticed. Some patients make us feel indispensable, or even just significant. Sometimes they excite our voyeurism. Culturally and emotionally, they arouse affinity. Or inversely, they excite our curiosity about difference. Here race, culture, ethnicity, sexual diversity are all big players and may go unanalysed as they evoke shame in us. Collegial discussions often lead to feelings of inferiority in therapists when the patient is richer, better read, more travelled. All too often we are being seduced, intimidated, patronised, and such engulfing feelings blind us.

Or do we choose because one person is more apparently needy than another? That is, do we secretly indulge our omnipotence? Or do we choose a patient who is from our fraternity? Someone who will help others?

An ambition to help the patient is inadequate, Bion (1967) observed. For if we do that, this will be quickly grasped by him and swept into his system of attack. If the psychoanalyst has formulated any other aim, Bion writes warningly, then he is no better off. The patient knows and will demolish this or use it to attack him. If someone is taken as an obligation to someone or something, this too often becomes a source of great hostility.

So all our well-meaning beliefs—to spread the word, to help a friend's family member, to help a patient's friend are stood on their head. In one such effort I made to oblige a colleague, the patient became convinced that I was in cahoots with his sister and thereby his parents to keep tabs on him. He may well have been right. Not because I was breaching confidentiality, but in so far as his family's design was concerned and my being a part of this apparatus in his mind. Perhaps the family had wanted an ally to bring him back into the fold. This treatment did not last. My blindness to his fantasies certainly did not help our relationship. Naively, I imagined I was agreeing to a colleague's request and this would have no consequence.

Another instance I am thinking of was a patient who passed on the number of her therapist to her friend. An everyday occurrence. This patient was a very quiet, docile woman who spoke so softly that the therapist could not hear her. The patient she referred turned out to be violent and homicidal/suicidal. The latter treatment did not last. In a subsequent session, the therapist felt decimated by her old docile patient in a way that she could not understand. She could not understand because the verbal exchange had been very civil. But when we discussed this later, it emerged that the patient had referred a violently rejected part of herself and this was really her way of bringing that into the transference. However, when this violence could not be tolerated in the analysis, the original patient had no choice but to bring it to my colleague. This was a strange, uncanny experience for both of us to observe. It made me retrospectively aware of many such referrals that I had failed to observe analytically.

Is it possible we decide based on their symptoms? Are we put off by their symptoms—too aggressive, too boring, too psychotic? I remember being caught by John Steiner's (2015) mention that considering that we are psychiatrists and psychoanalysts, we actually hate psychosis and are always wanting to get rid of it. We unthinkingly encourage our patients to go to psychiatrists, so they can take pills that suppress their symptoms and make it easier for us to deal with them. How many times may this have influenced our work with our patients? Which patients do we refer out? At the beginning of my career when I was quite eager to start, I recall wondering if certain colleagues were dumping the "undesirable" patients on me. Equally, it must be said that there were the generous colleagues, thanks to whom I had patients who I felt were "good" patients. What or who then qualifies as a good patient?

These very questions of our criteria become a lot more intense when we have students who come to us with stated and unstated hopes of becoming analysts. When we take on somebody who is also interested in training, it is altogether tricky territory. The chances of a pseudo-analysis are greater, as perhaps all my colleagues know.

In the case of such patients, what Meltzer (1990) calls the "preformed transference" is a lot stronger. He describes the preformed transference as that "which has gathered its expectations from literature, films, friends' accounts. It is generally either austerely institutional or wildly romantic and is set aside fairly promptly when the setting has been clarified" (p. 97). This should give way in due course to the gathering of a transference that is not coming from inherited ideas but is rooted in the specificity of the transference that takes shape in the analytic field. Both analyst and patient unconsciously may deviate from analysis into pedagogy.

I recall a colleague who took on a patient who happened to be a student and was taken aback when, after two years, the patient asked about the next step. The next step to what, my colleague asked? In the patient's omniscient projection, the analyst "knew" that she wanted to train, but this had never been spoken of. This is an instance of omniscience on the part of the patient of course, but it makes me think that this is one of those unstated aspects in the transference which we may—I certainly feel this true for me—fail to address as it may never present itself—until it actually does.

Analysts may find the pressure of such unstated and even stated hopes quite intolerable or even offensive. They may also develop a mentor-like relationship with their trainees. In the latter case, there may be areas of omnipotence, as when analysts have any relations outside the analytic arena—these could be seemingly innocent areas like sending readings, suggesting possibilities for doing better analysis, etcetera. Many of these interventions in the external life of our patients may come from unanalysed areas of our mind and we also know that we can never be fully analysed. Are we always able to separate our omnipotence and narcissistic investment in our patients, so we can continue doing psychoanalysis, or do we slide unnoticed into becoming omnipotent mentors? It is of course not so much about dispensing with these, as it is to do with bringing them into the realm of the transference. It is not so much about finding a pure motive for taking on a patient, as it is about bringing this into the field of transference and countertransference.

A second set of questions is around the other thorny issue—termination. We have learned that the unconscious is not governed by time and having an artificially prefixed term period is not a workable model. We also find that becoming more functional is an overvaluation of the external world and rather "superegoish" as a model. But when work with a patient becomes too strenuous and or too tedious, do we unconsciously try to terminate it?

Let me give an example—a patient I will call Amita with whom I suddenly began to feel a hostility and boredom. This was very strange as for many years I had felt very protective towards her. How I remember her is as someone who communicated an internal world with the relentless cruelty of her objects. She had first come when she was grieving the death of her young child; that was what brought her to a crisis.

One detail that sticks in my mind from the early years is that every time her mother got angry, she would say to her daughter in vigorous Punjabi: "Why were you ever born?" After Amita lost her young boy, her mother said, "Now just think of his life as a dream and stop mourning, get on with your life." The sessions would be mostly a litany of indescribably cruel and yet repetitive events in her week. It struck me that this mother—not unusually—felt that giving birth to a daughter was a defeat and she seemed to be overcome with rivalry, rather than maternal tenderness.

To go back to my question at the beginning—why did I find it hard to empathise with her? I was alarmed at the hostility I felt in the room with her. I started having fantasies of terminating work with her. I thought of getting more interesting patients. In my irritation with her, I would find myself thinking of her as unable to think, to take in analytic interpretations, and it took me a very long time to realise that the toxic wish to expel her had entered our relationship and I had become the mother who wanted to expel an unworthy daughter, who felt that her milk should nourish worthier children. Somehow, before it was too late, this struck me. For better or for worse. But I cannot say with any certainty how many times I may have acted unconsciously to make this happen.

The issue of termination raises the final set of preoccupations I want to touch on. How do we conceptualise psychoanalysis when we decide on the question of termination? Would we be right in thinking of psychoanalysis as a cure for mental illness? Is a medical model appropriate for psychoanalytic thinking? Or are we restricting psychoanalysis when we use improvement and cure as criteria? Bion suggests that often the individuality of a mind is at the cost of the group. The group or family wants the patient to be more endurable. This acts as a pressure on the analytic dyad to show improvement. Does this compromise psychoanalysis? Moreover, does the idea of a cure put a pressure on the analysis to hurry through? Is it a disguised fear of one's own psychotic parts? I know how disturbing it can be when I am with an old patient

and we are having a satisfactory conversation which is suddenly interrupted by a hallucinatory moment. One attempts through interpretation
to smooth it over. But such an interpretation may be born from a fear of
my own psychotic part. How does one respond so as neither to encourage the psychosis nor to stymie it?

Or should we be thinking of the growth of the mind? And in that case,
can we imagine helping our patients grow without growing ourselves?
The patient goes to the analyst because he is not able to think of his life
in a way that makes it bearable. If the mind has to grow, can it be without
the simultaneous growth of the analyst? How can we hope for change
unless we are ready to change ourselves? I would like to bring in a line
or two from Bion (1967):

> Progress in psychoanalysis is inseparable from a need to tolerate
> the painful concomitants of mental growth; of which the
> immediate revelation of further problems requiring solution is
> not the least. For the psychoanalyst the problem presents itself
> for solution not only by the analysand but by the psychoanalyst
> as part of their own growth. He may develop contemporaneously
> with his patient or independently or not at all. (p. 137)

In the somewhat oracular voice he often employs, Bion warns that if we
stop growing, we may be a "part of the sociology of psychoanalysis, but
we are no longer doing psychoanalysis" (ibid.).

But then again, perhaps success and failure are not analytic concerns.
For if we are able to embody Bion's ascetic stricture of being without
memory and desire, failure and success feel weighed down by barometers
of verifiability and quantifiability. Nevertheless, Freud's writing arises
phoenix-like, from the ashes of his failures.

Learning from failure

Freud we know learned as much from his failures as he did from his
successes, if not more. *Beyond the Pleasure Principle* (1920g) is just
one instance of how a lifetime of work—premised on the centrality
of the pleasure principle—is acknowledged as limited. Here is a small

passage where he concedes the priority of something over the pleasure principle, and in one fell blow, cuts away at an entire body of work that had so far relied upon its centrality:

> These dreams are endeavouring to master the stimulus retrospectively, by developing the anxiety whose omission was the cause of the traumatic neurosis. They thus afford us a view of the function of the mental apparatus which, though it does not contradict the pleasure-principle is nevertheless independent of it and seems to be more primitive than the purpose of gaining pleasure and avoiding unpleasure. (p. 32)

Transference, as we well know, is the other big cornerstone that arose from Freud's first failure—with Dora. The structure of analytic work itself is derived from his observing the inefficacy of the original structure. In "Analysis Terminable and Interminable" (1937c) he reiterates the story of the Wolf Man who needed to go back to Russia. They had a finite time to work together, so a date had been set for him, and initially it seems to work well. But then the symptoms recurred and he returned to Vienna.

Freud writes, "The patient has stayed on in Vienna … his good state of health has been interrupted by attacks of illness which could only be construed as offshoots of his perennial neurosis …" (p. 218). So even as he speaks of it in terms of success, he adds provisos that qualify any such uncategorical success. From the title itself, Freud writes a meditation on the impossibility of finitude, certitude, and endings. As mentioned in the previous chapter, Meltzer (Meltzer et al., 1986) delineates two strands of opinion on the nature of therapeutic engagement—one which is surer and moves towards tangibility and the other that remains shrouded in intangibility.

When Bion (1967) writes about his work with patients, his highly condensed writing embodies an agility in his thinking that forms a rapid to and fro between recognising his failure and modifying his technique. Crucial to his writing is the rapidity with which failures are observed; and here by failure, I mean when the analyst intuits that his intervention is not received and he needs to modify something in order to be heard. For instance, in "On Hallucination" (1958b), he observes about his patient:

> On previous occasions I had interpreted his behaviour to mean
> that he saw my words as things and was following them with his
> eyes. (p. 75)

This line itself condenses a process. We understand that this must have
been through Bion's observing the failure of words to communicate. Up
to this point, he is using Kleinian ideas of concrete use of language. He
then imagines the sojourn of these words, as if they are objects, that they
could be doing things, following the patient around as attacking objects.
The passage continues:

> He had shown relief, almost amounting to amusement… I said
> that he was again seeing objects passing ahead … This time he
> became anxious and said, "I feel quite empty. Better to close my
> eyes … I have to use my ears …" This association brought it to
> my mind that he was not observing a direct relationship between
> myself and the opposite wall, as … on previous occasions. My
> interpretation was being taken in by his ears, but … cruelly and
> destructively. (p. 75)

Again in a very succinct description, Bion describes the fate of his words.
They are not a means of communication; they are not attacking, not following, but are entering the patient "cruelly and destructively" through
his ears. This is one small moment to point to a whole metapsychology
Bion built on learning from the frustrations of failing to communicate
with the psychotic part of the personality, which has a tremendous intol-
erance of frustration. He is not engulfed by his frustration but actually
uses it to hallucinate the patient's experience, and here he arrives at the
idea that the psychotic part may be evacuating beta elements through
the sensa and thereby hallucinating reality.

Bion recognises the crucial need for concomitant growth in the analyst in order to sustain the analysis. By growth here, I think Bion means
a constant need to keep the muscle of the mind active to be able to
withstand the darkness until you can discern some shape. This is an
area that to my mind remains relatively underemphasised—that it is
our inability to travel to places in ourselves that may lead to unsatisfactory endings:

> Progress in psycho-analysis is inseparable from a need to tolerate the painful concomitants of mental growth … He (psychoanalyst) may develop contemporaneously with his patient, or independently, or not at all. (1958b, p. 137)

These are three possibilities that we can explore at each moment in our sessions. To what extent does the encounter deepen our sense of what is going on? Is the patient able to mobilise areas in our mind that lie inaccessible to us? Are we able to explore this for ourselves or bring it into the service of the patient? Perhaps these latter two possibilities are not mutually exclusive. In fact, I suspect Bion means to suggest that as long as the analysis enables us to arrive at surprising places in our mind, the analysis is alive. The absence of this is tantamount to sterility.

Some time ago, a patient of mine, after several years, stopped coming. Over the next few weeks, I sent him messages that went unanswered. I then informed him—with no small relief—that I would not be able to hold on to his slots. Needless to say, he neither replied nor paid his outstanding bills. I have not heard from him since. I had undergone a change of supervisors at the time and I feel he reacted to my inability to contain some of the changes in my own thinking. I felt more severe and uncannily he commented on it.

At the time, I recall looking on PEP-Web for material that could help me make sense of the failure I felt. I found that very few papers spoke of failure. The closest I found at the time was Kernberg's (2007) paper discouragingly (to my purpose then) called "The Almost Untreatable Narcissistic Patient". This increased my sense of failure and shame. I am aware as I write this of the fear of exposing myself to the judgement of my seniors and my peers. Revealing our thoughts in group supervisions—in my limited experience—can also devolve into defensive posturing and falsifications. Since then I have come across a growing acknowledgement of writing about failure. I would like to mention Schellekes' (2019) paper in particular where she writes very movingly about a patient who left her very early and how she carries him in her mind and the need to write as originating from something that went incomprehensibly wrong.

My own primitive islands notwithstanding, I do think much of our work is indeterminate and unpredictable and that our writing does not embrace adequately enough the tenuousness of our endings, the indeterminacy of our links. It is with this in mind that I selected a case for writing here. The clinical fragment that follows is from my work with a patient with whom I spent six years of intense, turbulent, and enriching work. This came to an unfortunate and grinding halt.

Rehana

We met Rehana in the first chapter which was written before I knew this is how it would end. It feels very strange to write about her now, as though I were writing an obituary. I suppose she will haunt me for many years yet. Of all the patients one has worked with, there are some one keeps writing about and seeking supervision for—Rehana was such a one. This was emotionally a very powerful encounter and over the course of our work together, I felt challenged in many different ways.

Rehana came with no sense of time, memory, or history. Retrospectively I think I sensed some danger in working with her and I offered other referrals. But she barely listened. She texted me that same night saying she had collapsed and was being rushed to the hospital. There was something striking about her unique blend of thinness and delusion. "I am Aphrodite," she said banging her slender, white fists on my table. Naively, I had searched for irony or metaphor, and found none. Her looks matched her words. She looked and behaved like she was from a world very far from the small town she had grown up in with her light golden hair and fair skin. She would stay in my mind after sessions in an unsettling way—I could see her trembling as the sessions would end.

"What should I hold onto?" She would ask this with such stirring helplessness, I would find myself scrambling through things we spoke of, and give her some word or idea to physically hold. She would seize whatever I offered and would either hold it as a crutch, or as a blanket she could wrap around herself, to last till the next session. This was long before I had heard of autistic objects.

I would imagine her return to her lonely flat and the make-believe world of the "friends" she spoke of. I would dread the next day when she would return to tell me about her cutting herself again. I have no memory, she would keep repeating. "I was told that as a baby I would cry and nobody could comfort me." This was the only image she carried. Her growing up sounded shadowy, as if she were an apparition to herself. The only person she spoke of was a coach in high school who told her she could be a great artist. She had trusted this woman J for many years but later she realised J had been wanting a relationship with her all the while, and she severed all contact with her. I felt there was something proleptic (late Middle English: via late Latin from Greek *prolēpsis*, from *prolambanein* "anticipate", from pro "before" + *lambanein* "take") about this. Perhaps I would prove to be like J, I had said. She disagreed vehemently. Nevertheless.

We forged a language for her states of mind, which felt mostly "vaporous". The first couple of years were tough and I felt lost and scared with her repeated cutting, and ecstasy, and alcohol binges. She would party late with hard drugs, and drive after drugs and alcohol.

A dream I mention now is to be able to give texture to the violence in the work with her.

> I am walking away in a forest. I'm like an ascetic, given everything up. I feel quite good—dark. Blah! Blah! Am alone among a lot of trees. There's my best friend—getting married. We grew up together and were very close. I've come back for his wedding. Father's giving a speech, happy that I'm back. I've come back and it means something. Nothing makes me angrier than his celebration of this false thing. Fucking idiot! Fucking stage! Idiot! Walking away, towards an open area. I'm walking with mother, telling her he's spoiling everything. She's my confidante ... I want to fucking kill him.

The violence never felt close then, as she had walled me off and placed me in a split far away.

Rehana: You are different. You are the only one who wants nothing from me and who gets me.

My mind was lulled and seized by an omnipotent phantasy of being able to soothe an inconsolable baby. She would huddle in corners of my room, hiding her face from me. Over the next couple of years she stopped cutting herself. She set up a very successful business too and got very rich. This reinforced by omnipotence—and I will here invoke Chapter 4 where I have written about analytic arrogance. Arranging her thoughts was not always easy, but she liked to struggle and think with acuity.

Analytic foreclosure

I have written down in some detail a session from the fourth year. This one had disturbed me then. I had felt moved by Rehana's appetite for truth. In this session, she talks about her inability to feel for anyone else. She tried hard to feel and I think perhaps I could not see a certain "sociopathy" in her eyes (Alvarez, 2012). I find I took refuge in the romantic idea that it is the dread of closeness, dependency, and abandonment that makes people aloof. The truth of this theoretically learned belief notwithstanding, I failed to address Rehana's truth. This genre of mistakes is not uncommon in my work and I daresay in a lot of therapeutic work.

In this session, she wants to look at her cold, ruthless, uncaring side, while I end up making excuses for her. This was her inability to feel for others, her visceral hatred for people who were needy (father, mother, boyfriends), her ease in using others and feeling nothing for them, an absence of gratitude, guilt, remorse. She would lead many men on with her easy charm: "Nice to have all that attention, so I thought why not ..."

I do not know how much ordinary sociopathy there might be in each of us. I don't know how much evasion of emotional contact we encounter in ourselves and others. (The proliferation of dating apps that locate you geographically and offer you possibilities of neighbours you can "hook up" with makes such evasion of emotional contact the stuff of everyday life. In fact, breakdowns are seen as pathological and mourning as requiring medication. There is a kind of aversion to emotionality that is evident in so much of our culture. But this merits another discussion.) Here, my point is that psychoanalytic theories may tend to "romanticise" sociopathic tendencies which then become a bulwark against the experience of the moment. The following is an instance of a "psychic foreclosure" (in the sense of excluding prematurely) on my part.

Session

Rehana: I left here last time and thought about how angry I have been. I read something and spoke to B and it struck me that I am a sociopath. I just don't feel for anyone. Not you, nor A, nor N. I just feel disconnected. What it seems we do here is either we say that I am really afraid of being left alone and so I can't connect or I have so much that I am afraid of loving. I met N [the partner she has just broken up with after trying very hard to make it work] on Wednesday. I could see how much N felt for me. It's normal, like you are going to meet an ex. Texted me before the date and checked, "Do you really want to meet me?"

    The truth is I don't care. I am not like everyone else. I tried telling N that. And then everything made sense; why I can never keep you outside of here. I would write down notes here [for a few months, she went through a phase of writing notes in sessions] and read them later, but it wouldn't do anything for me. What do you think?

Me: I hear your fear that I may have made excuses for you, that I could not bear to see the truth that you don't feel any love …

Rehana: Isn't it true? Suddenly I don't need to pretend. This is my secret. I have always known I have a secret somewhere. I thought and thought about being gay. But, really, women don't excite me physically at all. I think of men sexually all the time, never of women. So it's not about being gay. This was the secret. I have had to conceal the fact that I have no feelings for people.

Me: No positive feelings …?

Rehana: Yah. No positive feelings. I just don't care and I have been pretending all my life. Now there's this relief that I don't need to. But I need to know what you think.

[*My mind goes to how warmly I feel towards her and how much her friends seem to love and care. What does she manage to evoke in others? Is she projecting her loving parts into us? I am also aware that I have been making such "romantic" interpretations for a long time but seem not to be able to stop. Later I will learn I was engulfed by her omniscient belief that all her objects fail to keep boundaries and fail in their duty to her.*]

Me: You do seem to have a lot of people who care for you.

Rehana: Yes and I'll tell you why. It's because I am intelligent and I can ask questions and say things because I am not like others. Because I don't care about anyone. They find that attractive. This is my truth. [*But her capacity to think is a recent development.*]

Me: It feels true but scary?

Rehana: True. You think so too?

Me: It feels true here at this moment. But for now and in this moment only. It may change later. [*Afterwards I realise this unnecessary point of technique was to defend us both from her "sociopathy".*]

Rehana: That is what I want to know—is there going to be a change? Should I think of that as a goal that we are working towards or should I work towards accepting that this is who I am and this is about accepting that? I want to know how you think about this.

Me: [*really feeling caught out*]: Even though it feels true for the moment, there is a terror of it staying this way forever. So there must be a small part wanting and hoping it would change ... I say this because while we may recognise certain difficult unchanging things about us, we find ourselves holding on to the slender hopeful parts ...

Rehana: Or will it be like it has been that for about two weeks I will feel despair, feel myself falling apart and then after two weeks, I will get used to it and may begin to feel hopeful again? [*pause*] What is it like to be Rehana? What do you think? Fuck! Shiftiness ... and gargantuan efforts to stay stable, speak slowly, and mean what I say ... [*I see her constantly strain with effort.*] Fear of invasion. I like to show off my life. But there is nothing quintessentially me. I oscillate between being kind and arrogant. It is a jihad [holy war] constantly against that arrogant side. [*This I feel is very true and I find myself connecting strongly with her and as often feeling her helping me to locate things in myself. I admire this new capacity for truth.*]

Me: Yes ...

Rehana: It feels small. I find it small. I met Q [*new love interest*] after work, we kissed, went out for drinks. I thought I'd have one, but I had four. Became very wobbly. I know I shouldn't drink so much, it's probably the meds. She mentioned this other guy. [*Both she and Q are bisexual.*] I felt very dispensable. She has a boyfriend, and then there's me. Earlier, I would have said something to belittle this guy, but I fought it. If Q is ever to be with me, it shouldn't be because she needs me. That is what I would always do earlier. Felt very wobbly. Then in the car, on the way back, I felt better. But … who am I? It feels so unstable.

Me: Rehana feels unstable … [*She's restless and thinks time is up. I say there are three or four minutes.*]

Rehana: Yah. Volcanic. Like I am on a raft in choppy water. Just holding on. It's boring … I see trees and I know they are beautiful. But I can't feel the beauty … do you know what I mean?

Me: It is difficult to feel the beauty when you are trying to hold on to a raft …

Rehana: Yes. So does it change? Is this a process? I need you to tell me something. [*This has become a clamour.*] That is the thing with this place. You really don't know … So is there a shore? [*She looks at me. I feel cornered again and smile weakly.*]

Rehana: Noooooo [*half-playfully as she leaves*].

The end

In the last two years, I began to feel her grow away from me. I began to find it increasingly hard to be able to say things which made sense to her. I would feel despair and sadness at losing her. The last months the atmosphere of the sessions was thick with violence. She wanted me to tell her to go and I found myself under a lot of pressure from her on the one hand, and my "internalised" supervisor on the other. I had the occasion to encounter what I have termed as "lateral inversion" in the field. The "fearful symmetry" could not be contained by me and it all ended rather badly. For almost a year, she had been straining at the leash. To leave analysis, make her own choices, and not depend on me, while I did not think her ready yet.

Rehana: You are unable to revise the photograph of me in your mental album.

This was her analysis of the situation and it felt woundingly true. Had I really become a mother who can't let go off her needy little baby? I could see the changes but could also see the fragility. She says she has grown, and the rest of it she wants to do by herself. While I am around, she feels her creativity gets consumed by our talk. All her thinking happens here with me, and there is no desire to think away from me. She says I don't accept that this is who she is, and she won't change, and nor does she wish to. I felt this was true. I wondered what moment I was waiting for, despite all my disavowal of goals? Am I too attached to the helpless infant who came to me? She feels that and it rings true. Is her confidence true? I really am lost.

Rehana: I am bored. Tired of you, tired of myself. I feel like I am coming here for you. It has become about your needs.

I would begin to feel everything I said was tired and just a way of showing her how she still needed analysis. The sense of being old, boring, and stupid would engulf me completely.

Rehana: I am very cognisant of how vaporous I am, how fragmented …

It felt like she had learned my way of thinking and even my vocabulary. And her mind, now sharpened, shreds mine into minute particles. The atmosphere of those last months became very violent—wrestling with internal objects who want her to stay adhesively in a oneness. I must not be those objects. I sought supervision.

"But of course she is not ready, it is obvious." This was my supervisor's voice. Rehana had always been adept at learning languages and carried an arrogant self-reliance alongside an apparent haplessness. Every session felt stormy, but I felt the demand for termination was precocious and premature. There was a deep cleavage between a sharp and cutting side of her mind which has developed like a sword and a rather thin sheath which still needs to thicken. As though she had sharpened her cutting side against me and now wanted to try this edge on others.

Fearful symmetry

This analysis engendered a very unique experience for me. I thought there was something undecipherable happening where the analytic field began to feel like a combat zone in which the two opponents have identical experiences:

Me: I cannot think with a gun to my head.

Rehana: [*sarcastically*] Funny you saying that. I feel like you have put a gun to my head.

I would feel stunned by the symmetry. And I should add here that whereas the demand for symmetry by patients is usually linked with a denial of dependency, here it was not a demand, it was an assertion of parity. In hindsight, it was her superiority. Rehana would often arrive armed with a precise "recall" of the previous day's session.

Rehana: Yesterday I told you I saw a movie and I felt how similar the life of this dancer was to mine. Now you could have taken the conversation in any direction, but you chose to talk about my need to get into another's skin. Really? That's new? How come you never talk about the changes in me?

She had turned the tables on me and could ask me questions as though she could penetrate my insides. The field became a mirror, which inverts all images laterally, even as it reflects all it sees.

I would try to give it some meaning:

Me: It feels like there is a thick wall between us and my words bounce back at me frustratingly distorted.

Rehana: That is exactly how I feel. You are so deaf and blind. It's like everything I liked here with you is taken away with violence. You had this way of observing earlier. I could never know what you wanted. But then suddenly it's become about you wanting me to stay. I am coming here because I feel guilty and afraid.

Uncannily she was giving words to my feelings. How was this experience replicated as also laterally inverted? We were having the same experience. Would it be fair to say that the field was like an axis where one became the negative of the other? *Mendacium* and *veritas*, K and -K? We were experiencing the same thing, but like a mirror image it felt laterally inverted. I felt like I still sought to know and to experience what made her so violent; she felt like she knew what she needed to and now I was being self-indulgent. She felt I had both memory (of her needy past) and desire (for her not to terminate her analysis). Bion writes that the primitive part of the mind does not resist interpretations, instead it stimulates memory and desire in the analyst to retain omnipotent control and evade growth (1965, p. 22).

> Me: It feels like I keep harping on the same boring, tired things. I am not seeing how cognisant you are.
> Rehana: This is where we part, the dissonance. You said this earlier …

It felt like she was stimulating me to repeat myself and we would both feel frustrated by the repetitiousness. In her last session, she says: "I just can't go on." I had felt this anguish acutely.

From a phase when she would scribble notes in a thin diary during the session, her capacity to think had grown, but she steered it away from leaning towards life, dependency, and vulnerability. Instead it felt like her capacity to think was colonised by her deepest urge to free herself from her dependence on me. I felt deeply moved by her efforts, and the uniquely meditative quality of the sessions. But what moved me alongside my dread of the sessions, only terrified her. The emotional quality of our relationship threatened her. Now she could think and that was her attribute. And I may have aided it, but she had acknowledged that, as also that I had nothing more to give her.

This always felt like a negation of the need for gratitude. Gratitude as we know is difficult to bear with its lack of symmetry. She was enraged at finding I had nothing more to give. I sought more supervision in order to survive this destructiveness. She would unerringly manage to say wounding things that would make me smart. I would feel as though my child were saying: "You are being selfish by holding on to me." This was a fraught time for me as in fact my son was leaving home. Was it really my transference?

> Me: I see you come in with your fists clenched, and then as we go on, they unclench. You feel moved by my real presence. Not the me in your head, but the me you encounter here. You want to go away from the real me that moves you.
> Rehana: [she is quiet for a bit] This is true. [her voice again full of suppressed rage] That is why I can't do this anymore … I can't go to work after this …

This was her last session as I remember it now. I had followed my supervisor's advice that I treat her wish to go as a free association; she was far from ready for termination. But perhaps my timing was all wrong. It was an abrupt departure and had the feel of a clumsy exit, rather than a timely end. Tustin writes, "Autistic techniques are reactions to avoid becoming conscious of the 'black hole' of separation of, partings, of endings, and ultimately of death." (Tustin, 1986, p. 282) Was this what Rehana had dreaded? The autistic techniques included adhesive identification to begin with, then a gradual growing of the second skin through that, and finally a cruel rejection of the object whose skin had been extended. Now she was me, but a cruel and destructive internal world raged under the skin. She could sound like me, but it was with a very different internal reality, and this must have terrified her.

Thinking about Rehana continues to teach me a great deal and in surprising, unpredictable ways. I was left troubled, shaken. Maybe it wasn't such a failure, I tell myself. Perhaps one can only go as far as one has been in one's own analysis, and beyond that we can try to write, as the epigraph borrowed from Winnicott (1949) says. Rehana, to her credit, took me to places in myself that I may have been too afraid to go to alone, and perhaps she left when I could no longer do so. I tried to go further than I had been in my own analysis, but obviously not far enough.

Perhaps she could feel an emotional connection that was different from the creeper-like connection she had had with me in the beginning, and this was terrifying. And perhaps there was always a script of attaining autochthony that she carried and it made her want to leave urgently. But eventually she went away feeling I had failed her. I can see how blind I was in those early years when she brought me her violence, when she spoke of her mentor J. She foretold how it would end. Was her "foreknowledge" a part of her omniscience? I have left this open-ended. Was that the danger I sensed in working with her?

I had been afraid of my ability to contain her delusions and her brittleness. Rehana had managed to control the analysis and made me a scarecrow in the garden. "Why don't you tell me how much I have grown?" she would plead. I would feel controlled and afraid she would be confirmed in her manic grandiosity. This was her internal object perhaps—who never felt she could contain the madness. And omnipotently, she made me another version of that same mother she knew only too well. But eventually I do think she left because I reached the limit of my capacity to think about the island we inhabited. And it has taken me very long to see that while I may have enabled a journey, she had outstripped me.

* * *

While discussing the "prospects of analytic treatment", Freud (1937c) concedes the significance of the "individuality of the analyst". He writes,

> Ferenczi makes the further important point that success depends very largely on the analyst's having learnt sufficiently from his own errors and mistakes and having got the better of the weak points in his own personality … Among the factors which influence the prospects of analytic treatment and add to its difficulties in the same manner as the resistances, must be reckoned not only the nature of the patient's ego but the individuality of the analyst. (p. 247)

This is not elaborated much. But we can see this as opening up the space for more bipersonal models of psychoanalysis. To what extent are we able to learn from our failures, to what extent do we grow with our patients, and manage to forge new languages for them? Intuitively we recognise such limitations in ourselves, and so unsatisfactory outcomes like Rehana's linger on in our minds as reminders of these.

Bion (1958a) insistently cautions against the analyst's omniscience which he almost equates with arrogance. He mentions an analyst who thought the analysis was going just fine, till one day the patient went and killed himself. While perhaps factually true, there is often something apostolic in his tone and allegorical in its ramifications. To be able to expand on our thinking, it seems we have to confront failure. Bion was finding an inability to work with patients who did not have shared tools of communication. Tiresias-like, the analyst must blind himself to what is accessible to the senses, in order to make contact with the "infra-red and the ultra-violet" (Bergstein, 2019, p. 55) ends of the spectrum. Here is an instance: "It had emerged gradually over the years until finally it was borne in on me, and the patient in due course confirmed it, that he felt his sense organs to expel as well as to receive" (Bion, 1958a, p. 67).

In this short passage, years of observation are compressed, as well as years of not knowing. In this penumbra between unknowability and truth lies Bion's idea not of epiphanic truth, but rather of emotional truth. This is an intuitively arrived-at moment where it feels that something in the analyst's unconscious has caught a glimmer of something in the analysand's, to give rise to a thought that is nascent and imbued with "nowness". Such a truth is fleeting and suffused by its transience. And it is this process that most defines the psychoanalytic one. Bion's writing of his clinical work is embedded in a nowness which is amongst other things, a reminder for us to be in the analysis without memory and desire, and to evolve a form sans chronos and telos. The passage below from "On Hallucination" (1958b) is luminous with such a quality:

> The patient has arrived on time and I have asked for him to be called. As he has been with me in analysis for some years and a great deal of work has been done, I am not surprised when he appears without further ado, though such unceremonious progression has not always been the rule. As he passes into the room he glances rapidly at me; such frank scrutiny has been a development of the past six months and is still a novelty. While I close the door he goes to the foot of the couch, facing the head pillows and my chair, and stands, shoulders stooping, knees sagging, head inclined to the chair, motionless until I have passed him and am about to sit down. So closely do his movements seem to be geared with mine that the inception of my movement to sit appears to release a spring in him. As I lower myself into my seat he turns left about, slowly, evenly, as if something would be spilled, or perhaps fractured, were he to be betrayed into a precipitate movement. As I sit the turning movement stops as if we were both parts of the same clockwork toy. The patient, now with his back to me, is arrested at a moment when his gaze is directed to the floor near that corner of the room which would be to his right and facing him if he lay on the couch. This pause endures perhaps for a second and is closed by a shudder of his head and shoulders which is so slight and so rapid that I might suppose myself mistaken. Yet it marks the end of one phase and the start of the next; the patient seats himself on the couch preparatory to lying down. (pp. 65–66)

The description begins in *medias res* (Latin: in the midst of things), without a prelude. Regardless of reasons (such as confidentiality), history in the conventional sense is dispensed with. The writing style here embodies Bion's technique. There is definitely a memory at work here (not a recall but an impressionistic texture) which makes Bion say "development of the past six months". However, when he banishes memory, he forbids assumptions of continuity and when he banishes desire, he challenges the grammar of development. Even in his earliest writings on groups, he unfussily moves the idea of working with groups to being about the here-and-now links prevailing in the group:

> I had, it was true, had experience of trying to persuade groups composed of patients to make the study of their tensions a group task, … (p. 121)

This emphasis on the links in the here and now become more evident in his style of writing about clinical work where the focus is on the emotional truth of the here and now. There is no history while he asks the analyst to blind himself to the sensuous background. This is about being able to intuit the emotional connection through the session and, through that, enrich his capacity to think about his emotions. So it is not divorced from therapeutic concerns but it does ask for them to be suspended from the foreground.

Inscape

The English poet Gerard Manley Hopkins (1844–1889) brings to nature poetry a kind of detailing, *haecceitas*—a distinctive "thisness" of things that was influenced by the medieval Franciscan scholar Dun Scotus (*Cambridge Encyclopedia of the Jesuits*, 2017).

Powerfully shaped by the Oxford Movement with its call for a return to earlier (purer) Catholicism, Hopkins privately wrote poetry in praise of God. He did this by noting the details of God's creation. This microscopic specificity that he records is in itself "evidence" of God's presence and attentiveness. "Pied Beauty" (1877) is a good instance of how he brings together a theme in nature—the theme of pied or dappled things ranging from "brinded cow", to "fresh-firecoal", and "finches' wings". God it seems, is in the detail:

Glory be to God for dappled things—
For skies of couple-colour as a brinded cow;
For rose-moles all in stipple upon trout that swim;
Fresh-firecoal chestnut-falls; finches' wings;
Landscape plotted and pieced—fold, fallow, and plough;
And áll trádes, their gear and tackle and trim.
All things counter, original, spare, strange;
Whatever is fickle, freckled (who knows how?)
With swift, slow; sweet, sour; adazzle, dim;
He fathers-forth whose beauty is past change:
Praise him.

But it is the look of the poet that binds together disparate things in nature. This common attribute of "dappled" creations is for him the inner essence of the thing and the music booms with an internal chiming: "Landscape plotted and pieced—fold, fallow, and plough". There is a dense visuality communicated through the strides of consonant-heavy rhythms.

This "inscape" or heightened attention to the uniqueness of each experience with nature creates a way of looking. In the language Hopkins uses to speak about his method, he mentions "inscape" to describe this inner essence. I borrow it as a description of Bion's clinical writing which is reminiscent of Hopkins' intimate recordings. This intimate observation is an act of devotion to the presence of the other in the here and now.

Bion's observation of the link between him and his patient may be read as notes on technique, and through this, he profoundly embodies both his metapsychology and his technique in the manner of his case writing. His body of work restores a radical emphasis back to psychoanalysis with his ascetic strictures. The analyst is looking intently at the moment—every small movement, posture, gesture—"shoulders stooping", "knees sagging"—is being recorded. The room is rife with the force of a magnetic field: "inception of my movement to sit appears to release a spring in him".

This is instructive—such observation is based on foregrounding the present. Much like a portrait artist who focuses on the subject's face ignoring the background, Bion trains his gaze to the now. He is also describing his own somatopsychic responses to the patient: "as though we were both parts of the same clockwork toy" (1958b, p. 66). Even the motion of "tuning" is felt in the analyst's body. This is a highly trained eye scanning the link between the patient and analyst, an at-one-ment. Through this intense recording, Bion illustrates technique that follows a new metapsychology. The psychotic part of the mind does not have the capacity for thought and verbal language fails. But with an intensified gaze, the analyst can reach into his own perceptual shifts and understand the relaxing or tensing of the link. This he can communicate to the patient who may then introject this capacity for thinking. The syntax of Bion's case has a dense texture of "nowness". In this sense, Bion's notes on his sessions are more like Hopkins' "inscape", rather than the panoramic landscape of Lorrain or Turner. The syntax is shorn of memory (no concrete history) and desire (we do not know how the analysis is developing)—this is not just a reminder of analytic abstemiousness, but an act of devotion to detail.

On a related note, Civitarese (2016) expands the analytic stance from Freud's freely suspended attention to including very minute and almost intangible somato-psychic pulsings. Sensations, flutters, tiny movements by the analyst if observed can help in recognising what is afoot in the field. This may help transform what is un-dreamable by the patient into dreamable experience if the analyst can hallucinate the patient's experience and then wake up from that. These experiences that go by unnoticed in the session are unthought and often unthinkable (pp. 53–83).

While this book purports to be about liminality and the fertile area of the caesura, "Sometimes there are walls, frontiers, barriers, ditches: the caesura can no longer be crossed, and we understand that it has been transformed into censorship" (Civitarese, 2018). One such space is the idea of the ending of a psychoanalysis and to think of it beyond ideas of success and failure that carry in them a sense of ineluctable truth and knowability.

Epilogue

Solitude or blank desertion? Haunted by ancestors: writing psychoanalysis

There is something predatory about writing—after our ancestors have laid the groundwork. When Coetzee was awarded the Nobel Prize, he spoke of imagining an aged Robinson Crusoe musing on all those writers who wrote stories of being marooned alone on an island:

> But now, reflecting further, there begins to creep into his breast a touch of fellow-feeling for his imitators. For it seems to him now that there are but a handful of stories in the world; and if the young are to be forbidden to prey upon the old then they must sit for ever in silence. (2003)

If this captures the older generation's experience, for me as I conclude this book, I am only too aware of the anxiety of the upstart—of having to justify a book that may not have anything new to say, that stands on the groundwork done by a long line of ancestors who make it both possible to think of what has been unthought, and impossible to say what perhaps remains unthinkable. And puts me in the unfortunate position of the predator.

The Muses in classical literature served as an antidote to the hubris of the writer by having "provided" the inspiration. The contemporary practice of writing acknowledgements can be seen as a continuation of the same tradition. The first chapter of *The Interpretations of Dreams* (1900a) can be read as a conflation of the acknowledgement section and a history of literature. Each writer must bear the oedipal burden of what Bloom (1973) called the "anxiety of influence". There must be a good enough reason to write. One has to justify one's impulse to write, as most do not have a Miltonic project of "justify[ing] the ways of god to man" (Milton, 1795, *Book 1*, line 4).

What I am concerned with here is whether this book can emerge from the shadow of the ghosts that inhabit it. And by ghosts I mean an elusive and changeable set of hovering presences, shaped and inflected by our objects in an idiosyncratic combination that is peculiarly our own. This book has reflected on the limits of our tired idioms. If we wish to expand the analyst's own capacity to tune in to his feelings, it is a truism that this requires language to correspondingly expand itself. Accordingly, I think as analysts we need to keep un-learning the "mother" tongues and relearning "foreign" languages. Every generation of analysts grows up in a familiar language of analysis (mainly the school of the analyst and the pedagogy she is subjected to). This could be the language of cathexis, libido, ego. Or it could be of breast, penis, envy. Or it could be dissociation and enactment. Or beta elements and reveries. Every sect has its own vocabulary. In my own country, psychoanalytic writing has also been dominated by an insistence on cultural difference and an unconscious post-colonial anxiety. This confused desire with its facile binaries often tends to overwhelm the psychoanalytic project.

It is in the nature of language to get oversaturated and for the mind to take refuge in its favourite places.

However, there are obstructions to this in the analyst and her mental braces, which may include her favourite language, her particular idiom, school of thought, and, most fundamentally, her own analysis. These create a bastion that she may be unable to evict as they may be too threatening to her own psychic economy. "Reveries" for instance may be used rather generously by us. This may at times overlook our own unformulated experience, our beta elements, and often assumes that our experience of the patient is coming from a non-psychotic part, while the patient's is from a psychotic part. What gets named "reveries" can become rather self-indulgent on our part, even though Bion (1962) clearly defines he means a particular sort of reverie. Much writing on this subject has been intuitive and pervasive—it has offered a technique to bail us out from the everyday feeling of being blocked. But like most vocabularies, this one too has spread itself rather wide and thin.

It is not enough for us to have associations/reveries but to be able to read them in the context of the transference. Much gets written about how miraculously analysts have reveries and these become the points of breakthrough in the analyses. However, to "read" closely one's associations in order to use them in the field is harder to put in words. Words that are overused and oversaturated with meaning—such as autonomy, regret, arrogance, truth—are always in danger of appearing transparent. Some of the chapters are sojourns with and into such words, exercises in un-saturating the meanings.

Some chapters, by tracing the use of a single word, reveal the translucent screen of verbal language which conceals an unyielding opacity of language. We may read some of these chapters as exercises that attempt to establish a "commensal" relationship between the container (words) and contained (meaning), so that they can take turns—that is, so that changing meanings can alter the shape and use of words (autoimmunity, parasitism, arrogance, autonomy, regret). These words looked at closely expand and give way to altering meanings. This accommodates historically and psychically shaped changes in thinking and feeling.

In addition to the symbolic, concrete, and adhesive uses of language discussed previously (Chapter 1), emotions can be avoided in the analytic encounter when language is used in a deadened, functional way. What Alvarez (2012) calls the "why because" syntax creeps in at such moments: "You were so angry with me because I went on a break", "You felt that last time I was hostile because you were pushing me away".

It is used intellectually by patients who may have acquaintance with psychoanalytic language as well—"I think I was projecting this or something …" Language instead of enabling an emotional connection is then used to obfuscate one. This may happen especially in training analyses. There is a devaluation of analytic process through a fetishisation of its form. This appears to be (over)valuing, but in fact hollows the process by ritualising it and results in being an as-if or pseudo-analysis. But from my ongoing experience, it feels like the verbal content of the patient offers a beguiling screen which is all too often liable to take us away from the difficult waters of the here and now.

We have looked at syntax (circular, linear), vocabulary (rehearsed, intellectualised, functional), tense, parts of speech (pronouns either missing or misleading), and figures of speech (paradox, hyperbole). We looked at Bion's seminal use of caesura—a poetic device. The rhythm of narrative itself—with its own demands of closure, chronology, and development—may shape the analysis (Chapters 1, 3, 4, and 7). The syntax of language imposes a certain kind of ordering that overdetermines communication (Chapters 1, 4, and 7). The belief in telling a story like it is overlooks the long-standing marital history of form to inherited ideas, such as chronos, telos, morality, arrogance. How do we speak without a pre-existing template? Bion's writings caution against the perils that surround the psychoanalyst, including the seduction of beauty or the impulse to aestheticise. Invoking Plato's warning against poets:

> ... it is possible to hope that the capacity of the artist, though useful may not be essential to the psycho-analyst. Indeed it may be a disadvantage in so far as the artist's capacity may enable him to provide, as Plato feared, a substitute for the truth. (1970, p. 2)

In Chapter 2, I mention a patient who always arranges the session as "before analysis" and "after analysis". This syntax is so embedded that it is nearly impossible for him to speak to me without this scaffolding. This haunts our own writing. I have reflected in Chapter 6 on the difficulty in selecting the form for clinical vignettes. Should I use them to "illustrate" some predetermined theory? Or can I write them and see what emerges? I had hoped to do the latter, however it is hard to banish narrative as it binds the material. Eventually, what emerged was the idiosyncratic nature of these attacks and the thinness of the sessions. I would suggest no causal link but a co-incidence (constant conjunction) of these. The treatment relies upon increasing the elasticity of the psychic experience in the here and now. It is the repeated act of trying to give names to sensations, to attach them to feelings, to associate feelings with thoughts, and to try to learn to give meaning to what may be happening in the here and now. At any rate, the two case histories follow two different styles of writing as they are designed to illustrate different points.

By way of contrast with my own conventional writing, I examine Bion's inscaped writing of his cases. In his work, increasingly, psychoanalysis which had a preconception of giving shape to the unconscious untangles itself from the prison house of language that is shaped by Christianity, morality, abnormal psychology, psychiatry, pedagogy, and psychoanalytic jargon itself.

Bion's use of the caesura opens up the idea of psychic punctuation which can be explored. More commonly used than a caesura is the humble hyphen. I have touched upon but not taken up more fully the correspondence between punctuation and psychic significance. The building blocks even of verbal language need our attention, as much as the words that carry them. For instance, a patient observed, "How wonderful the English language is! Which other tongue would allow me to say the sky was the colour of 'plum-red-menstrual-stained-satin-pyjamas'?" It occurred much later to me that what she also illustrated to me was the uniqueness of an object. It is this set of attributes that distinctively defines my object and makes it unsubstitutable.

I have briefly discussed Bion's writing of his cases as a discourse on his method. Having banished memory (genealogy) and desire (to see changes and improvement in the patient), he writes in *medias res*, creating a syntax of nowness. This is one way to evade an overarching but unconscious teleological impetus of most narrative, what Kermode (1966) called a "sense of an ending". Resisting this powerful impulse is linked to relinquishing, for some moments, a knowable universe.

To say this better, it would have to be in someone else's words:

> For last year's words belong to last year's language
> And next year's words await another voice. (Eliot, 1962)

This book started out as an exploration of the liminal spaces that constitute the domain of psychoanalysis, but eventually it began to narrow down to the impediments (roadblocks, bastions, and walls) that emerge in the analytic link.

It seems that the primitive part of the mind is always looking for ways to evade psychic pain and emotional truth is always in peril. The links between us and our patients, and more importantly within us ourselves are always fraught with danger. All too often omniscience and arrogance threaten K: melancholia poses as grief, adhesiveness as introjection, sentimentality and nostalgia replace emotionality, horror takes over terror, while sensationalism robs mysteriousness, romantic love acts as an alibi for terrifying intimacy, empathy conceals deadness, obsequiousness sounds like gratitude, collusions and *folie à deux* dissemble as mutualism. In these liminal moments the links between analyst and analysand slide away from the emotional truth, rather than towards it.

References

Ahumada, J. L. (2016). Is the nature of psychoanalytic thinking and practice (e.g., in regard to sexuality) determined by extra-analytic, social and cultural developments? Insight under siege: Psychoanalysis in the "Autistoid Age". *International Journal of Psychoanalysis, 97*(3): 839–851.

Akhtar, S. (1996). "Someday …" and "If only …". Fantasies: Pathological optimism and inordinate nostalgia as related forms of idealization. *Journal of the American Psychoanalytic Association, 44*(3): 723–753.

Akhtar, S. (2002). Forgiveness: Origins, dynamics, psychopathology, and technical relevance. *Psychoanalytic Quarterly, 71*(2): 175–212.

Akhtar, S. (2015). Where is India in my psychoanalytic work? *Psychoanalytic Review, 102*(6): 873–911.

Alvarez, A. (1998). Failures to link: Attacks or defects? Some questions concerning the thinkability of Oedipal and pre-Oedipal thoughts. *Journal of Child Psychotherapy, 24*(2): 213–231.

Alvarez, A. (2010). Levels of analytic work and levels of pathology: The work of calibration. *International Journal of Psychoanalysis, 91*(4): 859–878.

Alvarez, A. (2012). *The Thinking Heart: Three Levels of Psychoanalytic Therapy with Disturbed Children.* London: Routledge.

Amir, D. (2010). The split between voice and meaning: The dual function of psychotic syntax. *International Forum of Psychoanalysis, 19*(1): 34–42.

Anderson, W. (2014). Getting ahead of one's self?: The common culture of immunology and philosophy. *Isis, 105*(3): 606–616.

Angum, F., Khan, T., Kaler, J., Siddiqui, L., & Hussain, A. (2020). The prevalence of autoimmune disorders in women: A narrative review. *Cureus, 12*(5): e8094. Published online May 13. doi: 10.7759/cureus.8094 PMCID: PMC7292717 (last accessed May 30, 2021).

Araújo, A., Jansen, A. M., Bouchet, F., Reinhard, K., & Ferreira, K. F. (2003). Parasitism, the diversity of life, and paleoparasitology. *Memórias do Instituto Oswaldo Cruz, Rio de Janeiro, 98*(Supplement I): 5–11.

Aristotle (c. 330 BC). *Poetics.* Ann Arbor, MI: University of Michigan Press, 1970.

Arvanitakis, K. I. (1998). Some thoughts on the essence of the tragic. *International Journal of Psychoanalysis, 79*(5): 955–964.

Balter, L. (2005). Nested ideation and the problem of reality. *Psychoanalytic Quarterly, 74*(3): 661–701.

Baranger, M., & Baranger, W. (2008). The analytic situation as a dynamic field. *International Journal of Psychoanalysis, 89*(4): 795–826.

Beckett, S. (1946). *The End.* In: *First Love and Other Novellas.* London: Penguin, 2000.

Beckett, S. (1953). *Watt.* New York: Riverrun.

Benjamin, J. (1990). An outline of intersubjectivity: The development of recognition. *Psychoanalytic Psychology, 7S* (Supplement): 33–46.

Benjamin, W. (2003). On the image of Proust. In: H. Eiland, M. W. Jennings, & G. Smith (Eds.), *Walter Benjamin: Selected Writings Volume 2, 1927–1930* (pp. 237–247). Cambridge, MA: Harvard University Press.

Bergstein, A. (2009). On boredom: A close encounter with encapsulated parts of the psyche. *International Journal of Psychoanalysis, 90*(3): 613–631.

Bergstein, A. (2013). Transcending the caesura: Reverie, dreaming and counter-dreaming. *International Journal of Psychoanalysis, 94*(4): 621–644.

Bergstein, A. (2014). Beyond the spectrum: Fear of breakdown, catastrophic change and the unrepressed unconscious. *Rivista di Psicoanalisi, 60*(4): 847–868.

Bergstein, A. (2015). Attacks on linking or a drive to communicate? Tolerating the paradox. *Psychoanalytic Quarterly, 84*(4): 921–942.

Bergstein, A. (2019). *Bion and Meltzer's Expeditions into Unmapped Mental Life.* London: Routledge.

Bergstein, A. (2020). Violent emotions and the violence of life. *International Journal of Psychoanalysis.* https://doi.org/10.1080/00207578.2020.1796492 (last accessed May 30, 2021).

Bick, E. (1968). The experience of the skin in early object-relations. *International Journal of Psychoanalysis, 49*(2): 484–486.

Bion, W. R. (1953). Untitled, pp. 256–258. Original unpublished work undated.

Bion, W. R. (1954). Notes on a theory of schizophrenia. In: *Second Thoughts.* London: Karnac, 1993.

Bion, W. R. (1955). Language and the schizophrenic. In: M. Klein, P. Heimann, & R. Money-Kyrle (Eds.), *New Directions in Psychoanalysis: The Significance of Infant Conflict in the Pattern of Adult Behaviour* (pp. 220–239). London: Tavistock, 1955.

Bion, W. R. (1957). Differentiation of the psychotic from the non-psychotic personalities. In: *Second Thoughts.* London: Karnac, 1993.

Bion, W. R. (1958a). On arrogance. *International Journal of Psychoanalysis, 39*(2–4): 144–146.

Bion, W. R. (1958b). On hallucination. *International Journal of Psychoanalysis, 39*(5): 341–349.

Bion, W. R. (1959). Attacks on linking. *International Journal of Psychoanalysis, 40*: 308–315.

Bion, W. R. (1961). *Experiences in Groups and Other Papers.* London: Tavistock.

Bion, W. R. (1962). *Learning from Experience.* In: *Seven Servants.* New York: Jason Aronson, 1977.

Bion, W. R. (1965). *Transformations.* In: *Seven Servants: Four Works.* New York: Jason Aronson, 1977.

Bion, W. R. (1967). *Second Thoughts.* London: Maresfield.

Bion, W. R. (1970). *Attention and Interpretation.* In: *Seven Servants.* New York: Jason Aronson, 1977.

Bion, W. R. (1976). Evidence. In: *Clinical Seminars and Other Works.* London: Karnac, 2008, pp. 312–320.

Bion, W. R. (1977). *Two Papers: The Grid and Caesura.* London: Karnac, 1989.

Bion, W. R. (1979). *A Memoir of the Future.* London: Karnac, 1991.

Bion, W. R. (1992). *Cogitations.* London: Karnac.

Blake, W. (1794). Tyger. In: *Songs of Innocence and Experience: Shewing the Two Contrary States of the Human Soul.* New York: CreateSpace, 2011.

Blomfield, O. H. (1985). Parasitism, projective identification and the Faustian bargain. *International Review of Psycho-Analysis, 12*(3): 299–310.

Bloom, H. (1973). *The Anxiety of Influence*. New York: Oxford University Press.

Bollas, C. (1984). Loving hate. *Annual of Psychoanalysis, 12/13*: 221–237.

Bollas, C. (1992). Why Oedipus? In: *Being a Character: Psychoanalysis and Self Experience*. New York: Hill & Wang.

Bollas, C. (2000). *Hysteria*. London: Routledge.

Botella, C., & Botella, S. (2005). *The Work of Psychic Figurability: Mental States Without Representation*. Hove, UK: Brunner-Routledge.

Britton, R. (2013). Commentary on three papers by Wilfred R. Bion. *Psychoanalytic Quarterly, 82*(2): 311–321.

Brody, S. (1995). Modern psychoanalysis and the immune system. *Modern Psychoanalysis, 20*(1): 67–78.

Bromberg, P. M. (1998) Staying the same while changing: Reflections on clinical judgment. *Psychoanalytic Dialogues, 8*(2): 225–236.

Bronstein, C. (2011). On psychosomatics: The search for meaning. *International Journal of Psychoanalysis, 92*(1): 173–195.

Bronte, C., & Davies, S. (1847). *Jane Eyre*. London & New York: Penguin, 2006.

Burke, S. G. (1992). Chronic fatigue syndrome and women: Can therapy help? *Social Work, 37*(1): 35–39. www.jstor.org/stable/23716539.

Burton, R. (1628). *The Anatomy of Melancholy*. Oxford: John Lichfield.

Butler, D. G. (2015). Falling through the cracks: Precarity, precocity, and other neoliberal pressures. *Fort Da, 21*(2): 33–52.

Butler, J. (2003). Violence, mourning, politics. *Studies in Gender and Sexuality, 4*(1): 9–37.

Bychowski, G. (1960). Symposium on "Depressive Illness"—in the structure of chronic and latent depressions. *International Journal of Psychoanalysis, 41*: 504–508.

Cambridge Encyclopedia of the Jesuits (2017). Worcester T. (Ed.). Cambridge: Cambridge University Press.

Cather, W. (1911). The Joy of Nelly Deane. In: *Coming Aphrodite! and Other Stories*. New York: Penguin, 1999, pp. 205–220.

Civitarese, G. (2008). "Caesura" as Bion's discourse on method. *International Journal of Psychoanalysis, 89*(6): 1123–1143.

Civitarese, G. (2011). Exploring core concepts: Sexuality, dreams and the unconscious. *International Journal of Psychoanalysis, 92*(2): 277–280.

Civitarese, G. (2016). *Truth and the Unconscious in Psychoanalysis*. London: Routledge.

Civitarese, G. (2018). Hymenality in psychoanalysis: A reading of *Boundaries and Bridges: Perspectives on Time and Space in Psychoanalysis. International Journal of Psychoanalysis, 99*(1): 275–286.

Civitarese, G., & Ferro, A. (2013). The meaning and use of metaphor in analytic field theory. *Psychoanalytic Inquiry, 33*: 190–209.

Coetzee, J. M. (1992). *Doubling the Point: Essays and Interviews.* D. Attwell (Ed.). Cambridge, MA: Harvard University Press.

Coetzee, J. M. (2000). *Disgrace.* London: Vintage.

Coetzee, J. M. (2003). He and his man. Nobel lecture at the Swedish Academy, Stockholm, December 7. https://nobelprize.org/prizes/literature/2003/coetzee/ 25261-j-m-coetzee-nobel-lecture-2003/ (last accessed May 30, 2021).

Coetzee, J. M., & Kurtz, A. (2015). *The Good Story: Exchanges on Truth, Fiction and Psychoanalytic Psychotherapy.* London: Harvell Secker.

Coleridge, S. T. (1817). *Biographia Literaria. Chapter XIV.* Oxford: Clarendon, 1907.

Darbishire, L., Ridsdale, L., & Seed, P. T. (2003). Distinguishing patients with chronic fatigue from those with chronic fatigue syndrome: a diagnostic study in UK primary care. *British Journal of General Practice, 53*(491): 441–445.

Derrida, J. (2003). Autoimmunity: Real and Symbolic Suicides: A Dialogue with Jacques Derrida. In: *Philosophy in a Time of Terror.* G. Borradori (Ed.). Chicago, IL: University of Chicago Press.

Dimen, M. (2000). The body as Rorschach. In: *Studies in Gender and Sexuality, 1*(1): 9–39.

Edelman, G. (1989). *The Remembered Present: A Biological Theory of Consciousness.* New York: Basic Books.

Eigen, M. (1997). A bug-free universe. *Contemporary Psychoanalysis, 33*(1): 19–41.

Eliot, T. S. (1922). The Wasteland. In: *Collected Poems.* London: Faber and Faber, 1999.

Eliot, T. S. (1925). The Hollow Men. In: *Collected Poems.* London: Faber, 1931.

Eliot, T. S. (1962). Four Quartets. In: *Collected Poems: 1909–1962.* London: Faber.

Encyclopedia Britannica (2020). Symbiosis. https://britannica.com/science/ symbiosis (last accessed May 29, 2021).

Erikson, E. H. (1946). Ego development and historical change—clinical notes. *Psychoanalytic Study of the Child, 2*(1): 359–396.

Erikson, E. H. (1995). *Childhood and Society.* London: Vintage.

Faber, G. (1925). *Poetry Diary 2019.* London: Faber.

Ferenczi, S. (1988). Confusion of tongues between adults and the child—the language of tenderness and of passion. *Contemporary Psychoanalysis*, *24*(2): 196–206.

Ferro, A. (1999). *The Bi-personal Field: Experiences in Child Analysis*. London: Routledge.

Ferro, A. (2002). Some implications of Bion's thought. *International Journal of Psychoanalysis*, *83*(3): 597–607.

Freud, A. (1963). The concept of developmental lines. *Psychoanalytic Study of the Child*, *18*(1): 245–265.

Freud, S. (1888). Letter from Freud to Fliess, August 29. In: *The Complete Letters of Sigmund Freud to Wilhelm Fliess, 1887–1904*. Cambridge, MA: Harvard University Press.

Freud, S. (1899a). Screen memories. *S. E.*, *3*: 299–322. London: Hogarth.

Freud, S. (1900a). *The Interpretation of Dreams*. *S. E.*, *4–5*: ix–627. London: Hogarth.

Freud, S. (1912–13). *Totem and Taboo*. *S. E.*, *13*: 1–161. London: Hogarth.

Freud, S. (1914c). On narcissism: An introduction. *S. E.*, *14*. London: Hogarth.

Freud, S. (1914g). Remembering, repeating and working-through. *S. E.*, *12*: 145–156. London: Hogarth.

Freud, S. (1916a). On transience. *S. E.*, *14*: 239–259. London: Hogarth.

Freud, S. (1916–17). *Introductory Lectures on Psycho-Analysis*. *S. E.*, *15–16*: 241–463. London: Hogarth.

Freud, S. (1917e). Mourning and melancholia. *S. E.*, *14*: 237–258. London: Hogarth.

Freud, S. (1918b). From the history of an infantile neurosis. *S. E.*, *17*: 1–124. London: Hogarth.

Freud, S. (1919h). The "uncanny". *S. E.*, *17*: 217–256. London: Hogarth.

Freud, S. (1920g). *Beyond the Pleasure Principle*. *S. E.*, *18*: 1–64. London: Hogarth.

Freud, S. (1925a). A note upon the "mystic writing-pad". *S. E.*, *19*: 227–234. London: Hogarth.

Freud, S. (1925d). *An Autobiographical Study*. *S. E.*, *20*. 1–74. London: Hogarth.

Freud, S. (1926d). *Inhibitions, Symptoms and Anxiety*. *S. E.*, *20*: 75–176. London: Hogarth.

Freud, S. (1926e). *The Question of Lay Analysis*. *S. E.*, *20*: 177–258. London: Hogarth.

Freud, S. (1927e). Fetishism. *S. E.*, *21*: 147–158. London: Hogarth.

Freud, S. (1930a). *Civilization and Its Discontents. S. E., 21*: 57–146. London: Hogarth.

Freud, S. (1933a). *New Introductory Lectures on Psycho-analysis. S. E., 22*: 1–182. London: Hogarth.

Freud, S. (1937c). Analysis terminable and interminable. *S. E., 23*: 209–240. London: Hogarth.

Freud, S. (1937d). Constructions in analysis. *S. E., 23*: 255–270. London: Hogarth.

Freud, S. (1950a). A project for a scientific psychology [1895]. *S. E., 1*: 283–397. London: Hogarth.

Frosh, S. (2014). Temporal vertigo: Mourning, loss, and survival. *Studies in Gender and Sexuality, 15*(3): 223–227.

Gandhi, M. K. (1925). *My Experiments with Truth*. Ahmedabad, India: Navajivan, 1957.

Gargiulo, G. (1998). Meaning and metaphor in psychoanalytic education. *Psychoanalytic Review, 85*(3): 413–422.

Geertz, C. (1973). *The Interpretations of Culture*. New York: Basic Books.

Giard, A. (1913). *Oeuvres Diverses, Volume 2. 1911–13*. Paris: Laboratoire d'évolution des êtres organisés.

Godwin, R. W. (1991). Wilfred Bion and David Bohm. *Psychoanalysis and Contemporary Thought, 14*(4): 625–654.

Goldman, R. P. (1978). Fathers, sons and gurus: Oedipal conflict in the Sanskrit epics. *Journal of Indian Philosophy, 6*(4): 325–392.

Green, A. (1999). *The Work of the Negative*. London: Free Association.

Grotstein, J. S. (1997a). *A Beam of Intense Darkness*. London: Karnac.

Grotstein, J. S. (1997b). Mens sana in corpore sano: The mind and body as an "odd couple" and as an oddly coupled unity. *Psychoanalytic Inquiry, 17*: 204–222.

Harris, A. E. (2009). You must remember this. *Psychoanalytic Dialogues, 19*(1): 2–21.

Harris, M. (2007). *Your Teenager: Thinking about Your Child during the Secondary School Years*. London: Karnac.

Hartmann, H. (1939). Psycho-analysis and the concept of mental health. *International Journal of Psycho-Analysis, 20*: 308–321.

Heisenberg, W. (1971). *Physics and Beyond: Encounters and Conversations*. [German original: *Der Teil und das Ganze*.] New York: Harper & Row.

Heisenberg, W. (1989). *Physics and Philosophy: The Revolution in Modern Science*. Introduction by Paul Davies. London: Penguin.

Homer (c. 500 BC). *Homeric Hymn to Aphrodite*. G. Nagy (Trans.). http://uh.edu/~cldue/texts/aphrodite.html (last accessed May 30, 2021).

Hood, E. (2003). The environment-autoimmune link. *Environmental Health Perspectives, 111*(5): A274–A276. www.jstor.org/stable/3435079 (last accessed May 30, 2021).

Hopkins, G. M., & Smith, K. E. (1976). *Gerard Manley Hopkins: Poetry and Prose.* Exeter, UK: Wheaton.

Jameson, F. (1970). Walter Benjamin, or nostalgia. *Salmagundi, 10/11* (Fall 1969–Winter 1970): 52–68.

Joseph, B. (1982). Addiction to near death. *International Journal of Psychoanalysis, 63*(4): 449–456.

Joseph, B. (1985). Transference: the total situation. *International Journal of Psychoanalysis, 66*(4): 447–454.

Joseph, B. (1989). *Psychic Equilibrium and Psychic Change: Selected Papers of Betty Joseph.* London: Tavistock/Karnac.

Kapadia, S. (1998). On borderline phenomena. *International Journal of Psychoanalysis, 79*(3): 513–528.

Kayser, M. S., & Dalmau, J. (2011). The emerging link between autoimmune disorders and neuropsychiatric disease. *Journal of Neuropsychiatry and Clinical Neurosciences, 23*(1): 90–97. https://ncbi.nlm.nih.gov/pmc/articles/PMC3086677/ (last accessed May 30, 2021).

Keats, J. (1818). *Complete Poems and Selected Letters of John Keats.* New York: The Modern Library, 1958.

Kermode, F. (1966). *A Sense of Ending.* New York: Oxford University Press.

Kernberg, O. F. (2007). The almost untreatable narcissistic patient. *Journal of the American Psychoanalytic Association, 55*(2): 503–539.

Klein, M. (1946). Notes on some schizoid mechanisms. *International Journal of Psychoanalysis, 27*: 99–110.

Klein, M. (1955). *On Identification.* New Directions in Psycho-Analysis. London: Tavistock, pp. 309–345.

Klein, M. (1961). *Narrative of a Child Analysis: The Conduct of the Psycho-Analysis of Children as Seen in the Treatment of a Ten-year-old Boy.* London: Hogarth and International Psychoanalytic Library.

Klein, M. (1997). *Envy and Gratitude and Other Works 1946–1963.* London: Vintage.

Klein, S. (1980). Autistic phenomena in neurotic patients. *International Journal of Psychoanalysis, 61*(3): 395–402.

Kristeva, J. (1992). *Black Sun: Depression and Melancholia.* L. S. Roudiez (Trans.). New York: Columbia University Press.

Laplanche, J. (1997). The theory of seduction and the problem of the other. *International Journal of Psychoanalysis, 78*(4): 653–666.

Lasch, C. (1979). *The Culture of Narcissism: American Life in an Age of Diminishing Expectations.* New York: W. W. Norton.

Lawrence, D. H. (1948). *Sons and Lovers.* London: Penguin.

Lerner, A., Jeremias, P., & Matthias, T. (2015). The world incidence and prevalence of autoimmune diseases is increasing. *International Journal of Celiac Disease, 3*(4): 151–155. DOI: 10.12691/ijcd-3-4-8. Available online at http://pubs.sciepub.com/ijcd/3/4/8 (last accessed June, 13, 2021.

Loewald, H. W. (1960). On the therapeutic action of psycho-analysis. *International Journal of Psychoanalysis, 41*: 16–33.

Lowental, U. (1986). Autodestruction and nonexistence: Two distinct aspects of the death drive. *Psychoanalytic Review, 73C*(3): 349–360.

Mahler, M. S. (1958). Autism and symbiosis, two extreme disturbances of identity. *International Journal of Psychoanalysis, 39*: 77–82.

Mahler, M. S. (1971). A study of the separation–individuation process and its possible application to borderline phenomena in the psychoanalytic situation. *Psychoanalytic Study of the Child, 26*: 403–424.

Mahler, M. S. (1974). On the first three subphases of the separation—individuation process. *Psychoanalysis and Contemporary Science, 3*(1): 295–306.

Mahler, M. S. (1975). On the current status of the infantile neurosis. *Journal of the American Psychoanalytic Association, 23*: 327–333.

Maiello, S. (2000). Broken links: Attack or breakdown? *Journal of Child Psychotherapy, 26*(1): 5–24.

Marty, P. (1967). Régression et instinct de mort: Hypothèse à propos de l'observation psychosomatique. *Revue française de psychanalyse, 31*: 1113–1133.

Marvell, A. (1681). Dialogue between Soul and Body. In: *The Metaphysical Poets.* London: Penguin, 1972, p. 245.

Matthews, B. E. (1998). *An Introduction to Parasitology.* Cambridge: Cambridge University Press.

McClelland, R. T. (1993) Autistic space. *Psychoanalysis and Contemporary Thought, 16*(2): 197–231.

McDougall, J. (1974). The psychosoma and the psychoanalytic process. *International Review of Psycho-Analysis, 1*(4): 437–459.

McDougall, J. (1989). *Theatres of the Body.* London: Free Association.

Meltzer, D. (1967). *The Psycho-Analytical Process.* London: Karnac.

Meltzer, D. (1975a). Adhesive identification. *Contemporary Psychoanalysis*, *11*(3): 289–310.

Meltzer, D. (1975b). Dimensionality as a parameter of mental functioning: Its relation to narcissistic organization. In: D. Meltzer, J. Bremner, S. Hoxter, D. Weddell, & I. Wittenberg (Eds.), *Explorations in Autism: A Psycho-Analytical Study* (pp. 223–238). Strathtay, UK: Clunie.

Meltzer, D. (1975c). The psychology of autistic states and of post-autistic states. In: D. Meltzer, J. Bremner, S. Hoxter, D. Weddell, & I. Wittenberg (Eds.), *Explorations in Autism: A Psycho-Analytical Study* (pp. 6–29). Strathtay, UK: Clunie.

Meltzer, D. (1990). *The Claustrum: An Investigation of Claustrophobic Phenomena*. London: Karnac.

Meltzer, D., Albergamo, M., Cohen, E., Greco, A., Harris, M., Maiello, S., Milana, G., Petrelli, D., Rhode, M., Scolmati, A. S., & Scotti, F. (1986). *Studies in Extended Metapsychology: Clinical Applications of Bion's Ideas*. London: Karnac, pp. 1–222.

Meltzer, D., Bremner, J., Hoxter, S., Weddell, D., & Wittenberg, I. (Eds.) (1975). *Explorations in Autism: A Psycho-Analytical Study*. Strathtay, UK: Clunie.

Meltzer, D., & Harris, M. (1976). A psychoanalytic model of the child-in-the-family-in-the-community. In: A. Hahn (Ed.), *Sincerity and Other Works: The Collected Papers of Donald Meltzer* (pp. 387–454). London: Karnac, 1994.

Meltzer, D., Milana, G., Maiello, G., & Petrelli, D. (1982). The conceptual distinction between projective identification (Klein) and container–contained (Bion). *Journal of Child Psychotherapy, 8*(2): 185–202.

Meltzer, D., & Williams, M. H. (1988). *The Apprehension of Beauty: The Role of Aesthetic Conflict in Development, Art, and Violence*. London: Karnac.

Meltzer, D., & Williams, M. H. (2010). Temperature and distance as technical dimensions of interpretation. In: *A Meltzer Reader: Selections from the Writings of Donald Meltzer* (pp. 21–34). London: Karnac.

Milton, J. (1795). *Paradise Lost*. London: Penguin, 2000.

Mitchell, J. (1996). Sexuality and psychoanalysis: Hysteria. *British Journal of Psychotherapy, 12*(4): 473–479.

Mitrani, J. L. (1992). On the survival function of autistic manoeuvres in adult patients. *International Journal of Psychoanalysis, 73*(3): 549–559.

Money-Kyrle, R. (1978). The aim of psychoanalysis. In: *The Collected Papers of Roger Money-Kyrle*. Strathtay, UK: Clunie, pp. 442–449.

Munro, A. (2001). What is remembered. In: *Hateship Friendship Courtship Loveship Marriage*. New York: Vintage.

Munro, A. (2011, June 27). Gravel. *The New Yorker*. https://newyorker.com/magazine/2011/06/27/gravel-alice-munro (last accessed May 30, 2021).

Nissen, B. (2008). On the determination of autistoid organizations in non-autistic adults. *International Journal of Psychoanalysis, 89*(2): 261–277.

Nissen, B. (2013). On psychic elements in a case of autistoid perversion. *International Journal of Psychoanalysis, 94*(2): 239–256.

Ogden, T. H. (1989). On the concept of an autistic-contiguous position. *International Journal of Psychoanalysis, 70*(1): 127–140.

Ogden, T. H. (1992). *The Primitive Edge of Experience*. London: Karnac.

Ogden, T. H. (1997). Some thoughts on the use of language in psychoanalysis. *Psychoanalytic Dialogues, 7*(1): 1–21.

Ogden, T. H. (1998). A question of voice in poetry and psychoanalysis. *Psychoanalytic Quarterly, 67*(3): 426–448.

Oxford English Dictionary (2009). Second edition on CD-ROM (v. 4.0). Oxford: Oxford University Press.

Oxford English Reference Dictionary, The (1995, 1996). Oxford: Oxford University Press.

Pamuk, O. (2005). *Istanbul: Memories and the City*. London: Faber and Faber.

Phillips, A. (2010). *On Balance*. London: Hamish Hamilton, 2011.

Phillips, A. (2012). *Missing Out: In Praise of the Unlived Life*. New York: Farrar, Straus and Giroux.

Plato (c. 380 BC). *The Republic*. London: Penguin, 1987, pp. 421–439.

Proverbs 16:5, 18–19. *The Bible*. King James Version.

Pullman, P. (2010). *The Good Man Jesus and the Scoundrel Christ*. New Delhi: Penguin.

Ramanujan, A. K. (1999). *The Collected Essays of A. K. Ramanujan*. V. Dharwadekar (Ed.). Delhi, India: Oxford University Press.

Rapp Learn, J. (2017, December 19). Genital parasite crabs are struggling to find sex partners. *NewScientist*.https://newscientist.com/article/2157002-genital-parasite-crabs-are-struggling-to-find-sex-partners/#ixzz6wKIm9wzv (last accessed May 30, 2021).

Richards, I. A. (1936). *The Philosophy of Rhetoric*. Oxford: Oxford University Press.

Rosenfeld, H. (1964). The psychopathology of hypochondriasis. In: *Psychotic States: A Psychoanalytical Approach*. London: Hogarth, pp. 180–199.

Rosenfeld, H. (1983). Primitive object relations and mechanisms. *International Journal of Psychoanalysis, 64*(3): 261–267.

Rosenfeld, H. (1987). *Impasse and Interpretation: Therapeutic and Anti-therapeutic Factors in the Psychoanalytic Treatment of Psychotic, Borderline, and Neurotic Patients*. New Library of Psychoanalysis, 1. London: Tavistock, pp. 1–318.

Rosenfeld, H. (2001). The relationship between psychosomatic symptoms and latent psychotic states. In: F. de Masi (Ed.), *Herbert Rosenfeld at Work: The Italian Seminars* (pp. 24–44). London: Karnac.

Sadedin, S. (2014, August 4). Why pregnancy is a biological war between mother and baby. *Aeon.co*. https://aeon.co/essays/why-pregnancy-is-a-biological-war-between-mother-and-baby (last accessed May 30, 2021).

Sartre, J.-P. (1943). *Being and Nothingness*. New York: Gallimard.

Schellekes, A. (2019). Arid mental landscapes and avid longings for human contact: Beckettian and analytic narratives. *British Journal of Psychotherapy*, 35(1): 91–106.

Segal, H. (1957). Notes on symbol formation. *International Journal of Psycho-analysis*, 38: 391–397.

Shakespeare, W. (1606). *King Lear*. R. A. Foakes (Ed.). London: Arden, 1997.

Showalter, E. (1987). *The Female Malady: Women, Madness and English Culture: 1830–1980*. London: Virago.

Showalter, E. (1997). *Hystories: Hysterical Epidemics and Modern Media*. New York: Columbia University Press.

Skelton, R. (2016). *PEP Consolidated Psychoanalytic Glossary*. http://pep-web.org/document (last accessed May 30, 2021).

Smith, D., & Germolec, D. (1999). Introduction to immunology and auto-immunity. *Environmental Health Perspectives*, 107, October: 661–665. doi:10.2307/3434323.

Sodre, I. (2015). Addiction to near-life: On pathological daydreaming and the disturbing ambiguity of faking true-love. In: *Imaginary Existences: A Psychoanalytic Exploration of Phantasy, Fiction, Dreams and Daydreams*. London: Routledge.

Sophocles. (429 BC). *Oedipus Rex*. In: *The Three Theban Plays*. R. Fagiles (Trans.). New York: Penguin, 1982.

Steiner, J. (1985). Turning a blind eye: The cover up for Oedipus. *International Review of Psycho-Analysis*, 12(2): 161–172.

Steiner, J. (1989). The aim of psychoanalysis. *Psychoanalytic Psychotherapy*, 4(2): 109–120.

Steiner, J. (1993). *Psychic Retreats: Pathological Organisations in Psychotic, Neurotic and Borderline Patients*. London: Routledge.

Steiner, J. (2015). Melanie Klein's technique then and now. Melanie Klein Trust. https://vimeo.com/174515650 (last accessed May 30, 2021).

Strenger, C. (1989). The classic and the romantic vision in psychoanalysis. *International Journal of Psychoanalysis*, 70(4): 593–610.

Teitelbaum, S. (2008). Allergic to people: Building bridges in a ripped psychic-soma. *American Journal of Psychoanalysis*, 68(2): 177–188.

Tennyson, A. (1859). Tithonus. In: *Collected Poems*. London: Oxford University Press, 1946.

Thoreau, H. D. (1908). *Walden, or, Life in the Woods*. London: J. M. Dent.

Turner, V. (1969). *The Ritual Process: Structure and Anti-Structure*. New York: Aldine D. Gruyter.

Tustin, F. (1969). Autistic processes. *Journal of Child Psychotherapy*, 2(3): 23–39.

Tustin F. (1972). *Autism and Childhood Psychosis*. London: Hogarth.

Tustin, F. (1980). Autistic objects. *International Review of Psycho-Analysis*, 7(1): 27–39.

Tustin, F. (1984a). Autistic shapes. *International Review of Psycho-Analysis*, 11(3): 279–290.

Tustin, F. (1984b). The growth of understanding. *Journal of Child Psychotherapy*, 10(2): 137–149.

Tustin, F. (1986). *Autistic Barriers in Neurotic Patients*. Oxford: Routledge, 2018.

Tustin, F. (1988). The "black hole": a significant element in autism. *Free Associations*, 1(11): 35–50.

Tustin, F. (1991). Revised understandings of psychogenic autism. *International Journal of Psychoanalysis*, 72(4): 585–591.

Tustin, F. (1994). Autistic children who are assessed as not brain-damaged. *Journal of Child Psychotherapy*, 20(1): 103–131.

Valabrega, J.-P. (1954). *La conversion psychosomatique*. Paris: PUF.

Van Gennep, A. (1960). *The Rites of Passage*. Chicago, IL: Chicago University Press.

Webster's New World Dictionary (1987). New York: The World Publishing Company.

Wharton, E. (1900). The duchess at prayer. In: R. W. B. Lewis (Ed.), *The Collected Short Stories of Edith Wharton Vol. 1* (pp. 457–474). New York: Charles Scribner's Sons, 1968.

Wharton, E. (1917). *Summer, Novellas and Other Writings*. C. G. Wolff (Ed.). New York: Library of America, 1990.

Willett, C. (2001). *The Soul of Justice: Social Bonds and Racial Hubris*. New York: Cornell University Press.

Williams, M. H. (2005). *The Vale of Soulmaking: The Post-Kleinian Model of the Mind and Its Poetic Origins*. London: Karnac.

Winnicott, D. W. (1949). Hate in the counter-transference. *International Journal of Psychoanalysis, 30*: 69–74.

Winnicott, D. W. (1956). On transference. *International Journal of Psychoanalysis, 37*: 386–388.

Winnicott, D. W. (1969). The use of an object. *International Journal of Psychoanalysis, 50*(4): 711–716.

Winnicott, D. W. (1971). *Playing and Reality*. London: Penguin.

Winnicott, D. W. (1974). Fear of breakdown. *International Review of Psycho-Analysis, 1*: 103–107.

Woolf, V. (2015). *The Waves*. eBooks@Adelaide. Adelaide, Australia: University of Adelaide Library.

Wordsworth, W. (1798). The Prelude. In: *English Romantic Writers*, 2nd edition. San Diego, CA: Harcourt, 1995.

Yeats, W. B. (1921). *Collected Poems of W. B. Yeats*. London: Macmillan, 1956.

Yeats, W. B. (1936). What then? In: A. N. Jeffares (Ed.), *Selected Poetry*. London: Macmillan, 1968.

Index